A Coat of Many Colours

JMTurner.
1989.

From
Michael Townsend.

Other books by Michael Wilson

Christian Marriage (jointly with Mrs M. Wilson), Scottish Mission Book
Depot, Accra 1951
Health Talks by a Radio Doctor, Scottish Mission Book Depot, Accra 1960
The Christian Nurse, Edinburgh House Press 1960
Sickness and Society, Sheldon Press 1961
The Church is Healing, SCM Press 1965
The Hospital – A Place of Truth, University of Birmingham 1971
Health is for People, DLT 1975
Editor, *Explorations in Health and Salvation – a Selection of Papers by Bob
Lambourne*, University of Birmingham 1983

All except the last mentioned title are out of print

A Coat of Many Colours
Pastoral Studies of the Christian Way of Life

Michael Wilson

EPWORTH PRESS

British Library Cataloguing in Publication Data

Wilson, Michael, *1916*–
A Coat of many colours.
1. Christian life
I. Title
248.4

ISBN 0–7162–0453–3

First published 1988
by Epworth Press
Room 195, 1 Central Buildings,
Westminster, London SW1H 9NR

Typeset by The Spartan Press Ltd
Lymington, Hants
and printed in Great Britain by
The Camelot Press Ltd, Southampton

Contents

Contents

Acknowledgments

The author and publisher are grateful to the copyright holders for permission to include the following extracts:

James K. Baxter: A story from *Jerusalem Daybook*, 1971, reproduced by permission of Price Milburn, New Zealand.

Archbishop Michael Ramsey: Extract from his final speech to the General Synod of the Church of England in the debate on *Church and State*, 1971. Reproduced with his permission.

K. C. Norton: Extract from an address to a conference on *Current Issues in Child Psychiatry*, at Lake Couchiching, Canada, given when he was Minister of Community and Social Services in the Government of Canada, 1978. Reproduced with his permission.

The Rev Phillip Than, an Anglican priest in Brunei: for permission to quote from a private letter.

Stan Windass and Dr Michael Chance: material from an unpublished manuscript, reproduced with permission.

Abbreviations

AGM	Annual General Meeting
AV	Authorised Version of the Bible
BAC	British Association for Counselling
BCC	British Council of Churches
CMC	Christian Medical Commission of the World Council of Churches, Geneva
CND	Campaign for Nuclear Disarmament
DLT	Darton, Longman & Todd
DPS	Diploma in Pastoral Studies
GNC	General Nursing Council
GP	General Medical Practitioner
IQ	Intelligence Quotient
NEB	New English Bible
NHS	National Health Service
NT	New Testament
OT	Old Testament
OUP	Oxford University Press
ROSPA	Royal Society for the Prevention of Accidents
RSV	Revised Standard Version of the Holy Bible
SCM	Student Christian Movement
SPCK	Society for the Promotion of Christian Knowledge
SSJE	Society of St John the Evangelist
TUC	Trades Union Congress
USPG	United Society for the Propagation of the Gospel
WCC	World Council of Churches
WSCF	World Student Christian Federation
YMCA	Young Men's Christian Association

Preface

. . . the time has come when people can only truly communicate with one another out of what they themselves have experienced and suffered. For they can no longer speak to one another out of pure knowledge alone (C. G. Jung).

If you try to convey your meaning by a series of logical arguments, it is like a chain of links: if one is broken, the sense is lost. If you try to convey your meaning by a variety of methods – story, argument, case studies, poetry, parable, prayer, picture, or sermon – then one broken thread does not lose the meaning which is carried forward by other threads, like a rope. I believe this to be the method of the writers of the Bible, and that it is an excellent way to convey meaning across cultures, both within the Western world and more widely. In writing this book I have preferred the method of the rope to the chain. I explore human life from two points of view – as scientist and as artist. Science can provide what we call a factual account of the way things are; but no one would imagine that a scientific account of human behaviour (how we love one another, for example) could be anything but laughably inadequate! We would quickly call a poet to come and help. An artist may give us deep feeling for people, and also tell us parables to disturb us if we get too set in our ways. My writing is therefore interspersed with stories and experiences to stimulate the imagination.

It has taken several years to write this book, but a lifetime to prepare. It has been shaped by twelve years of teaching the Diploma in Pastoral Studies course in the University of Birmingham (see Appendix 2 pp. 223–4). But the previous twelve years as a priest (seven of those years in city parishes), and the twelve years before that as a doctor (ten of those years in Africa and four of them as a soldier) provided the experience of faith and life in many human situations which composes the raw material of the book. My indebtedness to others is therefore great.

I would like to thank the late Dr James Mathers, friend and colleague, for reading the first draft and helping with suggestions. But that is only a small part of his contribution which has extended over the years in cooperation with the university course. To him, and to the late Dr Bob Lambourne and the late Revd Charlie Browne, I owe much, for their writings and for our joint explorations into the subjects of this book.

I would also like to thank my wife, Jean, and my eldest son, Christopher, for reading the first draft and making many helpful suggestions. I am grateful also to the Revd Dr Anthony Bird who read the material about the experimental general practice, and gave me further information and ideas.

Beyond this special help, I owe an immense debt to all kinds of people who have worked with me in situations of joy and sorrow. In particular I must mention the students of the D.P.S. course in Birmingham who shared their experience and laboured with me in study and exploration.

There is a custom in Ghana that when you are given a gift you return thanks for it on the following morning at sunrise. However if you cannot appear in person, then you say '*When the cock crows tomorrow morning, that will be me giving you thanks.*' May there be a great crowing of cocks at sunrise tomorrow, and may thousands of my fellow pilgrims-in-learning hear my voice saying 'Thank-you'.

Note

I have given much thought to an appropriate term for the so-called 'First' and 'Third' worlds. I have rejected these descriptions; also the terms 'developed' and 'developing' worlds as too patronizing. The 'North/South' labels of the Brandt Report are now commonly used of the economic and social divisions within Britain itself. So I have chosen to speak of 'Western' and 'Two-Thirds' worlds as the least objectionable descriptions.

Quotations from the Bible are (unless otherwise stated) taken from *The Jerusalem Bible*, DLT 1966.

Introduction

'Hush, don't speak about it' is the name of an African village – in the local dialect 'Achimota'. Across the wooded hill above the village runs a path trodden by slaves as they were driven down to the castle of Christiansborg, seven miles away on the Gold Coast of West Africa.

This hill was the last chance of escape before they reached the dungeons of no return whence they were shipped across the Atlantic. Escaped slaves hidden in the bush were fed by the villagers: it was a secret hiding place. 'Hush, don't speak about it.'

Achimota was chosen as the site for the first great college of higher education in the country, where boys and girls were educated for the future life of the free state of Ghana. On this symbolic site there grew up not only the college but also the seedlings of the new universities at Legon and Kumasi.

The first vice-principal, James Kwegyr Aggrey,[1] was known internationally for his work of reconciliation between black and white races. The crest of the new college (above) was designed to one of his parables: 'On a piano you can play a tune of sorts on the white keys and a tune of sorts on the black keys, but for real harmony you need both black and white.' And its motto, *'Ut omnes unum sint'* (That they all may be one), points the way to one family of diverse races and beliefs which is God's long-term plan for humanity, and which was Achimota College's immediate plan for its own country's common life.

The story of Achimota is a parable of this book, which is about human relatedness, rescue from disintegration, and the building of a learning community where apprenticeship for life and work in the values of the kingdom of God is served.

It is right to begin in Achimota where I myself served an

apprenticeship among African peoples from whom I learnt the heart of what I have written about pastoral care. In accordance with Akan custom, I pay tribute to the wisdom of the elders whose proverbs and tradition I wish to use:

One tree cannot make a forest.[2]

PART ONE
All Change

It helps if you consider yourself to be an immigrant into the future (Margaret Mead).

In Part One we describe the vast social changes going on in Western countries and the world-wide spread of cities. There is an accompanying change in Western ways of thought and language.

The new post-Christian culture has relegated religion to a private sphere of moral choice and personal behaviour, while public issues are settled pragmatically. There is therefore a loss of connection between theory and practice, faith and life in the modern world.

Increasingly the church finds itself in conflict with the values of a society dominated by secular science and technology, but this is the milieu in which the Christian church today must think, speak and act to enable people to live fuller lives together.

1 Life in Cities

In 1950 just over one quarter of the world's population lived in cities. By the year 2000, if present trends continue, it is likely that almost half the world's peoples will be settled in cities.³ The rate of expansion of cities and towns in the Two-Thirds world is now such that their population will have multiplied by eight in the second half of this century. The huge growth in world population and the increase in city dwellers throughout the world are trends of our time.

It is in this situation that the church finds itself. It is in this situation of change that the church is itself changing because we as a people, individually and socially, are changing. Before discussing the Christian life, however, and the problems created by change for theology, mission and pastoral care, some survey of those changes which are particularly disturbing our lives may be helpful, especially for readers in other countries. I find it impossible to talk about the work of the church without first describing the situation within which its work is carried out: the people of God are responsible for the whole of the society within which they are placed.

Although the growth of populations and the crowding into cities is one of the most obvious changes of the second half of the twentieth century, there are many other complex changes going on in our lives at the same time. The stability of people's lives is being lost. We are a people on the move like nomads. All over the world the settled village communities are being disrupted by the drift of people to the towns. Increased travel facilities bring tourists from outside, and increased communication through wireless and television brings instant news of events and ideas.

People not only migrate to cities where a higher standard of living has been glimpsed, imagined or sometimes attained, but also commute in and out of cities, to and from work, all over the world. The rich escape each night to dormitory suburbs where gardens and relative quietness make living pleasant. The poor travel by overcrowded public transport from one grey area where they live to another grey area where they work.

The extended families that used to live close to one another and gave support in times of illness or unemployment are being broken up and scattered widely by re-housing schemes, the decline of manufacturing industry and the search for work. We have not yet succeeded in building a close-knit society, in which local community is based on a high degree of individual independence, supported by social services rather than family ties.

People are on the move not only within nations but internationally. Immigrants and refugees from India, Kenya, Vietnam and the West Indies have sought to escape overcrowding, poverty or oppression by settling in Britain. Here they find, for example, educational and health opportunities for their children which are beyond the wildest dreams of their own countries. Consequently most big cities are multi-racial with a diversity of peoples, cultures and faiths. Certain areas of a city may contain a high proportion of settlers from India, China, Pakistan, Ireland or the Caribbean.

Nevertheless the generation of strangers born in their country of adoption find the scales weighted against them. Unemployment amongst black teenagers is higher than amongst whites. 'The new black presence'[4] in cities has not imported our many social problems, but has exposed to public gaze pre-existent weaknesses in the social fabric. Unemployment, poverty, bad housing, the evils of landlordism and class conflict were already present in our cities before the second world war.

In the Western industrialized countries, unemployment particularly dominates the social scene. The human cost of joblessness in terms of despair, apathy, loss of sense of worth, mental sickness, broken family life and delinquency, is borne by a multitude of social services both statutory and voluntary.

Why, then, are cities spreading and people from rural areas and far countries migrating into them? Opportunities for a higher standard of life and choices of work, education and leisure are far greater in cities than in rural areas. Transport, medical services, safe water supplies, schools, leisure activities are better, and wider choices are available. In a city, the mixing of peoples, the variety of goods in shops, entertainment through art, theatre, discos and clubs, music, sport, skating rinks and swimming baths, the lights and night life, libraries, cathedrals and museums, parks and pubs, all form an exciting cosmopolitan place full of diversions from boredom. All over the world, people have glimpsed the possibilities of an alternative life-style to the grinding poverty of peasant subsistence farming.

But the city has another face. The opportunities elude the grasp of many. In a time of economic expansion when work is plentiful and money more freely available, all those doors to which money is the key are open. But in times of economic depression, unemployment and poverty spread. Doors close. Overcrowding, lack of housing, the search for jobs, rising costs of food and transport, violence and broken community life, lead to low morale and despair. Life is very unfair, and those for whom life is always a struggle – the poor, the old, the shanty dwellers, one parent families, the handicapped, strangers and the emotionally crippled – become a burden to the many voluntary and state agencies who shoulder the responsibility of the vanished extended family which was a people's first source of social security. Many fall victims to loneliness and meaninglessness: and symptoms of urban stress are there below the surface in times of prosperity as well as depression. In the last twenty years there has been revealed a whole generation of young people, black and white, who feel they have no personal future and no stake in society. Open injustice in the distribution of national wealth between North and South within Britain, and between the developed Western world and the Two-Thirds world is like a running sore. Some would say that the cost of living the way we do live, with particular regard to pollution of oceans and rivers, acid rain, desertification, and social alienation, is too high. Over all lies the threat of nuclear, chemical or biological accidents and war. Indeed the future is bleak.

On the other hand there is a new world consciousness growing and in the last fifty years humankind has assumed a far greater responsibility for the development of a world community of nations, for the quality of human life, and for the conservation of the natural world. International organizations like the United Nations, World Health Organization, World Council of Churches, World Wildlife Fund, Red Cross, Amnesty International and Greenpeace are characteristic of our day. God is at work through these great movements.

The growth of population, the spread of cities, homelessness, the mobility of workers and the uprootedness of peoples, together with the constant development of technology in industry means a profound change not merely in everybody's lifestyle but a change in us and our values – the way we see things, the way we do things, the way we understand ourselves and others, and the kind of good life that we desire. *We are a changing people.*

Certain consequences follow these changes, and they are an important part of the fluctuating situation in which Christians live and work and bring up their children. Nelson[5] invites us to imagine a cartoon in which two seekers after wisdom reach a mountain top to see a guru in pursuit of the secret of life. Their comment to him is: 'If these are the secrets of life, why are they in a loose-leaf binder?'

2 Understanding our World

Thinking and speaking of God today in terms of the categories of causality is the main source of atheism (Gabriel Marcel).

I have always had a profound respect for aboriginal superstition, not as formulations of literal truth, but as a way of keeping the human spirit obedient to aspects of reality that are beyond human articulation (Van der Post).

A whole group of giant thinkers lie behind the modern development of a city, its life and industry: Darwin, Freud, Marx, Matthew Boulton, Watt and many others. As a result of their ideas, people in Western countries like Britain, France and Germany generally no longer make sense of themselves, their society or their natural environment through religious explanations. The drought in Britain in 1984 was not explained as a punishment for wickedness inflicted by an angry God. We looked for reasons to the weather men. For the solution of practical problems most people turn to science and technology, not prayer: and most people today recognize that lightning strikes cathedrals and brothels indiscriminately. (However in 1984 the fire in York Minster was considered by a significant minority of both Christians and others to be an act of God in retribution for the consecration of the Bishop of Durham.)

A delightful example of this change in understanding which science brings was given by John Townroe:

Let us go back exactly one hundred years, to March 19th 1866 . . . The Vicar of the small market town of Warminster in Wiltshire was on holiday in Rome . . . he wrote to his parishioners from the Piazza where he was staying and this is what he said: 'I was so thankful to hear that the days of Humiliation for the Cattle Plague were so well observed in Warminster. May we all own this chastisement as a loud call to us to mend our lives and to walk more closely with our God.' Signed, J. E. Phillips.

Can you imagine a Vicar today writing like that to his people in his parish magazine? We have the Cattle Plague today, and call it foot-and-mouth disease . . . Clearly something here has gone on the bonfires, something concerning both belief and practice.[6]

In speaking of scientific methods one is aware that our explanations constantly change in the light of new discoveries. But for explanations of the movements of comets, for the understanding of the migration of birds and peoples, for the causes of leprosy and war, for the ways of bringing up children, for the management of birth and the delay of death, most people look to the sciences such as astronomy, ornithology, anthropology, medicine, sociology and psychology, not religion.

This change in our understanding is described as 'secularization' and a society so described as 'secular'. The old traditional way of understanding was religious, and the world so understood as 'sacral'. In secularism it is human beings who take the centre of the stage and begin to dominate nature.

Although there are still catastrophes when earthquakes and typhoons devastate, yet the hope is that we will eventually learn to control the whole of nature. Moon landings and the elimination of smallpox from the world give reality to such hopes, and everywhere people have caught a glimpse of new standards of life which promise that poverty and disease can be overcome. Secularization spreads because it offers better explanations of the way things are than the old sacral view – better explanations of how the body works and how crops grow, upon which to base methods of healing and farming. Such knowledge gives a better chance of bringing up healthy children who are less likely to die before their first birthday.

Before the 1939/1945 war, if someone in Britain fell ill with pneumonia, there were several days of high fever while the patient fought for life against the infecting germ. Everything was done to maintain the patient's strength, but no specific cure existed. Then, if the outcome was favourable, about the sixth day the body produced an out-pouring of antibodies into the blood, the skin poured with sweat, the temperature came down and the patient sat up and asked for food. The 'crisis' had come. But the outcome was often death where apathy or weakness could not match the invasion. Pneumonia was called 'the friend of the aged'.

Then came the discovery of the Sulpha drugs, and soon after, antibiotics. The treatment of lobar pneumonia was dramatically changed. *Its cure now lies in the hand of the doctor.* The crisis can come within a few hours: it is swift and predictable. Even very old people can be saved time after time from death by pneumonia.

Previous to these medical discoveries it was common to pray for the healing of a patient with lobar pneumonia. Earnest intercession for the patient was made day after day by families and congregations, until the crisis came – or death. Today we do not need to pray for the crisis; we give penicillin and it comes.

Our understanding of the relationship of God to the people involved in a pneumonia event has changed. God has, as it were, stepped back and put full responsibility for life or death into the hands of human beings. We could say that God has taken pneumonia off the intercession list and put it on the thanksgiving list instead. But in practice God tends to slip out of our thinking altogether in relation to pneumonia. All the facts and explanations, the diagnosis and the cure, can be given in terms of medicine, epidemiology, biochemistry and pharmacology. We do not need to look further, unless we are one of those people who wants to ask a deeper 'why?'. Why make a world in which pneumonia exists? What meaning has it?

Religious explanations for everyday joys and sorrows therefore no longer carry conviction. Talk about God has little meaning for the public affairs of life. Religion has been relegated to the private choices and personal behaviour of individual lives. Although the nineteenth-century parent could put *'Thy Will Be Done'* on the tombstone of a child who died of diphtheria, the twentieth-century parent no longer believes in that kind of God and gets her children immunized. But people may *think* that those who still believe in God, believe in a God of that kind: and not without reason.

Secularization involves a revolution in *thought* and *values* which has deeply affected our understanding of ourselves, our social organization and our world. Scientific understanding and the ability to act on it (to cure pneumonia, to build cars with robots and to prevent soil erosion) has given human beings a new kind of responsibility with far-reaching consequences for the development of Christian spirituality and pastoral care.

This new responsibility is God's gift to us and invites our response. We can become *co-creators with God* in curing pneumonia, immunizing our children, feeding the hungry in Ethiopia, or writing letters on behalf of prisoners of conscience. God does not rescue us if we refuse to take up this new form of responsibility. A devout Christian patient of mine died in Nigeria from malarial blackwater fever because he trusted his Lord and Saviour to protect him and refused to take anti-malarial pills.

The scientist seeks to find and control the causes of whatever problems disturb society. This means a constant backward probe into causes and effects rather than a forward thrust towards a goal of fulfillment. Secularism has given us a new sense of human responsibility but also robbed society of that sense of purpose for the future which follows from belief in God. One consequence of loss of belief in God (who holds all things together as a whole) and loss of belief in a divine goal of fulfillment towards which humanity strives purposefully, is loss of wholeness – disintegration between theory and practice (chapter 3), between people (chapter 4) and within the self (chapter 5).

The effect on language

> Reality is neither 'in here' in the mind, nor 'out there' in the world; it is the interplay of both mind and world in language (Crossan).

Religious words which were used in common speech have now lost significance. One of the favourite biblical images of the *shepherd* and his sheep no longer fires the imagination of urban peoples. Campbell[7] has tried to rekindle the usefulness of the shepherd image because it is well loved among Christians and deeply rooted in both Bible and art. The word 'pastoral' still lingers on in (mostly) professional speech. But less and less does a modern shepherd in Western countries illustrate the qualities which a Palestinian shepherd of the biblical era showed: modern shepherds have some of the age-long qualities of patience and care for animals, but also have veterinary, nutritional and economic skills appropriate to a technological and commercial society. We can get at the original meaning of the Bible by sympathetic study, but kindle no fire in the modern heart. The notion of shepherd and sheep is more a matter of sentiment today than of motivating power.

The word *health* in common speech means something very different to its meaning in the Book of Common Prayer ('and there is no health in us'): and the word 'heal' is unlikely to be used by a doctor. *Sin* no longer describes an experience or an observed behaviour in most people's lives. More often today we describe people as sick rather than as sinful, and psychology has become more important as a way of explaining people's behaviour. The battered wife or abused child becomes a problem for the social worker rather than a clergyman, the alcoholic a medical problem, the delinquent a child guidance problem (or perhaps in 1988 many people regard all three as matters of law and order). Knowledge of the social factors which play a part in such situations has modified popular ideas of responsibility and remedy.

The myths, models, nursery rhymes, images, stories and patterns, through which a whole community grasps and makes sense of its experience, have changed. The stories of science have taken over from religion the task of building our image of the world. But we tend to forget that what we call 'scientific facts' are also stories, and are only *one* way of 'seeing' the way the world is. The stories of science constantly change (can facts change?) as research disproves the old myths, models, and stories: who today has ever heard of the 'ether', or 'phlogiston'? Scientific myths which constantly change cannot be absolutized. Christians who live in a society whose way of understanding life is scientific need to be open to light from the biblical myths so that our own cultural assumptions are challenged.

The way in which religious language used to form the basis of everyday speech has changed since the Enlightenment. There are, therefore, gaps between our Christian ways of thinking/speaking, and our everyday ways of looking at the world: between our faith and our place of work: between Christian values and social values.

The meaning of the term 'pastoral care' has also been affected by secularization. Pastoral care was defined by Clebsch and Jaekle as consisting of:

> ... helping acts done by representative Christian persons, directed towards healing, sustaining, guiding and reconciling troubled persons whose troubles arise in the context of ultimate meanings and concerns.[8]

But such a narrowly religious definition does not fit our situation today. For example, at a state comprehensive school in an inner city area, the headmaster appointed a deputy head for pastoral care. The term 'pastoral care' is understood secularly in the context of education. Its use in this way so confused a visiting Christian clergyman from Africa that he asked the deputy head of pastoral care: 'I suppose you take classes of instruction for admission to church membership do you?' She was so non-plussed that she actually ignored the question and spoke of other matters. But that question could have been put to my housemaster when I was at public school before the second world war and he would have replied: 'Of course.'

There is a loss also of the religious rhythm of life. The Christian calendar, with its seasons of Advent, Christmas, Lent, Easter and Pentecost, is not only built into worship, but is also related to the seasons of nature, and so used to regulate a pattern of common life in celebrations, holy-days, days of rest for family-building, and periods of solemn self-appraisal and charity towards others. Such a rhythm is now at the mercy of commercialism. In London, one Christmas, I saw the three wise men in a gas company showroom advertising the wisdom of choosing a certain model of cooker. Christian festivals like Good Friday have become secularized and are no longer kept as holy-days. Hot cross buns can be bought soon after Christmas in London: in New York you may have difficulty in finding any. In the Christian tradition, Sunday was always the first day of the week in celebration of the resurrection. Recently in diaries and calendars it has become customary to put Sunday at the week's end: and it begins to resemble other days in matters of work and commerce.

However, religious ideas lie at the foundation of the way a people thinks and lives: they are the cement of a culture and mould its values. The tension between the old and new ways of belief was put by the Duke of Edinburgh in this way:

> Until it can be demonstrated that science, technology and economic growth can take the place of religion and provide that essential inspiration and motive which has created all great civilisations in the past, it would appear that our culture is simply free-wheeling on our Christian inheritance ... The very essence of most religions ... is that they provide the only satisfactory alternative to expediency in making judgements and decisions on the important issues which each generation has to face.[9]

It is a constant struggle for Christians to hold their faith and life together while trying to think and act in a society where there is a division between theory and practice. It is difficult to live a common life with others whose values conflict with those of Christianity. We will go on to explore how separation between theory and practice expresses itself in society.

PART TWO
Loss of Wholeness

The true state of affairs of the material world is wholeness.
If we are fragmented, we must blame it on ourselves (D. Bohm).

In Part Two we consider the disintegration of Western culture in thought, word and deed. For example there has developed a separation between faith and life in the everyday: and between theory and practice both in theology, social sciences and nursing.

The several areas in which this separation between theory and practice is explored (ch. 3) are not really distinct areas, but are like several expeditions into a disturbed territory in order to report back on the findings. In such reports both the scientist and the artist have complementary reports to make.

There is a stark choice between treating people as objects or relating to them as persons. This particular crisis presents society with a new way of perceiving illness (ch. 4).

Loss of wholeness in Western culture is reflected by a rift in the self of Western peoples (ch. 6). The invasiveness of Western culture means that disintegration and loss of hope are global problems, not just Western problems (ch. 5).

3 Things Fall Apart

If the poet tries to split himself in two between the man and the poet, he will inevitably commit suicide as an artist (Yevtushenko).

For while in the outward man, as technician, man come of age is optimistic and confident, the inward man remains profoundly unsatisfied, alienated from his culture, his personal self-hood and his God. A rift runs right through secular man's consciousness (F. R. Barry).

Theory and practice

A chaplain who lives and works in a village community with mentally handicapped adults wrote as follows:

> I am writing to invite you to a symposium which we are planning this year in order to talk over the problem of the gap which appears to exist between the needs and experience of those working in the field of social service and the training which many of them receive in colleges and universities . . . It would seem to us here that with the stress now being put on theoretical knowledge and professional certification this gap is widening.[10]

This letter arrived shortly after I had read a study of the loss of connection which exists between what student nurses are taught in schools of nursing and what they learn when they work in hospital wards.[11] Almost three quarters of the students were described as 'non-correlators' – that is, they could not bring together and make a sensible whole out of their theory (school of nursing) and practice (hospital ward).

A student will be faced in an examination with a question phrased on the lines 'Describe the nursing care required by a middle-aged man, who has been admitted with a diagnosis of coronary thrombosis.' She may well remember such patients: she may have undertaken different items of nursing care for each of them: she may have been in charge one night when one such patient was admitted and become aware of her lack of expertise at coping with his fear, his wife's tears and the doctor's demands. This cannot easily be put together to answer the question and she will fall back on the memory of an excellent lecture on the subject (in Training School) which bore little relationship to what she had ever done.[12]

This gap between theory and practice is not a situation confined to social work and nursing. The same problem besets those who work in education for many professions such as medicine, the police and the church.

I found it useful to discuss the research described above with a group of nurse tutors and to compare their situation with my own as a theological educator. We had common difficulties in bringing theory and practice into a wholeness of professional art.

In order to prevent the development of a theory/practice gap, these nurse tutors had given up a period of introduction for new students in the school, and begun their training with a period on the wards from the first day. More recently the students have started their training outside the hospital and first learn to know 'well' patients before encountering ill people later. To avoid a similar theoretical introduction to academic theology, my own group of pastoral studies students began their university course with work in the city (in a hospital, city planning or industry).

The very word theology has been used more than once in a TUC annual conference as a pejorative word meaning irrelevant. The arguments being put forward were dismissed as 'mere theology': that is, the arguments in the speaker's mind did not connect with the practical situation. Theology in the mind of a secular society stands for irrelevant theory, just as rhetoric now means irrelevant speech.

The beginning of this gap between theory and practice lies far back in history, and it was certainly an issue in the early church. The writer of James's epistle took to task those who emphasised faith at the expense of works. *Both* faith *and* works, he points out, belong to one another:

Take the case, my brothers, of someone who has never done a single good act but claims that he has faith. Will that faith save him? If one of the brothers or sisters is in need of clothes and has not enough food to live on, and one of you says to them, 'I wish you well; keep yourself warm and eat plenty', without giving them these bare necessities of life, then what good is that? Faith is like that: if good works do not go with it, it is quite dead.[13]

The title of a book *Waterbuffalo Theology*[14] was chosen to indicate that when the writer, Kosuke Koyama, preached the word of God as a Christian missionary in Thailand it had to connect with the daily life and work of his peasant listeners. The issues about which he spoke must be hot for them. What about a 'Housing Estate Theology' for Christians in Britain? Faith must connect with the hot issues in everyday life. Any attempt in this field to relate theory and practice is also caught in the professional separation between clergy and laity. This means, I think, that those who are involved in the daily thoughts, words and deeds of our cities – ordinary lay Christians – could be the key to the unity of theory and practice in theology.

Private and public

Another way of understanding this lack of wholeness is by considering the gap between private and public life. A working party of the Nurses' Christian Movement discussed the loss of connection between private and professional lives among student nurses:

> The very fact that we can divide a nurse's life into 'personal' and 'nursing' is a symptom of a changed attitude. For so many people in a technological society personal fulfillment is achieved in leisure hours, not at work. This can happen in nursing. For the nurse is also a technician and she has an increasing quantity of technical knowledge to acquire. She is rushed off her feet at work, and is often hardly able to be personal to her patients.[15]

Student nurses are quick to object to any infringement of their personal lives by nursing authorities. 'My life is my own, and my personal behaviour has nothing to do with my nursing' is a common attitude. On the other hand few would deny that a period of depression induced by the loss of a boy or girl friend's affection in one's private life would affect the public performance in nursing one's patients. A private experience of joy such as engagement or marriage, or of sorrow such as bereavement would likewise affect a nurse's sensitivity to others, simply because we cannot split up our lives into compartments and remain whole persons.

Questions of security have often been raised in political life when the private life of a Government Minister has brought him into intimate relationship with a woman other than his wife. In a recent case (1983) the Prime Minister drew a very firm line between public and private behaviour. Is this in fact possible? It denies the wholeness of a person. To be trustworthy is to be trustworthy both in public and private behaviour. It is a most divisive assumption about the nature of a human being that one can be moral in public but immoral in private matters: indeed the line of distinction between public and private life is difficult to draw. And what would one make of a testimonial for a job which described an applicant as 'trustworthy in some respects'?

This gap which we are describing between private and public life may also be regarded as a gap between skills (our functional role as miner, civil servant or teacher) and personhood (our natural capacity as a human being for relating to others – we are not robots). In the caring professions it is possible to use one's skill as a substitute for relationship. For example, a patient who has been recently bereaved may go to a doctor with some minor complaint, really seeking a shoulder to cry on. The doctor may not give this patient a chance to talk about sorrow but at once hands out a prescription. This is an understandable reaction because the doctor is a professional, highly trained in the use of drugs for the cure and relief of disease, and is extremely busy. As one doctor remarked to me: 'I dare not give my patients the chance to talk about personal problems. I haven't got the time.' But the grieving patient was looking for human support; and received a prescription as a substitute.

Personal care and political action

> When I give food to the poor, they call me a saint. When I ask why the poor have no food, they call me a communist (Helder Camara).

One of the particular strengths of Christian pastoral care arises from the value given to every *individual* person. This good tradition which secular society has inherited from Christianity is now being moulded by new values into an over-emphasis on personal autonomy and individual development (including often self-centred spirituality). Personal problems and suffering are then apt to be privatized. A current example of this is unemployment in our society. To discover the social cost of unemployment we need to talk to those who work with the Samaritans, the Marriage Guidance Council, Probation Service, Alcoholics Anonymous, and nurses on admission wards in psychiatric hospitals. Here is where the cost of unemployment is borne, individualized and private but never added up publicly. Thousands of professional and voluntary social workers carry heavy case loads of people whose individual and family suffering stems directly from unemployment.

The pastoral approach to unemployment fails to turn private problems into social issues. As a woman remarked in a discussion on probation work among delinquents, 'Can't we do something more radical, prevent it?' Too often a local church tries to respond to the human misery caused by unemployment only by establishing facilities for counselling, relief of need, setting up clubs or job centres. Attention is given to the pain of redundancy in terms of an individual's bereavement. Compassion for people and their families is certainly called for: but *both* private *and* public action is required. There is a basic political task to be done; and an educational task of changing the public conception of the nature of work and its place in personal identity and social life.

You cannot help people fully unless you also do something about the situation which makes them what they are. Even in the unique and very personal situation of bereavement there is not only the pastoral task of helping an individual, a family, or a neighbourhood to grieve, but *also* of changing the attitude to death in society. The failure of church members to engage in public and political changes of this nature requires further exploration.

In our individualistic society it is important to be seen to care. Hence the competition at a General Election to be known to be the most caring party – caring for individuals that is. So politicians often hold 'clinics' (*sic*) locally for solving individual problems. In Western culture personal care has become a common area of social agreement. All agree that it is good to love one's neighbour. The focus upon individuals is acceptable.

The problems of the individual and society are linked although different. Halmos in his book *The Personal and the Political* discusses these differences:

It is like the lion and the lamb trying to lie down together. The politician and the personalist are two different types of agent for change. The one who sets out to change society is a reformer, whereas the person who hopes to change an individual is a therapist, and if each tries to do both from their position as a politician or counsellor, they fail because they act inappropriately. Quite apart from the basic opposition of the two to each other, politicians are like dominant genes, all too easily taking over and excluding the personal, while counsellors and churchmen for that matter, tend to underestimate the problems of politics.[16]

Undoubtedly many Christians shy away from the aggression of politics, not only because they fear their own inner aggression but also because they mistakenly believe aggression to be sinful rather than an energy implanted in us by a good Creator.

This is a Western problem since it is in Western culture that the private and individual approach (which moulds Western patterns of personal care) has developed. The gap between the personal and the political approaches is such that there is public outcry and indignation among politicians when churchmen engage in politics: the Prime Minister's anger that the Archbishop exercised Christian restraint in the Thanksgiving Service for victory in the Falklands war in 1983 is an example; or the political brouhaha over the Church of England's report on inner cities[17] in 1985.

Ideal and real

This gulf between private and public life, between personal care and political action is rooted in different beliefs about God and the world and the relation between them. These different beliefs give rise to particular difficulties in doing theology and pastoral care because they result in a gap between an imaginary ideal world and the real world of everyday life.

An editorial in the Daily Telegraph reflected on this theme one Christmastide:

IDEAL AND REAL. There may be people for whom Christmas is little more than giving and getting, swilling and swallowing. They are in a way to be envied. For thoughtful people Christmas must always wear a double face. One is the face of an ideal world, never yet seen; a world of peace on earth and goodwill among men. The other is the face of the world as it actually is; never yet has Christmas come to a world without bitterness and misery, without war, hatred and want. The contrast between what is and what might be cannot be contemplated without anguish. Contemplated without faith or philosophy it could lead to cynicism or despair.[18]

Idealism in Christianity results in a gap between religious faith and practice on the one hand, and the real but broken world on the other. Religion may then tend to privatize 'spiritual' beliefs and actions. A division grows between the so-called 'spiritual' world and the material world which tends to bring them into opposition. An idealist religion is concerned with the 'spiritual' life and may actually despise material things (like bodies, for example) and try to achieve 'spiritual progress' at the expense of the material life. An idealist religion becomes other-worldly and may result in withdrawal from the world, because its primary concern is the cultivation of the 'spiritual'. Because it is opposed to the material life it becomes solitary, concerned with ideas and feelings, thoughts and imaginings. In religion it is romantic ideas which the idealist finds appealing, such as the moment of revelation, the feeling of ecstasy, a shift of attention to sacraments and another world, the fascination of miracle. All this is at the expense of the ethical task to be done, of obedience and of the rational understanding to be put to work. A temptation for the idealist is thus to become self-centred.

However religion is primarily concerned with two things: action and community. Idealism tends to withdraw from action into meditation; and from the anguish of the world as it is into the solitariness of one's own spiritual life instead of membership. It is sobering to think what an extensive influence Greek idealism may have had on Christian faith and pastoral care: the resultant private and 'spiritual' faith has favoured a false personalism which leads to a weak involvement in affairs of the world such as politics. Archbishop Desmond Tutu said: 'I sometimes wonder what Bible it is that people are reading when they say Christianity has nothing to do with politics.'[19]

And there is the nub of the matter. 'If you will tell me what you find in the Bible, I will tell you what kind of person you are.' Repeatedly, because of the way our perception of the world works, we read into the Bible what is already in our hearts, instead of reading out of the Bible what it is saying. Therefore private reading of scripture is partial, and can even be mistaken; we badly need the different viewpoints of others to correct our understanding, and our understanding to correct theirs. Realist and idealist are vital to one another for a more whole view than either can have on their own. The realist can earth the idealist; the idealist give the realist vision. Both are members of the one eucharistic community.

When a Chinese dance team visited Britain recently, in a conversation with the artistic director I asked him: 'Why are all your dances happy dances? Do you not have a tradition of dancing to express the sad side of life?' He told me: 'Of course in the villages we have a long tradition of dance to express sadness, grief and the like. But nowadays under communism we only dance happy dances.' Such denial of the shadow side of life is due to idealism.

Idealists have difficulty in coming to terms with sin, stubborn illness, handicap and death as continuing events in God's world. They strongly deny evil and their religion tends to defend them against the harsh imperfection of the world by developing a gap between the ideal and the real. In some Christian theology there are therefore said to be two kingdoms, of God and of Satan, locked in battle: but the victory is assured by the sacrifice of Jesus on the cross. The fruits of that victory can be realized by faith now.

For the realist the kingdom of God is both 'now' (in signs and foretaste of the abundant life) and 'not yet': the perfect fulfillment is still a promise and a hope. Human beings are co-creators with God in transforming chaos into order. For the realist the shadow side of both the person and society is the raw material out of which the kingdom is forged. Evil is not an enemy to be fought but clay for the potter's hand.

The particular significance of this gap for pastoral care is the attraction of the church's ministry of healing for the idealist. When I first took up work as chaplain to the Guild of Health I was surprised to find how many people concerned to help and heal others were themselves very broken people: and I would not wish to exclude myself from that description. Indeed it helped me to understand my own motivation for becoming a doctor and then working in the church's ministry of healing. This gap between idealism and realism is one root of the church's failure to bring wholeness to the disintegration of Western society: the same lack of balance afflicts both.

Left and right brain

> God guard me from those thoughts men think in their minds
> alone. He that sings a lasting song thinks in a marrow bone
> (W. B. Yeats).

Research on the functions of different parts of the brain[20] has shown
that the left and right sides of the brain work differently. The left side is
verbal, logical and analytical; whereas the right brain knows in
symbols, images and metaphors, and cannot put what it knows into
words. The right brain sees context and meaning; the left brain
organizes new information and correlates it with remembered facts
and concepts.

Both sides of the brain are connected by a living communication
system (*corpus callosum*) so that, for example, the holistic patterns
of the right brain need to be recognized and organized through the
left brain before the information is consciously known.

Traditional Chinese philosophy has always emphasised the complementary nature of intuition and rational thought, representing
them as a pair of archetypes *yin* and *yang*.

In Western society we are overwhelmed by left brain thinking.
Poetic and intuitive insight are devalued at the expense of logical and
linear thought. Ferguson writes:

> Every breakthrough, every leap forward in history, has depend-
> ed on right brain insights, the ability of the holistic brain to
> detect anomalies, process novelty, perceive relationships. Is it
> any wonder that our educational approach, with its emphasis
> on linear, left brain processes, has failed to keep pace with the
> times? In a way it makes sense that evolving human conscious-
> ness eventually came to rely on that hemisphere in which
> language primarily resides. Some theorists think, based on re-
> search data, that the left brain behaves almost like a separate
> competitive individual, an independent mind that inhibits its
> partner.[21]

Much of Two-Thirds world theology at the grass roots (where it is
relatively uninfluenced by Western modes of thinking) relies for its
expression on dance, proverbs, songs and rituals. Hollenweger[22]
contends that the great ecumenical dialogue of the next twenty-five

years will be between this mostly non-verbal theology of the Two-Thirds world and the academic theology of the West.

Pastors from the Two-Thirds world who come to a Western university to do theology have already learnt to think analytically in the Western way. In the process of Westernization some of our Pastoral Studies students had lost contact with aspects of their African or Oriental self. For example, European missionaries who train clergy for indigenous churches might entirely omit any consideration of healing, dreams or visions which play a significant part in local spirituality.

On the other hand, we meet students from overseas who are competent in both modes of theological thought, logical and non-verbal. They form part of a connecting pattern between the left and right brain approaches to theology which coexist within the world church. Already they are working for that synthesis which must come if we are to achieve a deeper wholeness of insight into truth. They are healers of theology.

When I left the university and said goodbye to my colleagues, I pulled their legs about the predominantly left brain approach to education. I felt that the left side of my head was safe in a Western university. But the right brain, on the other hand, was exposed to the chill winds of neglect and undervaluation. That, I explained, was why I always wore a beret in the university with the right side tucked well down over my right brain to protect it!

Faith and life

Several areas have now been discussed in which the division between theory and practice, as a result of secularism, is expressed. *Firstly*, in a divorce between faith and life because our whole way of understanding the world – weather, pneumonia or foot-and-mouth disease – has changed, and a new way of seeing how God relates to creation has not yet been grasped. This is especially obvious in work. As a parish priest recently remarked: 'Most lay people seem to leave their faith at the factory gate.'

Secondly, we noted how language about God has lost its base in the everyday, and faith-words like shepherd, sin and resurrection no longer connect with daily conversation: or worse still the same word (such as health) means different things in the faith and everyday contexts.

Thirdly, theological theory (like other knowledge such as the care of the body by doctors) is becoming so professionalized that it is left to theologians and clergy; and for practical purposes the more simple moral aspects of faith like 'loving one's neighbour', 'treating people as people', being honest or 'going the extra mile' claim a layperson's energy. Individual faithfulness goes less against the grain of present society than wrestling with public issues or political action which are more controversial.

Fourthly, matters of temperament may also play their part when idealism is found congenial and the realism of living in a violent society or suffering stubborn situations becomes unbearable: and coming to terms with one's own dark side is too painful.

Fifthly, we have also seen how Christian faith looks forward to the fulfillment of God's purpose for the world, while Western culture looks back for causes and effects in a constant effort to control the world. This is a potent cause of atheism.

The particular context with which this book is concerned is a modern city. It is in this context that so many Christians live and work. The present position was well summed up by the actor Alec Guinness in a special television interview (May 1987) at the Cannes Festival for his eightieth birthday. Asked about his conversion to the Catholic faith and what difference it had made to his profession he replied: 'No difference at all.' This is the disintegration between theory and practice, faith and life, which we are describing.

Another result of the division between theory and practice is that Christians may not see how their faith can be used as a *critical tool* for discerning the truth in daily life. For example, in the course of planning the Health Service for the new city of Milton Keynes, a seminar of doctors, social workers and clergy was called together. It was the first meeting between the church and the planners. At this stage, when the Department of Health and Social Services had *already* published its outline plan for the Health Service, the cooperation of the church was sought to help societies like Marriage Guidance and the Samaritans find volunteers. The church's role was seen as helping with social and medical problems. Obviously this is one of its tasks. But when the word 'health' was first uttered, no one – not even the Christians involved in the medical, nursing, social work and planning projects – thought that Christian faith or theology might have insight to contribute towards the kind of health for which the citizen of a future city might hope. This is an example of the division between theology and other disciplines whereby the church is trapped into problem-solving and casualty care by a secular understanding of what health is, and by the relegation of religion to a private sphere. (I have discussed a Christian understanding of health – a theology of health – in a previous book.[23]) This divided way of thought means that the Christian vision of the kind of society we could become goes by default – indeed may be positively resented as some kind of conspiracy to impose unwanted beliefs on people.

In the Church of England report *Faith in the City* there are good examples of how faith and life connect in a concern for justice. The very practical criticisms of the neglect of our inner cities are based upon the Christian belief in the dignity of human beings, and the equal worth in the eyes of God of people of different races, people of different faiths, people of different sexes, and people of different wealth. It was tragic comedy that a Government spokesman, when the report was published, should speak of 'communist influence' – exactly as Archbishop Helder Camara said: 'When I give food to the poor they call me a saint. When I ask why the poor have no food, they call me a communist.'

For Christians living in a thought climate in which theory and practice are divided, it is a constant struggle to discover the pattern which connects private and public issues, and to hold faith and life together in one whole way of thought, word and deed.

4 Objects

People as things

We can cure patients these days without even knowing their names (A surgeon).

For the truth is that development means the development of people. Roads, buildings, the increase of crop output, and other things of this nature, are not development; they are only tools of development (President Julius Nyerere).

One further consequence of secularization lies close to the nature of science itself. The scientist observes things. That is, he sets things at arm's length, dissects them, analyzes them and explains them. Those things become the objects of research and action. They may also become the objects of control, because the aim of research into causes is to enable a problem to be identified, remedied or prevented. The scientific method tries to distance object from observer and such objectivity has produced immensely rich fruits in the advance of human knowledge. But the knowledge so obtained is *knowledge about* things and people-as-things. Personal *knowledge of* people-as-people is of a different order based on reverence. To treat people as things — as a case of duodenal ulcer for example — may be dehumanizing. Nelson writes in Canada:

While shaping our world in the image of things, we have given enough recognition to persons as persons that the incompatability between these two understandings has been masked and not forced to consciousness. Those of us who complain about our mechanistic and inhuman world are reminded of the many areas in which persons are taken seriously as persons. This we are told should be enough. What is more, it is all we can have in a modern society — a society which must necessarily be run according to mechanistic principles. To recognise that persons are persons in all areas of life is simply not possible. You can't run a company or a government that way, or so we are told . . . But there is no clamour among us to have us understand that there is a fundamental conflict between man as person and man as thing, and that we must choose between them if we are to have life, and that abundantly.[24]

This process of dehumanization is real and important. It happens in industry (employees as objects to be 'shaken out'). It happens in commerce. It happens in hospitals. It happens in the church in spite of its intention to affirm our human worth, to expose dehumanization wherever it raises its head, and to forge a more humane society for the future.

One of the things which shocks some students from Africa and Asia is the development of professional caring in the British Welfare State. 'What extraordinary people you are!' remarked a Zulu student, 'You care for one another at arm's length.'

Richard Titmuss,[25] in his book on blood transfusion, points out that one of the principles of the Health Service is to provide services on the basis of *common human needs*; there must be no allocation of resources which could create a sense of separateness between people. Much of the world's suffering is caused by separation which has become institutionalized in terms of income, class, race, caste, colour or religion, rather than recognition of similarities between people and their common humanity. Shylock pleads:

Hath not a Jew eyes? Hath not a Jew hands, organs, dimensions, senses, affections, passions? Fed with the same food, hurt with the same weapons, subject to the same diseases, healed by the same means, warmed and cooled by the same winter and summer as a Christian is? If you prick us, do we not bleed? If you tickle us, do we not laugh? If you poison us, do we not die?[26]

But the very thing which Titmuss suggested the Health Service had been created to prevent, has happened. A separateness between staff and patients, between skill and humanity, between rich and poor, has been institutionalized in the system. An essential reverence for people has gone, because belief in a God in whose image people are made has gone.

African and Asian students recognize an arm's length approach in our professional/lay relationships in hospitals, universities, social work, voluntary societies and the church. They recognize in us a social difficulty in relating personally to others *except in a functional way*. Commonly this takes the form of relating in terms of one another's problems (something objective like loneliness, ignorance, old age or unemployment). But these problems do not exist in themselves. There are actually old *people*, lonely *people* and unemployed *people*. All too often we are concerned with the theory (problems), with the ideas of unemployment or loneliness, and thereby keep the reality – *people* – at arm's length.

When we concentrate on problems we divide people. Thus there are literally hundreds of voluntary societies in every city, each focussed around a problem. There are the Samaritans (suicide), Gingerbread (one parent families), Mind (mental health), two Marriage Guidance Councils, Age Concern, The Richmond Fellowship (emotional disturbance), Alcoholics Anonymous, Parents Anonymous (battered babies), Victim Support (for the victims of robbery, burglary, etc.) and many more. In 1985 the Mental Health Foundation completed a national *Someone to talk to directory*[27] which has 10,000 entries.

Organizations which offer counselling tend to arrange their separate training schemes, such as those of the Marriage Guidance Councils, a city centre church, Open Door, Cruse, British Pregnancy Advisory Service . . . There are not only practical reasons for this but also a social inevitability because more attention is paid to the problems which divide people than to the common humanity of the sufferers which unites people. We also inevitably produce experts, professionals and accredited persons to deal with the problems. If we concentrate on problems in this way, voluntary societies will continue to multiply (they are, and we all know some gaps where more are needed). 'What an extraordinary people you are!'

There are, of course, creative features: voluntary societies like the Samaritans offer friendship; and others, like Cruse Club, offer counselling and build group and community support. I do not have to enlarge on the love expressed in a multitude of ways by voluntary helpers. I am trying to explore a deeper matter which lies at the foundation of the ways in which we give and receive care in our society.

Professional caring is based on the arm's length objectivity with which scientists approach their material, whether comet, cabbage, cat or human being. They distance themselves from the object. Suttie[28] describes science as a *flight from tenderness* into a form of intellectual play. In this respect it is the very opposite of the Christian attempt to rebuild tender relationships between people. Kofi Appiah-Kubi of Ghana has written of Western-trained doctors: 'People ask why do doctors talk *about* us, but not *to* us?'[29] A group of hospital patients meeting together heartily agreed with this statement. At first people are affronted by such impersonal discourtesy. But when the gap has really become institutionalized, patients no longer feel dehumanized because alienation between doctor and patient is then complete: the doctor/patient relationship becomes entirely functional.

In the Christian understanding, it is care which forms the context in which competence and skills are exercised, not vice versa. By this I mean that nursing is the prime profession which provides the basic human care within which medicine can be practised. The comparatively detached way in which medical procedures of examination, diagnosis and treatment are carried out will not be experienced as inhuman if nursing care provides a context of human warmth. Nursing is not therefore a para-medical profession and must never become so: *it is medicine which is a para-nursing profession.* Clearly the Christian values which underlie such a statement are quite contrary to the para-medical developments in the nursing profession in the West based upon secular humanist values. The medicalization of nursing introduces the fatal (to nursing) possibility of arm's length caring.

At present it is often people who hold authority who may find that they have become cut off from their fellow human beings. The police are notable victims of inhuman attitudes by rioters and strikers. Bus drivers and nurses on duty may be assaulted.

In Britain we have become a society where it is possible for a nurse to write a book entitled *Patients are People*,[30] a most telling title. Who ever thought they weren't and why? The book is written to the point I am making. It is possible for the best-intentioned human relationships to be invaded by impersonal, functional, arm's length defences. One of the missionary societies[31] has issued a poster of a woman missionary cutting the hair of a tearful Amerindian woman. The caption reads:

We refuse to become the raw material whereby other people work out their own salvation.

Alienation

It is not only in formal caring relationships that distance may be kept but in neighbourly relationships also. The word 'alienation' means foreignness. It is now often used to describe this separateness, apartheid, aloneness, lostness, not belongingness which may affect city dwellers in their relationships with one another.

Our problem-centred approach to those who fall victims to illness, violence, drug abuse or unemployment may actually compound the problem. Our remedy is tainted with the sickness. At the heart of our Western culture is an alienating principle, an attempt to detach ourselves from others. Roszak writes:

> While the art and literature of our time tell us with ever more desperation that the disease from which our age is dying is that of alienation, the sciences in their relentless pursuit of objectivity raise alienation to its apotheosis as our only means of achieving a valid relationship to reality.[32]

Individualism is certainly one of our national characteristics. It has all the possibilities for variety and robust independence, as well as the weaknesses of competitiveness and isolation. Of course people rebel against being treated as objects, problems, patients, clients, voters or (as Beeching once described me and my fellow travellers) unprofitable weekend traffic! Young people in particular have protested at the whole system by widespread drop-out movements and violence.

When the wonderful uniqueness of every individual becomes cut off from the pool of human inter-relationships then alienation results and a society begins to face the nightmare of C. S. Lewis's fanciful description of hell in *The Great Divorce*: the further you went into the dull monotony of the place the further apart the houses got and the greater each individual's isolation from his fellows.[33] It is now a fact that loneliness is a major social problem in cities especially among elderly people.

There seems to be a close relationship between a loss of good neighbourliness in a society and the development of professional and voluntary carers. When the extended family and its network of care for one another, or the local community (a rural village, a street, or area in a city) with its neighbourly support disintegrates, it is replaced by statutory and voluntary services. A Minister of Community and Social Services in the Canadian Government observed at a conference in Ontario that

> . . . there is something inherently incompatible between community, in the sense that I have stipulated, and social services. It suggests that in a well-ordered community, social services (as they are currently conceptualized and organized) would not exist.
>
> This, of course, is not to say that the poor would not be cared for, or the aged, or the fatherless, or the retarded. It is to say rather that all of these and more would be cared for in a well-formed community as if those receiving care belonged there. They would be cared for by their friends and acquaintances with whom they feel a deep sense of identification. 'Services' in the organized sense would be supportive, supplementary and recessive.
>
> I am coming to suspect that the very creation of 'social services' is a sign not of social progress, but of disintegration; that creation of social services may not mark the existence of an enlightened community but rather represent the tombstone of community. It may mark the inability of a group of people to be a powerful enough community to care for one another without having to hire others to assume responsibility.[34]

When family, neighbourhood or community-solidarity fall apart, the gap is plugged but not healed by professional surrogate care. But it has been the realization that doing things *for* people may in fact make them dependent and rob them of responsibility, which has given birth to a whole new area of social service – community development. This takes seriously the need to work *with* people not simply *for* them. The rebuilding of community (or in village and rural areas the preservation of community) is a top priority for pastoral care. It is not enough to cure or rescue those who suffer from alienation. Christians must live a common life based on kingdom values which may leaven the society in which God has set them.

Perhaps what I have been discussing above is simply expressed in this poem. Behold an object!

The Handbag

An old and tattered handbag
With a hole and broken zip,
It's the only thing she salvaged
When she fell and broke her hip.
In a geriatric chronic ward
Sitting in a chair
She fumbles through the contents
With a melancholic air.
There's postcards from her nephew,
Some snaps and bills and chits,
A lot of empty envelopes,
Address book all in bits.
Her mirror (badly spotted)
Which she fearfully avoids,
A comb with several broken teeth,
A lump of pink jelloids.
Fifty-seven halfpennies,
And ninety-seven pence,
Thirty odd in tuppences:
Some spectacles (cracked lens),
A very faded photograph
Of her husband and her son –
Both are dead now many years
She's totally alone.
She's labelled 'SENILE DEMENT' –
'ARTERIOSCLEROSIS'
And 'FAECALLY INCONTINENT' –
Impressive diagnosis.
Which means she hardly speaks at all,
They call her 'love' and 'dearie',
She doesn't know what day it is
She only knows she's weary:
So fiddles with her handbag
And thumbs the contents through –
The postcards and the photograph
She's not sure who is who.

But the handbag is her very own.
It's her's and her's alone,
Without her battered handbag
Her whole world would be gone.

Change in our understanding of disease and illness[35]

Sometimes it is more important to know what kind of fellah has a germ than what kind of germ has a fellah (Shattuck).

In the area of sickness our society has moved from a pattern of *disease* where knowledge-about pathology shaped our responses, to a pattern of *illness* where knowledge-of the sufferer is more important. Both kinds of knowledge are needed, but we continue to try and treat illness as if it was disease because caring for ill people requires mutuality – the making of a costly relationship.

In rural areas of tropical climates it is diseases due to *disharmony with the natural environment* that most trouble people – such diseases as malnutrition, infections from dirty water like typhoid, and invasions by parasites such as malaria and worms. The diseases of poverty in fact.

In cities all over the world a new pattern of illness is emerging. As new standards of hygiene spread (improved housing, immunization programmes, clean water and food) many of the old diseases (cholera, diptheria, smallpox) come under control, but *new illnesses take their place.*

These city illnesses are due to *disharmony in the social environment,* that is, they are interpersonal in origin. They are illnesses due to urban stress (anxiety, nervous breakdown, high blood pressure, heart attacks), violence (suicide, wife and child battering) and addiction (tranquillisers, alcohol, smoking, heroin and overwork). During eight years in Ghana, I only saw one African with a duodenal ulcer and he got it while on scholarship in the United Kingdom! On a return visit twelve years later I saw as many Africans with ulcers in the hospital in Accra as you see in Western hospitals.

Of course some of the old types of disease persist in cities. Leukaemia and tuberculosis are still with us. New types of virus like AIDS appear. Poverty and its diseases still ravage city dwellers in the shanties. In a disaster situation like an earthquake, all the benefits of modern hygiene can be lost overnight and people plunged back into an era of the old pattern of disease with cholera and typhoid rampant.

Until recently we tended to understand interpersonal disharmony in individual terms such as neurosis or psychosis, using psychology to understand the *inward individual* aspects of the illness. But families and societies form a setting in which each individual person may be helped or hindered in making healthy relationships. Our individual health is rooted in the health of our family and society. Social studies have helped us to understand the *outward and shared* aspect of interpersonal illness. Understood in this way illness is called *psycho-social* and it is this pattern which dominates the Western world from North America to Britain, and Finland to New Zealand.

In the old pattern of disease we can often speak of a disease as if it was 'a thing in itself' ('there it is, that lump there'). But in psycho-social illness we are less certain what we are dealing with. People tell us how they feel ('I've got a pain here') but there may be nothing to see or touch. In fact we often cannot speak of disease at all, we must speak of *ill people*. Someone is ill (dis-eased) but has no disease.

A cancer or a parasite can be treated in one individual, but where can we locate the cause of anxiety, alcoholism, an ulcer, a heart attack, or an abused child? In the sufferer? The spouse? Work conditions? Debt? A broken home? Poverty, unemployment or the competitive society we have made together? These illnesses, like human beings, have fuzzy edges.

In the old pattern it is an expert who takes over and treats the disease: the doctor 'does something to' the patient. In the new pattern it is the victim who has to be persuaded to accept responsibility for 'doing something with' the helper. We might also see the approach of the helper in this new pattern as more feminine, cooperative and non-violent: whereas the medical approach is often masculine and violent.[36]

The new pattern of illness (I am using this word deliberately instead of disease) leads us to an understanding that human beings are not separate individuals. We are related to one another more like the members of a body. *Illness is shared*. It is not just the individual – viewed in isolation – who is ill, but the individual presents in his/her own body the symptom of the distress of his/her family, group or society of which s-he is a member.[37] Society expresses its distress in and through the body language of its individual members. Treatment must therefore look beyond the individual to the context – family, work and social relationships. *Growth towards health may lie not so much in the search for a specific drug as in determined efforts to change a style of life.*

A middle-aged man came for help to a city centre church.[38] He had had an anxiety neurosis for several years (that is, he felt anxious for no apparent reason: his heart would beat fast and he would break out into a sweat). When he underwent a sudden Christian conversion his anxiety neurosis cleared up. However within a few days of his recovery, his wife developed an anxiety neurosis – and it was on her behalf that he had come for help. Are we separate individuals? Or do we belong to one another so closely that we share our health and illness? Balint[39] gives clinical evidence of children presenting the illness of their parents. A child may throw an 'unexplained' temperature when there is friction between father and mother.

Hellberg[40] describes an incident in the casualty department of a hospital when four mangled teenagers, two girls and two boys, were brought in following a high speed car crash. 'Almost as if someone had touched a switch the hospital became alive' and all the resources of skill and technology were put to the task of first saving life, then mending bones and flesh, and finally to rehabilitation and discharge. But on the night of admission when the hospital chaplain contacted the parents of the four victims,

> they were either ignorant of what their children were doing, or did not care. He also found seven cases of divorce among the eight parents. No two parents were the natural parents of any one of the children. Most of the parents did not know that their son or daughter was out of the house . . . In a sense one can say that the tragic incident was less an accident than a predictable result of the situation. This also became obvious when a few weeks later one of the patients returned to the hospital with the same symptoms. Again her body was mangled as a result of a high speed car crash. The cure of the symptoms while constituting a technical repair, was not enough to solve the whole problem.

Slowly there are changes taking place in our understanding of what illness is. Howie[41] has pointed out that the Western medical approach to disease has developed a sophisticated system based on hospitals for diagnosing and treating disturbances in the human body. Today, particularly among family doctors (who see most illness in the community), there is developing a more 'behavioural' understanding of illness; that is, an approach which takes into account the way people live, their stresses, habits and attitudes as well as physical disease. This is an approach which does not draw hard and fast lines between physical, psychological and social factors in human disease; but sees illness as an attempt by a human being to respond to a *whole* situation which is experienced as hostile, and to re-establish harmony.

Basically it is *bòdies* (defined by a skin boundary) which are separate. *Persons* are centres of agency in a network of human relationships. If a change is taking place it is from seeing people as bodies to seeing people as persons-in-relationship. Such a change in our understanding of the person is likely to give rise to a better and more whole system of explanation of human illness than the traditional medical approach. However, the training of doctors proceeds on traditional lines, although the differences increase between training and the needs of people who go to their doctors (again the division between theory and practice).

In the army and police it is appreciated that a rising sickness rate may be due to low morale. If measures are taken to raise morale then the sickness rate falls. The traditional medical approach would be to train more doctors and to build more hospitals to treat the increased sickness. But tackling illness indirectly through raising morale is based on a different – 'behavioural' – understanding of the cause of illness: the emphasis is on the state of the person and their zest for life.

The passing of the first pattern of disease is a triumph. We know that no society will or should tolerate malnutrition and preventable disease. This is the autumn of materialism, rich with fruit.

But when the first pattern of disease has changed, the discovery that new kinds of illness take over has ushered in the winter of materialism. 'Man cannot live by bread alone'[42] is seen to be an iron exactment of life. Our humanity can perish amid plenty.

Salvation from sickness is always a triumph for which to give thanks but it is so often but one step in a long struggle towards fuller humanity. There are still the unresolved tragedies from which millions are not likely to be saved in the forseeable future. The middle-aged man, saved from his heart attack, may live on to experience the rejection of old age. The child, so brilliantly saved by a hole-in-the-heart operation, may fall a prey to urban stress or join the scrapheap of teenage unemployment.

Of course technology may bring further triumphs for millions, but a new pattern of illness awaits them and it is not one for which material solutions are likely to be found. It is not a pattern *from* which we are saved, but *in and through* which, often by suffering, we may grow towards fuller humanity. Siirala[43] has written a book entitled *The Voice of Illness*. Only as we listen to that voice and learn the lesson of the illness and change the conditions which gave rise to it, are we likely to grow individually and build a healthy society.

Many of the issues which I have raised could be explored by discussing: Is AIDS a disease or an illness? How would you prevent it?

In the whole area of psycho-social illness there are many people trying out different ways of coping (both individual and/or social). For example, giving emphasis to *prevention* (community development by social services, probation department, community policing); *treatment* (psychiatry, counselling, faith-healing); *care and problem solving* (social services); *long-term and crisis care* (voluntary societies); *punishment and rehabilitation* (courts and probation). Indeed it is the new pattern of illness that has brought into being new professions such as social workers, nurse practitioners and counsellors. But patterns of work in our Health Service tend still to be dominated by the traditional way of curing disease.

It is not enough to treat disease. We are in a new situation where the whole style of life is now recognized as contributing to health or illness. High morale is a sign of healthy human relationships. It is the building of human relationships, the building of healthy families, groups and nations, that requires more attention. It is essential to rescue pastoral care from its present one-sided concentration on remedial work (the old pattern of problem-centredness and treating people as things) to a new concern for building community (persons in relationship) in which ill and well people together may discover a sense of purpose and relatedness.

5 Culture

We do not experience things as they are: we experience things as we are (Talmud).

A further characteristic of present Western culture based upon secular humanism is its *invasiveness*. It is a dominating culture which is spreading worldwide. The reasons for this are complex. Clearly science and the technology dependent on it bring untold material benefits to humankind. To aspire to health care and clean water for all peoples of the world by the year 2000 is a great vision – and technically possible given the political will. The material prizes are great, but the spiritual dangers of cultural conquest are serious.

We have mentioned the motivation of scientists to control situations. Doubtless too there is an element of racism in our culture. For both these reasons we tend *to impose our own culture on others* as if it were universal. Yet we need other cultures with their different perceptions of the way the world is as a corrective to our own partial outlook.

When two cultures meet, as when European traders or missionaries went to Africa or when students from overseas come to Britain for study, there may be several possible outcomes:

Firstly, one people's ideas and ways of life may invade and destroy another people's culture: we would call this '*conquest*'. Writing before independence, Olivia Mukuna describes this process in Zimbabwe (then Rhodesia) which, apart from local details, has been part of the tragic history of Africa more generally:

> *Cultural invasion*, perhaps the most effective tool for oppression, is the imposition by the oppressor of his 'world view' on the oppressed. The oppressor's very strong ethnocentric attitude together with other conquest tactics manages to make the oppressed believe in his 'intrinsic inferiority'. (Early missionary attitude of condemning wholesale everything African as demonic and heathen made a significant contribution to cultural invasion in

Africa.) This belief in 'intrinsic inferiority' of one's culture leads to acknowledgement of intrinsic superiority of the oppressor who in this case is white. The result is not just alienation from oneself but from one's culture because the social 'I' has been challenged and upset. Manifestations of this 'intrinsic inferiority' include expressions of self-inadequacy. White or Western values became the standard measure, above all the white skin as a symbol of virtue and beauty (the latter especially exemplified by women using corrosive bleaching creams to make their skins lighter). Black becomes the accursed colour to the extent that God is condemned for having made one black. Doing things the Western or European way epitomizes this belief in the superiority of the oppressor's culture. Self inadequacy and degradation is expressed in statements like –Who am I, I am not a *human being*, I am only a *black* thing. The uneducated African speaking of his educated brother will say – He is educated, he is no longer a black man, he is 'white' or European. Thus, for the dehumanised African, to be is to be white. One can only be a human being of dignity when one is white and/or educated.[44]

It is in cities that Western culture is at its strongest. A pastor writes of the spread of Western values in Sarawak.[45] He describes three types of parish in the diocese: city, small town and village. In the *city* urbanization and secularism are deeply affecting the lives of the people. The young people have become money-orientated, resent authority, and the older generation has less and less control over them. This is contrary to the Asian cultural background and the old people get confused. In the *villages* life is still traditional and the old customs are observed. The elders have the final say and the young people observe the mores obediently. In the *town* there is an intermediate situation where depersonalization has not yet taken root and people still care for one another. Full exposure to the urban way of life has not yet eroded the traditional culture and the elders still have some control over the young people.

In many British cities young West Indians feel themselves under such kinds of white pressure to conform to acceptable social behaviour. They react violently against white society in order to preserve their own black identity and dignity, seeking rather their roots in Africa. Young Indian and Pakistani girls may find that their experience of more open relationships with boys in British schools conflicts with their own customs including arranged marriages. They may run away from home.

A tutor in a British nurse training school was taking a class of pupil nurses on the subject 'current affairs'. She decided to introduce a discussion on racism. Choosing a West Indian girl sitting in the front row she said: 'Now, imagine you are doing a dressing for a patient in the ward. You've just finished doing up the bandage and are putting things away when the patient in the next bed says in an unfriendly tone of voice: "Hey blackie, why don't you go back to the place where you were born?" – Now, what would you say, how would you handle that one?' At which the West Indian girl roared with laughter and in a broad local accent said: 'What! All the way back to Billesley?' (Billesley is a suburb in her city, just a bus ride down the road.)

When British people speak of the integration of immigrant cultures they often mean the slow conquest and assimilation of foreigners so that they become like us. A similar fate at the hands of invaders has threatened resident minorities – the Celts in Britain, the Maoris in New Zealand and the Indians in North America: but all these cultures have recently shown a resurgence of national pride in language, customs and spirituality.

Firstly, then, we have discussed how one culture may dominate, invade or conquer another. *Secondly*, when a people feels threatened by the strange ways of life which they encounter in another people, it may defend itself and its precious traditions by *withdrawal*. This can be a geographical withdrawal into a ghetto in a city or a 'promised land'. The ghetto may be a defended area within the mind when people become closed to new ideas (right or wrong) which are felt (often rightly) to be a threat to their own ways and sense of identity. Withdrawal may be the only way to preserve national pride, language and customs. It may be a healthy defence against a dominant and alien culture; or it may be a fanatical attempt to defend the indefensible by a deeply insecure people. The situation in Northern Ireland illustrates such deeply held divisions.

Thirdly, two different cultures may be strong enough to *inter-relate* in a mutual exchange of ideas and life style. Both peoples find they have much to give and receive from one another. Difference is experienced as an enrichment rather than a threat. This can be the strength of a united church of different denominations. Variation in traditions, such as styles of worship, brings enrichment: whereas any attempt at uniformity brings impoverishment.

In the world generally we are now in a period of sharp reaction to the invasiveness of Western cultural ideas (but not its science and technology). This has resulted, for example, in Black Theology being written by thinkers of African descent in South Africa and the USA. Asians have also developed their own viewpoint. Only when independence of thought is achieved may mutual exchange with the West become safe and creative, because people of different viewpoints may then enter dialogue in mutual respect. On the other hand, if a people withdraws itself too long from inter-cultural contacts it may become narrow, fail to realize itself as the people it truly is, and become unable to survive in a changing world.

It is not only theologians who have suffered from intercultural barriers to communication, artists have also made similar complaint:

> Speaking of the African dilemma in the area of artistic expression Olayinka observes that the African artist has a difficult time because his or her critics are in Europe and America; critics who expect the African artist to conform to conceptions which Europeans and Americans have of African art.
>
> In order to make it in the world of art, the African artist feels he or she is bound to those conceptions. But once the biases and prejudices are broken and the artist strikes an independent line, and once he or she has made it known that this is what he or she, as an African, feels should be one's expression as an artist, you will discover that they will take it as a shock. After some contemplation they start accepting you. The point is, at the initial stage you will have to suffer. But you have to be strong . . .[46]

The spread of the gospel has been involved in translation from one culture to another from the very first days when the sayings of Jesus, who spoke Aramaic, were interpreted into Greek. There was inevitably a loss of Jewishness – often untranslatable into a Greek framework of thought – in the ideas of Jesus.

Words taken out of their personal and cultural context become unreliable: translation is more than finding equivalent words in another language. It is the fruit of mutual knowledge of one another. Logical explanations have limitations with people whose communication is oral and more right-brain based. For them the story, ritual, drama and dance speak more deeply than logical argument. We know very little about the subtleties of inter-relationships between peoples of different cultures. Some fascinating research has been published in a New Zealand booklet entitled *Talking Past Each*

Other:[47] and Donovan's work with the Masai[48] is a vivid account of bringing the gospel to a strong pagan culture.

A pastor from Indonesia described the work of a member of her congregation with a gift of exorcism. Her consternation was great when she found herself in a group of Christians from many countries, few of whom believed in possession by evil spirits. The fact that her own belief accorded with beliefs recorded in the New Testament caused some discomfort to the disbelievers. Western culture has invaded many countries in the world. Indeed the very fact that students from Africa and India can come to this country to study theology indicates the extent to which they have adopted Western language, images and thought forms. Yet misunderstandings, bewilderment and hostility are not uncommon. There are wide gaps between cultures in attitudes to class, caste, foreigners, children, the elderly, and to evil, aggression, illness, authority, nature and death: in a word, to the understanding of what it means to be fully human. Perhaps we have made a significant step if we are honest enough to acknowledge such differences, to hold one another in mutual forgiveness and begin to find our differences *enriching* rather than threatening. Differentiation seems to be a pattern of God's working, rather than uniformity.

An illustration may be given of how differences between cultures can become fixed in structures. In the 1950s the first post-war influx of immigrants from the West Indies began to arrive in the UK. There was then a labour shortage and businesses like British Railways were recruiting workers in the West Indies. They came in their thousands and settled down to raise families in poor conditions in the big cities. The Christians among them got a shock: for they found that they were often not merely unwelcome to white congregations but actually the victims of racial prejudice. Separate black churches therefore began to develop alongside the white churches.

More recently the consequences of this separation became apparent. A meeting of some fifty black pastors was called together in a city to meet the Anglican Bishop of the Diocese. After listening to his address, the first question was put to him:

'You have in this city a Christian Council of Churches: why have you not invited us to belong?'
The frank answer was:
'Before this meeting I never knew you existed.'

6 Loss of Wholeness within the Self

It is no good asking what is the meaning of life because life isn't an answer, life is the question, and you, yourself, are the answer (Ursula Le Guin).

I 'come to myself' in relations with others (Ian Ramsey).

We have discussed the consequences of secularization in society, how it has affected the way we understand the world, and how it has resulted in loss of wholeness. We have described a division between theory and practice resulting in 'arm's length' relationships. At the heart of our search for health by scientific methods the limits of the new value system have been exposed: its methods can cure and prevent disease (a great blessing) but cannot imbue people with a sense of reverence, purpose or relatedness. We now speak in Britain of a *divided nation*. But the nation is a mirror of the inner world of its component members. The divided nation reflects a divided self.

When I was working at St Martin-in-the-Fields, I described[49] a situation which existed in the church on Sunday mornings. There was a soup kitchen in the crypt, to which eight hundred or more homeless people would come, depending on the weather. At 11.30, therefore, on a Sunday morning there were two congregations: a respectable one upstairs singing hymns, and a rather scruffy congregation downstairs (about twenty feet beneath the feet of the other) drinking soup, eating dry bread and (in wet weather) steaming off. Normally the congregations tended to arrive at different times, but a change of time for the service upstairs one Sunday led to the two congregations actually meeting by the doors. There were complaints.

I, of course, belonged upstairs; but I often wondered why. Maybe the only difference between 'us' and 'them' (for that is how apartheid corroded our views of one another) was that when I had a crisis I had friends: but when they had a crisis they were alone. So I stayed up and they went down. The difference could have been as narrow as that.

It was a stark and tragic separation between the haves and the have nots: a mini-mirror to the deep divisions between North and South in Britain, and between Western and Two-Thirds worlds. 'We', the upstairs congregation, out of our plenty provided badly needed food and shelter for 'them'. 'They', the downstairs congregation, represent the parts of ourselves that we either do not know or refuse to acknowledge. Our health, perhaps our sanity, depends upon others carrying the burden we refuse to carry. If I will not bear my own anxiety, I feed it into the common pool of our humanity, and someone more vulnerable than I am draws it out of the pool and lives it for me. Humanly speaking the vagrants in the soup kitchen are us.

Many of the volunteers for work in the crypt found it difficult to identify with the soup-drinkers. It remained 'us' and 'them'. Some of us found they held up a mirror for us to see ourselves. We might feel unaccountably angry with these good-for-nothing lay-abouts because within ourselves there is someone – a part of my very self – who would like to be a care-free truant, but I do not wish to acknowledge that stranger within. Or we might feel anxious because there is a stranger within my self who could become violent and what would happen if he surfaced and gained control? At least one volunteer retired to vomit; a most expressive way of saying 'This experience I cannot take into myself: I reject it.'

Every self which undertakes the task of integration – of becoming a whole person – has to come to terms with this shadow side of our nature; this dark man inside us. Jacob wrestled with his own shadow in the night, and – wounded – received a new name, Israel. Then and only then could he see the face of God in the face of his alienated brother Esau, instead of seeing his own projected hostility in his brother's face. Dewey writes:

> There is no other effective remedy for racism, religious or political fanaticism, or any of the other polarisations by which the world is torn apart at every level, from superpower confrontations to broken homes. 'Only when I have experienced myself as "dark" (not just as a sinner) shall I be successful in accepting the dark ego of my neighbour.'[50]

Only the integrated self can bear the pain and projected fears and hostility of others, transforming evil through suffering as Jesus did on the cross; thus assuming personal responsibility for part of the burden of being human – members one of another.

Underlying the above interpretation of the two congregations at St Martin-in-the-Fields is this Christian view of human beings as related to one another like the members of a body. We are like the different organs of a body which contribute variously and harmoniously to the whole. Our image of community in the Western world is very individualistic: we see human beings as related like marbles in a box. That is, those who live or work together are related because of proximity, but are 'really' separate and distinct. I mentioned previously how the corporate image of our human relationships makes more sense to a family doctor: experience in that field led me to suggest that illness is often shared.

It is we as members of society who together create our own social problems. The problem of the have-nots is our problem. The problem of psycho-social illness is our problem. The problem of violence is our problem. It is not a case of us and them, *we* are one humanity. That is the reality. But there are divisions within people and between people: that is the situation in which the church is called to heal.

In Part Two I have discussed the lack of wholeness due to secularism in Western society, and loss of belief in God's purpose for the world. In particular we have noted how this disintegration causes a division between theory and practice, faith and life. The objectivity of a scientific approach to people results in treating human beings as objects, and in concentration on treatment of disease at arm's length rather than on relatedness to ill people.

The dominance of Western culture and its powerful technology invades other cultures destructively and is spreading a one-eyed view of the world. The integrity of the self, which is at the heart of the wholeness of humanity, individual and social, is a free gift of God. But death and resurrection are the cost of receiving the gift, nothing less than the losing of life in order to save it.

Barbed Wire Men

It was Calvin who used the phrase 'the labyrinth of the mind'. Strolling through the labyrinth of my own mind I have tried to inspect the graffiti on the walls and have been surprised to find how often the subject of significant scrawls is *barbed wire*.

It is possible that the 1939/45 war helped to shape barbed wire as an image of *separation* in my mind. For me it sums up all the barriers and gaps which are erected to segregate, imprison or divide person from person. The word 'symbol' (=throw together) suggests association: but barbed wire suggests the opposite. Perhaps we should therefore speak of barbed wire as a '*diabol*' (=scatter), and its divisiveness as 'diabolic'. This poem sums up Part Two and points forward to Part Three.

Barbed Wire Men (A Holy Week Meditation)

I.

We are the barbed wire men!
Out! Out! Out!
Unsullied race of master minds,
Purest blood and whitest colour,
Here no defect mars perfection,
Here no dirt evades detection.
We are human, chosen race,
They are foreign, black of face,
We are barbed wire men!
We've built an iron curtain,
.Guard the frontiers! Man the towers!
None shall enter,
None intrude.
None shall rape our purity
None despoil virginity,
We are the barbed wire men!

2.

We are the barbed wire men!
In! In! In!
We are the ones who make the laws
Possess possessions, wealth and power.
Here no villain gets protection,
None here tolerates defection.
We imprison reds and spies
Guarding private enterprise.
We are barbed wire men!
We've built electric fences,
Guard the concentration camps!
None shall utter

None escape
None shall rob us of our peace
None disturb our life of ease,
We are the barbed wire men!

3.

We are the barbed wire men!
In! Out! In!
Wickedness is banned within,
Observe the ten commandments!
Black and white, divided minds,
Evil thoughts behind drawn blinds,
We are sane and able,
They are mad, unstable —
We are barbed wire men!
We've built secure salvation schemes,
Sin confessed and heaven insured.
Deny the shadows!
None obtrude!
None our model goodness spoil
None our upright virtues soil,
We are the barbed wire men!

4.

Barbed wire men your place is gone!
In *is* out!
Out *is* in!
Impure purity of heart
Lightens shadows, shadows light.
Tongues for the dumb! Eyes for the blind!
Free the Gulags of the mind!
Burst the bars! Unlock the mad!
Integrating good and bad.
Barbed wire men, the hour has struck!
Your diabol has lost its power
To symbol great with wholeness —
Veil of temple, rent in twain,
Shatters man-made separation
Twixt the good and bad creation.
Barbed wire men, the world is one!

PART THREE
Everyday Theology

In Part Three we go on to discuss how the pattern which connects all created life may be enhanced in Western culture through Christian faith and life. But first, *theology itself needs attention* because it is deeply marked by the secular disintegration of today. There is a rift between academic study and everyday practice.

We describe theology as a way of exploring life in the light of faith in God (ch. 7), rather than as a subject to be studied. Theology therefore needs rescue from the specialists, and the everyday use of theology by Christians living in the modern world could provide the thrust towards a new theology (ch. 8). The relegation of religion by secular society to the private sphere of life also gives theology a special responsibility for integrating personal care and political action (ch. 9).

When Western theology is viewed in a world context (ch. 10) it is seen to be limited in its perspective and in need of complementary views from other cultures to gain a more whole perception of God's purpose for the world.

7 What is Theology?

Many different writers have tried to define theology. Some selected examples will help to stir the imagination:

Martin Luther: Not reading books or speculating but living, dying and being damned make a theologian.

John Drury: The recipe for making theology is simple: God and man. A theologian is nothing more nor less than a person who is interested in these two beings and how they belong together.

Karl Barth: Theological work does not merely begin with prayer and is not merely accompanied by it; in its totality it is peculiar to and characteristic of theology that it can only be done in the act of prayer.

Kosuke Koyama: Theology is a reflection on history in the light of the word of God . . . There is no private theology. Our theology is a community production.

Ian Ramsey: Other disciplines will be judged primarily on the quality of their articulation; theology will be judged primarily on its ability to point to mystery . . . Eccentricity, logical impropriety is its life blood.

Margaret Kane: Theology is the continuing search for meaning.

John Austin Baker: Theology is interpreting existence in terms of God. There is therefore no private stock of subject matter.

'What is theology?' is a question which can deceive us into a wrong approach from the beginning. The use of the word theology is convenient but misleading because it suggests that theology is a subject, a collection of principles, concepts and history: whereas in reality theology is a way of exploring life which requires our whole involvement in thought, word and deed. The particular discipline of mind and action which is called theology (as I am inviting you to regard it) may also be described by a verb like 'theologize' to indicate an activity. I think the use of a verb theologize rather than a noun theology comes closer to the biblical way of thought. (In the Old Testament the Hebrews did not define an abstract concept like 'righteousness', but described the actions of their God as he *acted righteously* in matters such as rescuing the nation from slavery, feeding the hungry, caring for the fatherless and widowed.) We could say that there is no such thing as theology, there are only people doing theology. This would point to the risk of making a static object out of a living process.

I prefer to describe theology from different points of view rather than trying to define it. Bishop Westcott held that theology is only pure when it is applied. By 'applied' he meant the close relation between theory and practice. R. E. C. Browne wrote:

> In other words we do not theologize about theology but we think theologically about all men and all things; we think and speak and act theologically about such things as bread and stones, love and hate, death and life.[51]

Theology is thinking about life in the light of our faith in God. From the different descriptions by various writers given above we may describe two activities within theology which can be distinguished but must not be separated:

Firstly, there is the activity of *theologizing life* in the light of our trust in God. For example, when Peter visited the house of Cornelius in Caesarea the Holy Spirit was given to his Gentile listeners.[52] Such a cross-grained event caused questions in the church. At Jerusalem Peter had to put before the Jewish church 'the details point by point':[53] he told them the full story. The gathered church had also then to understand the facts told in the story, to make sense of them and to learn from them. After such a discussion they concluded:

> God can evidently grant even the pagans the repentance that leads to life.[54]

This was a lightning shaft from experience into the heart of traditional theology: salvation was believed to belong to the Jews and here was God giving it to Gentiles. Lessons had to be learnt from such a surprising event in which they discerned God to be at work, leading his people forward in a new way. The old theology was now rendered false by experience.

Experience.
— and theology.

In the Book of Acts (a significant title), God is understood to reveal the divine nature not in propositions but in events: those present theologize the event. Both event and story are rooted in language and soil, so that theologizing is a very local affair, closely related to particular situations, particular times and particular places. Hughes Smith[55] has used the term 'Open Cast Theology' to indicate this practical application to local situations. I have preferred the term *everyday theology* or everyday Christianity. There is a danger that everyday theology may become *too* local, and it always needs stories about experiences from the wider church for comparison and possible correction.

Secondly, there is *the study of theology*. What happened in the house of Cornelius came first, then the story (including the conclusions of those present), then the gathered church in Jerusalem theologized the material brought to them. But we are already in a different situation to the house of Cornelius. This is not where the event happened, but a long way away in a city. We are one step back, as it were, from the local situation: and the people discussing the story and judging the meaning and implications of what has happened were not themselves witnesses. When the theologizing is done there may be a new understanding which can be shared with others in some new action, a letter or a piece of theological writing. The story becomes part of the tradition of the church and is then translated and sent to Christian churches all over the world, and is also handed down to the next generation.

These kinds of second-hand reflections can then be studied at third hand (and so on) by other Christians who may or may not have experienced something similar in their own place. The purpose of 'telling the story' is to help the hearers to turn to the mystery themselves. They may have to change their own attitudes and behaviour in the light of new experience.

Luke's description of what happened at Caesarea and the subsequent reflections of Peter and the early church have become part of the theology which students learn about in a university or seminary today. It becomes part of the material studied for examinations and degrees in theology. Theology in this sense is necessarily more abstract. To tell the story, to communicate the fruits of local theologizing from one person to another, from one congregation to another, from one culture to another, from one generation to another, requires that concepts be thought out, principles enunciated and doctrines hammered out which can enshrine the experience of the church and the meaning of events for others. This abstract theology – a kind of shorthand account of the experience – enables inter-church and inter-cultural dialogue to take place, experience to be shared and affirmed or disagreed with, and stories to be passed on to the next generation. But it only bears fruit when related to life-experience again ('this is my story, too') and lived out in particular local situations.

This means that all theological statements are provisional; that is, they are bound in time and place to the age, culture, and language in which a Christian community struggles to express how the living God has impinged upon the lives of its members. It can also happen that in the light of changes in self-understanding or in a different age and culture, people might misunderstand the meaning or understand it differently. Peter has described what happened, Luke has recorded it. Peter and the Christians with him in Caesarea might have misinterpreted the event, hence the need for the church in Jerusalem to cross-check a local experience. Consequently it has become, in the Book of Acts, part of the history of the church in the scriptures, which has thrown light for all generations of Christians on God's way with 'strangers', immigrants or settlers. The incident quickens our own sensitivity to ethnic minorities and their needs in our own day and city: as a result of which Hollenweger[56] has pioneered theological research and reconciliation between black and white churches in European cities and elsewhere.

If theories and ideas are not referred to actual situations in contemporary life, then this kind of theology may become a game people play. It is possible for academic theologians to theologize theology: but such theology may be dead. One could write a thesis on forgiveness, but not know it as a life-experience. It is here that the gap between ideas and actions, academic study and practical application, the ideal and the real world, grows. Indeed one way of distinguishing between truth and fantasy is by action (that is, by exploring the everyday world).

The stories of the Christian church need to be made sense of in terms of each culture and situation where the church is at work: and to be made sense of by each generation in its turn. This involves theologizing life in the light of our trust in God. Theologizing life – closing the gap between theory and practice – is essential for the vitality of the study of theology.

Five things seem to me to be important in all this:

First, in the example given (Peter visits the house of Cornelius), it is not only an individual (Peter) who must make sense of his vision[57] and its relevance to what has happened and its effects on his own life-situation; but his experience and questions are also shared by the local groups of Christians in Caesarea and Joppa. Then Peter has to share the story of what happened and their deliberations on the matter to the church more widely. *The theological reflection and conclusions are corporate*: they are those of the community of faith, not just those of an individual. 'There is no private theology.' Our individual understanding needs the enrichment and/or correction of other different points of view.

Secondly, everyday theology (theologizing life), because it is undertaken by the community of faith, is a *Christian activity*. In the first instance we learn how to do it through our Christian apprentice-ship in the local church. It is part of our everyday Christianity. It cannot (I think) be done by an unbeliever. Studying the conclusions which Christians reach *may* be done by any scholar. In the account of Peter's experience in the house of Cornelius unless you read Greek you are dependent on someone to translate the original book in which this story is written. The translator needs to be a good Greek scholar but not necessarily a Christian (although this is arguable). In the study of scripture and tradition many people with secular skills and knowledge such as interpreters, historical critics, archaeologists, sociologists, and anthropologists may bring light to bear upon situations in which theologizing life has been done and recorded by our predecessors. Certainly if we take Barth's description of theology seriously – 'that it can only be done in the act of prayer' – the activity of theologizing life is part of a Christian's day to day spirituality as thought, word and deed are submitted to the inspiration of the Holy Spirit. There is an intuitive dimension to theology which makes use of the right side of the brain: the whole person is involved in response to God.

Thirdly, our ability to theologize varies with our *knowledge and experience*. New Christians may begin to theologize their lives as soon as they find faith. Their beliefs can be simple. They do not wait until they have read Augustine, Irenaeus, Thomas Aquinas, Kierke-gaard, Barth, Tillich and . . . Indeed many Christians are illiterate or belong to oral cultures and are well capable of theologizing their experience and telling others their conclusions. They theologize from the beginning according to their light, because it is the essence of Christian faith to live it every day. Christianity is a way of life, not an ideology. And our light grows as we mature in faith. This is not to repudiate those who are Christian thinkers, ancient and modern: nor to deny that Christians need to study and grow in their tradition to the end of their lives. It is to be realistic about where one begins and what is possible.

There will be Christian groups therefore who theologize their lives, believing in the verbal inspiration of the Bible because they have not yet encountered or have rejected modern biblical criticism. There are thousands of congregations in all parts of the world at this time who are unlikely in their life-time to have to wrestle with the problem of Genesis and Darwin: but their children may have to. This is not to deny the validity of their theologizing life, but it may well cause their clergy difficulty, particularly those who have undergone a Western-type seminary education: for it is clergy who nurture their congregations in the skill of theological reflection on the situation. There are likely to be people in one and the same congregation with very different amounts of knowledge to bring to the task: and different ways of thought. People who think magically do not cease to do so because they have become Christians. On the contrary they may now think magically (for example) about the sacraments.

The Bible stories, however, may be understood and used at different levels; and its history, songs, poetry and myths are understood differently by people of different cultures and at different times. The Bible communicates its message through *many different media*: some readers respond to poetry and myth, some to history and logical arguments, and others to proverbs, story or prayers. It communicates by a rope of many strands, not a chain of linked arguments.

Learning to be a Christian is not a matter only of taking a course of instruction; that is the way of the world. The Christian learns to live as a Christian 'in the Way' and therefore learns like an apprentice not a student.

Propositions about God and his purposes are always partial and provisional because the nature of God is revealed to fallible human beings who change over the centuries. God is therefore always working with people through partial truths – sometimes even through mistaken (as later generations subsequently discover) or disputed ideas of contemporary knowledge. Part of the burden of being human is our partial knowledge: but God accommodates his relationship to our very particular situation. The vital spirituality of mentally handicapped people is a constant rebuke to our over-dependence on written and spoken words in communicating our faith.

Fourthly, in the biblical tradition *word and deed* are seen as two aspects of one reality. God's first initiative was the word/deed act of creation. '*He spake the word and it was done.*' God's most detailed theological statement was made in Jesus – in living flesh and blood.

Likewise some of Jesus' most profound theological statements ('thinking about life in the light of his faith in God') were deeds: like the healing of the man with a withered arm on the Sabbath,[58] or the healing of a paralytic by the forgiveness of sins.[59] And this theology belonged to the crowds. The religious authorities stumbled over them, but the crowds understood. It was their language. They gave praise to God.[60]

Fifthly, the study of theology *and* everyday theology *belong together.* Lay Christians who seek to understand and live the Christian way will theologize their work, social issues, family life and citizenship. This is of first importance because this is what theology is for. Truth is lived truth as well as understood truth.

Theologians in university departments and seminaries, together with ordained ministers and lay people educated in theology, are resources for the laity to enable members of congregations to grow in their ability to theologize life (individually, with each other, and with unbelievers) in order to respond actively to God. Thus theology is seen to be an exploratory discipline to enable human beings to live effectively and gloriously. It is in pastoral studies that theology is re-discovering a connection between faith and life because acts of human care require both competent theory and practice.

The interdependence of study and everyday theology is like the interdependence of map makers and explorers. Academic theology is like armchair map-making, comparing, criticizing, questioning and re-drawing the always faulty sketch maps brought back by ex-plorers. But the revised maps need constantly to be checked, corrected and revised by explorers on the ground. If in this book I am giving primacy to the explorers' work, that is for three reasons: (*a*) Theology is for explorers: that is, for people who seek to live the Christian life: The map makers are backroom servants without whom the explorers may get lost. (*b*) In British society theology has been captured by the map makers and many explorers have forgotten the value of maps. There is a balance to be restored by developing explorers who are able once again to use the excellent modern maps to theologize their lives. (*c*) I am writing this book more for explorers than map makers: but because of their interdependence I hope map makers may also find the book helpful. Indeed I hope many of them will find my distinction offensive and will claim to be both map makers and explorers.

Unless theory and practice are seen to combine in the arena of Christian living, theology must inevitably become withdrawn from the personal, social, and political concerns of the day into an academic ghetto. It becomes a subject to be studied rather than a searching way of thought, word and deed. Study can become wrapped up in the past, just as everyday theology can become wrapped up in the present. Both are needed to discern how to respond to God now and in the future. One of the prime tasks of ministers is to mediate between theologians whose scholarly study of theology perpetually advances, and lay Christians who too often imagine that theology is an expert's business. *The study of theology* is certainly an expert's business: but the day by day use of theology to reflect on (*theologize*) living issues is every Christian's business.

In 1963 there was public controversy after the publication of Bishop John Robinson's book[61] about belief in the resurrection of Jesus: and again in 1984 after the enthronement of the Bishop of Durham. This raised the question of the nature of belief. Belief that the resurrection of Jesus actually took place – a unique event by any account – is not *only* a matter of accepting the story as told in the gospels. That is a 'yes' or 'no' matter to recorded events, a kind of believing from the outside. It is theoretical belief. It is arm's length theology. Many Christians are pressured into this sterile kind of belief because they are made to feel guilty if they have doubts about the details of the story. But what power has such outside believing by itself to influence our lives and behaviour? We are entitled to ask 'What practical difference would it make if we were to believe it?' If the answer is nothing, then the matter might as well be a meaningless fantasy.

There is also an *inside* believing of the resurrection which is not just 'head' belief but also 'heart'. We too can *experience* life-through-death in the everyday. Indeed baptism re-enacts that real Christian experience of painfully dying to old attitudes and ways of seeing the world, and rising to newness of outlook, newness of values, newness in belonging to others in the community of the church. It is a death of our old identity and a resurrection to new personhood. Head *and* heart belief in the resurrection, not only as a past event in the life of Jesus but also embodied as the key to suffering love today in the everyday, is part of my story too. I believe with head and heart – that is with my whole reason. I am a participant knower.

Everyday theology involves many interdependent activities. I find Deek's description[62] of the life of faith helpful. Writing of education in theology, he describes three main ingredients which must be pursued at the same time: the records of past theological thinking which we have received (*story*), the world around us (*context*), and knowledge of ourselves (*people*). To do theology, people have to make sense together of what is going on in their lives where they are (context), in the light of their trust in God. The scripture, worship and doctrines of the church (story) shape how people think about God. How people think about God shapes the nature of their trust, for fear or for love.

Let us consider these three points in turn:

1. Story

Dwell on the past and you'll lose an eye. Forget the past and you'll lose both eyes (Russian Proverb).

Lorenz in his study on aggression[63] has pointed out how the development of speech has changed man's evolution because it enables new knowledge and insight, with the changes that follow, to be passed down from one generation to another in story and drama. It is therefore equivalent to the inheritance of acquired characters which cannot (in biological evolution) be passed on in the genes. However the stories are not imprinted on blank minds: they are *learned* – often tacitly – by lively minds with different memories in a different context. No wonder our children come up with new perceptions of familiar stories.

I am using the word 'story' to cover all the ways in which Christianity (or any other religion) is handed down from one generation to another. In the light of what it receives, every generation wrestles with truth in its own time and place, learns more of God (perhaps), glimpses signs of the coming of his kingdom;

catches a vision of what the heart yearns for, and passes on to its own children some hardly won clue as to what being human means, some chink of light on the nature of God and people and their interrelationships. Or, of course, makes a thorough mess of life, misses opportunities and is swamped with suffering or blinded by apathy and becomes an awful warning to its children. In either case we hand on the scriptures which we received – a record of God's self-revelation and of God's purposes in another time and place. We hand on historical records and writings, church history, books of the early Fathers and of others down the ages. A great mass of written records, stories, teaching and testimony. In addition to written records there are oral history and stories, rituals, songs and dances which in some cultures are the main way of transmitting the tradition. There is also worship, whose drama tells a story both verbally and non-verbally; and there is the style of congregational and family life which may speak louder than any words because it forms the visible basis from which words are spoken and to which words refer.

It has been said that stories are like cash for ourselves, but like savings in the bank for our children. Each generation has to get them out of the bank and cash them in terms of their meaning for contemporary life. For example, what cash value has the story of the resurrection for a Christian of today working in industry or a hospice for the dying? Part of the process of everyday theology is to understand this life-through-death as a pattern for living today. However, doctrines are made for people not people for doctrines: and indeed there may be a generation for whom some of the stories are cold. But they will be passed on as received because in a new situation in another culture on another day they may become hot, and then their insights may be able to save a generation from mistakes and suffering, even death. In the wider Christian church, one of the important functions of the ecumenical movement is that we are able to supplement and correct one another's stories, and grasp a deeper meaning of life together. Inter-faith dialogue carries such search for meaning even deeper and wider.

In our own day, changes in culture are so great and so rapid that there is a very serious gap between the stories as received and life as it is being lived. In the West it is rarely possible for long past writings to speak directly to us in our day and age, for example about things like test-tube babies, computerization or worker participation in industrial management.

On the other hand, the traditions of prayer, healing, reconciliation and counsel reach back into biblical times. The human story has been painfully written through millenia in a continuous thread of suffering and joy. The thread is not broken.

There is a constant change in the context and in people. History grows. Century by century God reveals new aspects of the divine nature and purpose so that fresh discoveries in one age become the story of a succeeding age. For the Christian church this emphasises the skill and determination needed to bridge the gap between scholars, well versed in Christian tradition, and daily-life Christians. They need one another.

We are building history for our successors and they too will think differently from ourselves. Therefore, as Newbigin writes: 'Theology is a continuous conversation between the believers of today and the believers of yesterday.'[64]

2. *Context*

This is the living, changing world of daily life in which we theologize. In every age the stories handed down are there to be made sense of in terms of the context – for myself and my family, colleagues, fellow church members and citizens. The context of this book is a city in the Western world in the last part of the twentieth century; and because of its prime importance as a bit of the world which God loves, some description of this has been made in Chapter 1. We theologize in a situation both in time and place: in a particular culture, language and world view.

In the university of this city we have students on a Pastoral Studies Course from many different countries (see Appendix 2, pp. 223–224). They too have to make sense of the Christian tradition in their own situation, in their own particular culture, language and world view. This can result in very different interpretations of what the traditions and scriptures mean. For example, the Bible records quite a lot about speaking in tongues, about dreams, visions and miracles – notably the healing of the sick. In twentieth-century Western culture as well as in African and Asian cultures these things continue to happen. But there are different ways of understanding and explaining what happens. I have already mentioned the example of conflicting views about 'spirit possession' and exorcism between an Indonesian pastor and other Western Christians. I have tried to explain elsewhere[65] how two quite different ways of understanding the disturbed behaviour of someone – as possession or as hysterics – can exist side by side among Christians: and how the kind of pastoral care which is given will depend upon how you 'see' the sufferer's predicament. The conflict between different views is unlikely to be settled intellectually without some new light from the fruits of practical care – sweating it out, in fact, in the context where people suffer and rejoice together.

3. People

The Christian story however cannot be made sense of today in terms of life in a city, except in and through living people who are thinking and talking, loving and hating, working and playing, rejoicing and suffering, being born and dying, as members of the Body of Christ and as citizens of no mean city. It is *people* who make sense of the story for their own lives. People are young or old, stupid or sensible, selfish or self-giving: and people are fallible. Theologizing is a human activity, responsive to the good, and vulnerable to the bad in people.

In the New Testament much emphasis is laid on people's ability to 'see' or 'not to see', to 'hear' or 'not to hear'. We may see an event with our eyes but not really 'see' it (i.e. make sense of it) unless there is an inner readiness. An event can be like a seed falling into rich soil, or on to a tarmac road. Paul Valery has written:

> Nothing can seduce us, nothing can attract us – nothing makes our ears prick up, nothing arrests our glance – nothing is chosen for us among the multitude of things, and nothing disturbs our soul that does not in some way pre-exist in our being or is not secretly expected by our nature.[66]

Readiness or unreadiness to see or hear a truth is a complex matter. Inborn or acquired prejudice may block our understanding of people who are different from ourselves in religion, denomination, sex, class or race. One woman member of a national inter-church committee, for example, senses that some clergy simply cannot 'hear' a woman speaking. The opinion of a black person may similarly be disregarded. Our innate or acquired sense of authority may blind us to the human or inhuman nature of some action, belief or custom (like the Pharisees who were angered when Jesus healed sick people on the Sabbath, or like the behaviour of guards in a concentration camp).

Immaturity through lack of experience or slow personal development may hinder our readiness. People are strongly motivated to understand death when they have encountered it: before they see someone die, death is something to be known about with the head – it happens to other people – but it is not yet wholly grasped with understanding of head and heart that this is the way I shall go.

Everyday theology is not simply an intellectual matter but involves the whole of a person. An attack of flu may depress our insight because our bodies are involved in our fitness for intuitive activity. Our theologizing will always therefore reflect our own lack of wholeness, but it will also reflect our gifts and strengths. R. E. C. Browne writes:

> What a scientist does when he is not doing scientific things is as important as what the artist does when he is not painting. A theologian is a better theologian if he is something of a scientist and something of an artist because his task is to be an expert in living rather than an expert in theology. Theology depends on science and art to bring hidden treasures to light. Scientists and artists should be depending on the theologian's belief that it is possible to make sense of human experience despite frequent evidence to the contrary.[67]

Paulo Freire in his adult literacy work[68] in South America used the word 'conscientization': that is, the birth of new awareness in people, often in a community, about a situation and their involvement in it. The word also contains the element of 'conscience', which suggests that a person's sense of responsibility for some new behaviour is quickened. By learning to read they are enlightened and enthused to change their situation. There is in this process both an *inward* personal growth, and a new way of looking at the *outward* situation: both a personal and a political discovery. It is a true self-realization because it may involve both the growth of the individual and the group to which he or she belongs, and change in their common life. Learning to theologize is a similar awakening of a person and their group: it is akin to the conscientization which accompanies learning to read. Both involve the suffering of inward and outward change.

When Barth described the activity of theology as rooted in prayer he was referring to the work of a Christian community which is committed to God's work in the place of its calling. A group may pray together about the situation in which they find themselves. Prayer can put the whole matter into the long-term context of God's purpose in the world; action and understanding do not depend only on the local church – it is part of a wider purpose. Prayer also helps to retain a sense of responsibility before God, which is not always easy to keep in a discussion where information and intellectual argument command full attention. On the other hand prayer can include disciplined thought, sharp argument and responsible decision. It is not always easy to draw the line between what is prayer and what is not prayer. Often understanding and action in a situation is intuitive rather than logical, and intuition is formed by prayer and makes vision possible. When a group turns to discuss what to do, prayer (silent or spoken) may help the group to be obedient to what is so far clear about the will of God. The first step may be difficult but further clarity and power may well await the taking of the first step. Prayer may help a group to cope with anxiety in the face of such action.

A local church congregation in a city decided to form a group who would pray regularly for the sick. They met weekly and because there was a large psychiatric hospital in the parish they included its work in their intercessions. Praying for a hospital is pretty vague, so they discovered more about the place, and prayed for named members of staff and patients. Then they heard one of the psychiatrists saying that many of his patients were long-term inmates and one of their greatest needs was 'to be in touch with normal people'. So the group began to visit some of the patients who had no visitors. There followed the occasional return visits to the homes of the prayer group.

To the surprise of the prayer group (they had the grace to laugh about it) some of the people for whom they were praying became well enough for discharge to the community. The group found itself involved in befriending them, accompanying them shopping, and easing their loneliness and the anxiety of an open society.

The prayer group could now be said to be involved in the rehabilitation of mental patients. This was a long way from praying for the sick. But because they were obedient to an unfolding task to which God called them, they were led forwards from timid prayer to confident personal relationships – a step by step growth in maturity and Christian commitment. If you had asked them in the beginning to help rehabilitate mental patients, they would have run a mile!

This prayer group consisted, in the first instance, of members of the congregation who were interested in healing, and their theology of healing drew its inspiration from the healing miracles of Jesus. This is where they began. They were however open to see what the Holy Spirit was actually doing in their midst, and were realistic about their own contribution. *Their theology followed their experience.* If they set out with the expectation of miracles, they quickly discovered the demands of suffering love and the resources of prayer and mutual support with which to sustain their 'prayer and care' as they now described it: word and deed became one.

There is here an important change in the use of their theology. Their faith began with its centre in the Bible and hopes of 'greater works than these shall ye do'. But the reality of a twentieth-century psychiatric hospital provided them with immediate human needs to be met. Their faith became centred in the everyday and the Bible enabled them to see their responsibility in terms of prayer, then service, then friendship. Their theology had moved from head knowledge to a living faith of head and heart: from theory about *what God could do* to discernment of *what God was actually doing*.

The congregation then went on to theologize the whole notion of 'mental health' and how it might be promoted in the local community. Another theological shift from works of rescue to asking 'How can we build a community which enhances mental health?' . . . but that is another story.

I will conclude this section on 'people' by observing that the corporateness and right brain imaginativeness which are marks of many African people, and the individuality and left brain logic which are marks of many Western people, are both needed in theology. Both are differently gifted members of the wider family of nations.

Three areas involved in everyday theology have now been described; stories, context and people. In his original article Deeks described the third area as 'knowledge of ourselves'. I have put 'people' because I wished to discuss some wider issues of which self-knowledge is only one. I want to guard against individualistic tendencies in theologizing which can trap Western spirituality in a false self-centredness. I want also to retain the sharp insight which resulted in the Pastoral

Studies Course being called 'Pastoral *Studies*', so that it can hold up its head in a secular university and engage in the mutual criticism of disciplines between colleagues. Browne[69] suggests that a theologian must 're-create for his age the image of man, and must propose standards by which others may test that image'. This is a task which can only be undertaken if a theologian is learning as much as s-he can from artists, scientists and philosophers. It also requires that the theologian integrates thought and life. But theology needs *democratization* if it is to become a living theology for everyday use by lay Christians: its present development by specialists is a triumph of scholarship, but an impoverishment of everyday Christianity.

The tradition of the Christian way of life reaches forward from the past into people's lives in our cities today, and through us into the lives of our children and grand-children. I propose now to discuss further how theology may hold together theory and practice (ch. 8), political action and personal care (ch. 9) in one whole discipline of thought, word and deed. But this can only happen if theology itself is whole. Western theology alone is *not enough*. We also need the contribution of other peoples in a greater inter-cultural theology (ch. 10).

8 The Unity of Theory and Practice in Theology

Without both wings the bird cannot fly.

Everyday theology

When the old cathedral in Coventry was burnt down during a bombing raid by the German Air Force, the Dean walked round the smouldering ruins next morning, and standing where the altar had been – amid a tangled mass of charred beams fallen from the roof – he chalked on the blackened wall

'FATHER FORGIVE'

Tradition and tragedy met within the heart of a man who responded, as Jesus had, to the destructiveness of hatred with words of reconciliation.

On that morning the Dean faced the grim facts of the situation. But he also recognized the truth of the situation: that God, who is able to bring life out of death, is present in the facts of every situation. He therefore claimed the promise of forgiveness and forgave his enemies.

He then turned to share his insight with his colleagues and to work out with them over months and years what obedience to that insight meant for them in practical terms. To write his theological reflection on the wall was to start a determined and costly long-term plan of rebuilding not only a cathedral but also a post-war programme of reconciliation between citizens (especially young people) of Coventry and Germany: this was to include an International Conference Centre as part of the new cathedral's resources.

There is a growing literature from writers who theologize life. I mentioned before the book *Waterbuffalo Theology* which enshrines in its title the interwovenness of theology and daily life. Margaret

Kane in the UK[70] has explored the relationship between theology and industrial life; she concludes that the necessary skills for theologizing such situations in groups of Christian and non-Christian laity together hardly exist.

Simon Barrington Ward gives an example of such a situation[71] where a member of staff in a university in Africa found herself the only Christian on a small but courageous group set up to help the victims of a severe oppression. All the others – some of them among the most apparently fervid and vocal – had dropped out and vanished away. There she was with a small group of agnostics and atheists, her solidarity with them their common concern, their common humanity. Yet there seemed to be something they wanted of her – something that only she could give. 'What does the Bible say about that?' the chairman would ask her mockingly as each new issue arose. But behind the teasing there seemed to lurk somewhere a real desire to know. It was as if in her very presence she offered some curious kind of security, a wistful hint of some transcendent ground whereof perhaps she knew, and he was unaware. It was only gradually that she came to realize, as did the others in the group to a greater or lesser degree, that here was a genuine, if painfully searching, exchange. She needed the courage of their love; they needed the assurance of her faith.

Theologizing life may be very simple yet profound. For example, some peasants in the Philippines met and reflected on the land problem in the light of their faith in God.

When Jesus started his 'organisation', with all his wisdom, he chose as first leaders the peasants and the fishermen [not the famous or the powerful]. So, I say, the importance of the peasants is recognised not only before society but in the eyes of God too. The problem, however, is that, too often, the peasants themselves do not realise their own importance.

The voice of Mang Jose is emphatic: We must now wake up to our own importance and dignity, and unite in saying that we can forge our own destiny.

Another peasant in the same meeting objects: If God loves us so much that we have become his first favourites, how come we are so poor and exploited, how come we suffer so much injustice. Is this His way of showing us His love?

In answer Mang Jose says: The God who loves us is Creator. But we cannot pray to Him 'up there' and say: 'God, Creator, you love us; we have a land problem, please create more lands!' For, though He is indeed Creator, He wants us to co-create with Him.

He makes the crops to grow, but He will not make it grow unless we plant it. He will not even create a single human being without the co-creative help of a man and a woman. Neither will He create a just, humane society, unless we do our part and struggle for liberation from landlordism and usury and other oppressive forces.[72]

Such reflection leads to a conclusion about political involvement which is costly in the context of life in the Philippines.

In 1977 the Rev Dr Anthony Bird set up an experimental medical practice within the National Health Service (see Appendix 1 pp. 221–222). Theology and life together shaped the choice of site, the size and lay-out of rooms, and the style of medical work in his Health Centre. Because the work was thought of as 'medical mission', a terraced house in an ordinary street in an under-doctored area of the inner city was chosen, where the bulk of the patients are Asian immigrants. Dr Bird writes:

'They that are sick' is how the A.V. translates the Greek words . . . taken from Luke 5.31. 'Those who have it bad' is a more literal rendering, and points us to the evidence that Jesus' mission was not only to the outcast, but primarily so. If there be any truth in the frequent assertion that doctors are modern society's priests then the biblical insistence that the poor and outcast of society are the particular concern of God ought to be reflected in medical priorities. An inner city practice has the striking advantage that it caters for a rich variety of outcasts and is therefore well placed to sing the Magnificat of divine responsibility in such a setting. There are those ostracized by the religious and racial moralities and customs of their parents and peoples; those who by dint of unsocial illness like alcoholism, vagrancy or senile dementia say – cannot pay to technological medicine the danegeld of scientific allure necessary for 'worthwhile attention'; those whom the gospel-denying attitudes and practices of the established churches wither with silent condemnation or misplaced pastoral care; the unemployed; the illiterate and so on. Here are the outcasts, 'those who have it bad', whom Christ comes to heal.[73]

The way a doctor works and the attitudes of patients together shape the relationship between them. In Western medicine patients tend to put the doctor on a pedestal; and their approach is one of dependence upon an expert, of whom high hopes as a problem-solver are held. There is a change going on in this general attitude, but only a minority of people yet expect more share in knowledge and responsibility for what is being done for them. The doctor for his or her part either finds a pedestal comfortable (and a Western training predisposes to this), or has an uphill task persuading patients that doctors are fallible, humanity vulnerable, medicine limited and life temporary.

It is in this area of professional style that a bold attempt has been made to work *with* patients, rather than *for* them: to off-load some of the power associated with a doctor's work; and to promote healthy ways of living as a context within which to tackle any presenting problems. Two particular actions seem to me to express everyday theology in these connexions: *first*, the appointment of a nurse practitioner who can act as an alternative kind of person whom a patient may choose to see in preference to a doctor. And *secondly*, the granting to patients of free access to their clinical notes.[74] This matter continues to be controversial among doctors. However, because health promotion is the context within which treatment is given, the case notes are treated as potentially useful educational material. One of the unspoken assumptions here is that *illness may be a learning experience*, and an occasion for individual and family growth in understanding and responsibility. The notes become an important part of conversation between patient and receptionist, nurse practitioner or doctor. In writing up the notes, the nurse practitioner (for example) may *co-edit the entry with the patient*. This whole area of using the notes as educational material for the family's better health is felt to promote *interdependence* rather than dependence; and by fostering *choice and responsibility* it is felt to be giving practical meaning to the theological understanding of the word 'health'.

Further thought was given to the theological question of *human dignity*. Every patient coming to the surgery is a person of worth. So are the accompanying friends and relatives. So are those who hurry past the door about their own business. How do you preserve that human dignity in a doctor's waiting room, and not take it away, affront it or damage it, by what you say or do? But not only that: the very design of a waiting room may carry a message to those who enter. The white-coated receptionist behind a glass screen, the loud speaker, the light which flashes 'Next Please' – all entirely understandable and highly efficient; but it makes you feel like a foreigner (indeed that is what 'alienated' means). *If therefore you have a theology of the worth of every person, how do you embody that in the design of your practice waiting room?* Theology can and must affect bricks and mortar, wall posters, magazines and coffee mugs as well as human behaviour, so that we can remain human and not be cowed. *Humanity must prevail.*

In this practice human worth is affirmed by giving people plenty of space (relative to the size of the small house), and having a receptionist who is 'among the people', sitting in the waiting room, without uniform, and occupied in a way that can be interrupted constantly so that there is always time to listen and converse. The extra staffing involved to make this possible received priority over getting a second doctor. Receptionists were chosen as local people who were therefore able to be relaxed and communicative, not trained to be 'professional' and at 'arm's length'; not labelled 'Counsellor' and given an Appointments Diary. This did *not* mean that the necessary skills in filing records, writing letters, counselling and understanding a multiplicity of forms and benefits were given no priority. Indeed efficiency is essential because inefficiency hurts people. It is quite dehumanizing to experience the loss of your records and to have to wait for hours while they are found.

I still remember many years ago how surprised I was in Finland to be taken by a friend to a Health Centre for our mid-morning cup of coffee. But this is part of the respect due to our normality. So cups of tea or coffee can be had, and have their place as sacraments of relationship. 'I will set thy feet in a large room' says the psalmist.[75] (The Old Testament idea of health contains the meaning of *spaciousness*.) A large room is full of imaginative possibilities for human interchange in the face of the joys and sorrows which may be shared there. Ease of communication from patient to staff and patient to patient is part of what a healthy Health Centre is all about.

At least two aspects of the relationship between theology and life are illustrated by the experience of this General Practice. *First*, it was a Christian concern for 'those who have it bad' which initiated the project, and it was theologizing the situation which shaped it from the beginning. There were sufficient insights to begin the work. *Second*, once action is taken, new questions and new insights arise 'on the way'. Dr Lambourne [76] had suggested that God reveals the way step by step. We only see the next step ahead when we are obedient to what we know already.

At first it was thought that the close relationship with a university department of theology (which had contributed to the funding of the practice as a theological research project) offered the kind of expertise in theologizing which could help. What was now being sought were the theological insights which would help to make sense of daily experience. A theological group met in the university department of theology for a period. It consisted of all the practice staff (of whom Dr Bird is a theologian in his own right) and four members of the department. In order to provide a context for their reflections the theologians visited the practice to see its work: this of course could not involve them except temporarily in a limited way. A number of papers were read and discussed.

One of the difficulties was beautifully focussed when a professor had concluded reading his paper and a receptionist said 'I haven't really understood one word of what you are on about!' Slightly disconcerted, the professor replied, 'Well there are a few theological words in the paper, I suppose. Could you, for a start, point to any particular word which you don't understand?' However the problem was deeper than individual words and can best be summed up in the title of the pamphlet about inter-cultural relations, which I mentioned before, called *Talking past each other*.[77]

Theology belongs to the scene of action and to the Christians involved together in the job. It is one thing to invite a theologian to visit your general practice and help you to *formulate your own questions* and provide resource material towards answers: it is quite another thing to transport the practice staff into a theology department where university lecturers are not involved in the practice, and can really only provide material (excellent in its own right) which is academic to the coal face trials and tribulations. The receptionist referred to above was not stupid, simply suffering from culture shock.

Christian apprenticeship – learning and living theology

The proper question to ask of any people's religion is 'What have they experienced and how may we share in this experience?'

Christianity has single-mindedly pressed another question: 'What do they say they believe, and how does it square with our creed?' (D.E. Jenkins).

How can a man learn but from a friend? (Aristotle).

Because theory and practice are one in theology, they must also be *one from the beginning* in learning theology. It is sometimes suggested that when studying for a degree in theology the process is one of 'giving the students the tools' which they can then go out into the world to use. This is a disastrous theory because the study of theology then begins in a theoretical way *only*. I once asked a degree student who had gone on to train as a nurse how the theological tools she had acquired related to nursing. 'Well, they don't, actually!' she replied. She had the tools, but had not been taught how to use them: they still lay shiny and new in their box, labelled 'Theology, handle with care'. *True knowledge of theology lies in our ability to use it.*
A cerebral pattern of training for the Christian life is also far too common in the local church, because clergy have also been given boxes of theological tools and have not always had to learn as lay Christians how to use them in daily life. 'Training' for confirmation or service is often a matter of instruction. Lectures and courses are available for those who wish to deepen their spirituality. Even Bible study may remain in a biblical world and hardly connect with the modern world except through private faith, charity and personal behaviour. Christian training may actually deepen the division between theory and practice. No wonder this theoretical Christianity gets 'left at the factory gate'. That could be a very proper assessment of its practical value.

In a university the learning of theology is primarily the *study of theology*, but there needs at the same time to be some regular practical dimension so that theology may be experienced as an exploratory discipline in relation to the everyday world, not simply a theoretical subject to be taught.

Likewise in the local church where *everyday theology* is primarily learnt by linking faith and life, there needs to be some regular 'study of theology' so that a congregation grows in its understanding of Christian tradition and experience. Christian history is a gold mine but it has to be worked.

The relationship between the study of theology and everyday theology is at present subject to all the distortions of our Western culture, but a new model of study/practice is being born in Pastoral Studies which has important implications for both fields of learning.

Manson[78] described the relationship of the disciples to Jesus as *apprenticeship*. That is, they did not learn about God and the coming of the kingdom simply by instruction from the Lord as teacher, but they also learnt by sharing in work for the kingdom. Jesus was the master-craftsman who chose them, and to whose call they responded. Dyson[79] has questioned the notion of apprenticeship as likely to devalue serious study at the expense of a pragmatic approach. My intention in using 'apprenticeship' is not, I hope, open to this criticism. I have chosen it as a word which takes *both* theory *and* practice, theology and living, seriously.

There are many references in the New Testament to events sparking off questions, and to conversation between Jesus and the disciples, for example, a failure on the part of the disciples to exorcise an evil spirit: 'Why were we unable to cast it out?' was asked of Jesus 'privately'.[80] Jesus asked his disciples in the house 'What were you arguing about on the road?'[81] There was conversation between Jesus and his chosen three disciples as they descended from the mount of Transfiguration.[82] Also, on encountering a man born blind – 'Who sinned, this man or his parents, for him to have been born blind?'[83] Jesus also sent the twelve disciples out to preach the kingdom of God and heal the sick: following this experience they 'withdrew . . . where they could be by themselves with Jesus'.[84] Another time, Jesus was indignant when the disciples officiously sent away children who were being brought to him for touching.[85]

This is the biblical pattern of discipleship, learning to become a Christian by living 'the way'; action and then reflection on its meaning. *Apprenticeship is a pattern for the local church*. Reading, study, conferences and courses are complementary to learning by living. Christians need the opportunity to discuss with others, or with someone more experienced than themselves, the everyday events of life – where we have failed, where we have succeeded, the joys and sorrows, bewilderments, doubts and certainties. In fact, courses of training for Christian living which do not take learning by experience seriously may actually encourage an approach to the faith based on 'knowledge about' a subject, rather than a deepened 'knowledge of' how to live as a Christian in the secular world.

In courses for medical missionaries at the Selly Oak Colleges in the UK, I have noticed a profound change of outlook and values in relation to medical work between Christian doctors training to go overseas, and those on their first furlough after actual medical experience in a Two-Thirds world country. It is after experience that the serious theological exploration begins. Prior to experience lectures may remain unconnected with real life.

For example, it is possible to give a formal talk on death, which covers the sociological, psychological and theological aspects, leading to a basis for discussion about the care of the dying. This will give learners certain categories for understanding which will act as guidelines for future experience (prospective organizers). That is, when they have to care for someone who is dying, the information will provide a basis for coping with the situation.

However, when someone actually has to care for a dying person, then they *really* want to know about death. Previously it has been a cold matter dealt with by the head only, kept at arm's length: now it becomes hot, a matter for head and heart in which the observer shares. It now becomes possible to learn about death and the care of the dying in a new way. Information can be given, usually in answer to the learner's own questions, which will help the learner to put the living experience into some sort of framework of understanding (retrospective organizers). It also becomes possible to deal with fears and other feelings of threat or running away because these are real and near the surface.

Teaching and learning may be distinguished but not separated: they are interwoven processes. By 'teaching' I mean the area of education concerned with sharing of non-personal skills and information. By 'learning' I mean changes of attitude or behaviour due to the impact of experience. In learning the tutor shares in the process like the learner.

If a teacher imparts wrong information, this is relatively easy to correct, once awareness of error is established. But mis-learning is not so easily discovered, and the unlearning of attitudes and experience can be slow, painful and often incomplete. Some authorities contend that childhood learning is a *permanent* part of our make-up.

Learning by experience is also slow, as Mathers has pointed out.[86] Experience in a university over the years suggests that students on the Pastoral Studies course which I tutored did not become aware of the important things which they learnt on the course for eighteen months to two years afterwards. Other evidence (e.g. from psychotherapy) supports this observation. It has also been noted that in intensive group work with young constant offenders, it takes longer than one year for new attitudes to become established in habits and personal independence. New insight requires time to digest, and to work itself out into changed attitudes (=learning).

Learning is also *painful*. Colston[87] describes the stages of awareness and feeling through which someone who has experienced judgment passes. Clearly the experience of being under judgment brings us up sharply: it is really painful to have to admit we are wrong. Insight may result, hopefully, in consequent learning. The stages of learning (as Colston describes them) are closely parallel to those of grief following bereavement: this too is a learning experience where painful re-adjustment of the whole person may take place. (Perhaps it is time that many experiences of loss and change were all brought together into one common category as examples of *human learning by experience*: namely bereavement, redundancy, retirement, conversion, judgment, culture shock, homesickness etc.)

Theologically, we can also see these losses as opportunities for life-through-death regeneration. In learning, a part of our self dies, but a new part is quickened – a resurrection. In the Christian catechuminate of the early church, the intense residential training involved a thorough change of beliefs, attitudes and values, culminating in baptism (symbolic death and resurrection). Many examples of painful change are given in this book, and the repeated exorcisms of a catechumen indicate the authoritative power which was brought to the process of unlearning the values and habits of past life in preparation for new birth. The following examples of learning by apprenticeship are drawn from my own work with students on the course to which I have referred. However the *methods* of learning and living theology are just as suitable – if not more so – in a local church situation. There is a description of a similar course run for members of the congregation of St Martin-in-the-Fields (pp. 183 ff.).

Students were given practical work in various places in the city. In this way situations of possible learning were contrived. Whereas in teaching you can be fairly sure what points you wish to get across, in learning you cannot be sure either that students will learn anything, or if they do, what it is that they will learn. One prepares the soil, but cannot choose all the plants.

The main purpose of the practical work was to involve *the whole group* in the life of the city. This gave the theological, sociological and social work *a context for reflection*: the academic work was related to a specific situation and was not done in some 'ivory tower'. Each individual student shared their experience of practical work and theologized it with the group. Each student was apprenticed to the group and the group to each individual.

One value of practical work is the disturbance caused in a person by having to face a new and unknown situation. For example, a clergyman who has worked in a dog collar for ten years may become unaware of the effect this has on relationships with other people: it can come as a shock to have to drop this symbol of office and relate to others as a human being without distinction. A Catholic priest was devastated by his experience of working as a student in a hospital. It was the first time he had been in a hospital not dressed as a priest. He found himself unwanted.

Or a student may encounter a situation which is quite unknown previously, like the inside of a prison or a psychiatric hospital. The initial response to a strange situation is illuminating because old habits of relating or perceiving may prove inadequate: it becomes essential to experiment and find patterns of meaning in new aspects of life. Flexibility is required. This aspect of practical work also helps to train the will. Students have to learn to cope with situations beyond their imagined point of endurance; learn how to stay with it, and to discover that waiting can be creative – like Mary at the foot of the cross.

One young man arrived from overseas unable to speak a word of English (how this happened is a long story). On the first day in a probation service department he reported for work with his wife to interpret for him! The field work tutor and I gave the student a new priority (through his wife) 'to learn what it feels like to be a voiceless minority in the world'. His wife was then sent home and the timetable was re-drawn to give the student as much visual experience of probation work in the city as possible. Six months later in a discussion in the university on listening, this student burst out 'Ah, but I have had to learn to listen *with all my being*.'

Certain practical work had special value. For example, work in the probation service is useful for someone whose theology or practice has got too moulded into one-to-one skills such as counselling. Probation work is a sharp experience of the social roots and consequences of personal problems, and a healthy influence on too individualistic ideas about health and salvation. It can make one aware of the disintegrating effect of social policies and the complementary needs for both pastoral and political action.

Work with the Marriage Guidance Council had a particular impact on learners. They experienced the value of belonging to a support group of fellow counsellors with whom they were able to discuss their casework. In this way they were able to work through difficulties in their own handling of a situation, and they found that membership of such a group actually potentiated their ability to counsel. This was not entirely because of the particular help available in specific situations, but because membership of such a group increased their confidence through a sense of teamwork. Ministers often responded to this experience by asking: 'Why don't we do this in the church? All the structures exist, but somehow we don't achieve the depth of mutual trust which enables clergy to support one another in this way.'

In general the most congenial practical tasks were those which could be tackled by a range of pastoral *skills*. The student felt s-he had a recognized function. The most difficult tasks were those which threw a student back on his/her own resources as a human being; where there was no possibility of a functional approach. An example may help to make the point clear. An overseas student came on the course with considerable experience in counselling. In fact he had a Master's degree in the subject. For his practical work he attended a Drop-in Centre for young people near the city's courts. There he encountered a number of youngsters who were usually homeless, sometimes on probation, and frequently on drugs. The need for a wise counsellor was obvious. But the 'clients' were stubbornly and persistently resistant to help of this kind. They were just not interested. The student went through agonies of doubt about his identity and what he was doing anyway. He was on an expensive university course supposed to be learning things, and here he was wasting his time! He himself described to the student group how matters developed. One day he was trying to help a young man on drugs and probation (who was not the least bit interested in being counselled) when he (the student) suddenly burst out: 'Oh for God's sake let's go and have some lunch together.' For the student this was a moment of 'break through'. One human being recognized in another human being their common need to eat. It was a painful change of approach from service to friendship, from doing things *to* someone to doing things *with* them.

Apart from organized practical experience, uncontrived experience comes to any group of people who are working together. Mistakes are a valuable source of learning. Or someone may be bereaved. Black students from overseas usually experience racial prejudice on the buses or in the city centre. All experience is theological learning material when shared with the group.

Theological reflection on a past event can enable us to change and grow in preparation for future action. In the house of Cornelius, Peter responded to the Gentiles as fellow human beings *as he went in at the door*. He was 'ready' to 'see' the significance of what happened because, before he was summoned by messengers from Cornelius, he had gone up on to the housetop to pray: and there he wrestled in a vision with the Gentile problem.[88] It was a changed Peter who set out for Caesarea, 'ready' for the 'disclosure' which awaited the Jewish Church. Everyday preparation was the mother of his spontaneity.

It is to theology that we must turn to discover why both practical work and study – the model of the apprentice – play such a part in Christian growth and learning. There are at least three reasons: *first* because the understanding of truth in the New Testament is more than just correct facts. In John's gospel, Jesus, in the context of a conversation about his relationship with the Father, is recorded as saying: 'I am the way and the truth and the life'.[89] 'Truth' may therefore be thought of in terms of the living person of Jesus. God's clearest revelation of himself was not given in a book but in a person. The word became flesh. This had to be so because any description of something always falls short of the real thing. We know more than we can tell. Truth, then, is not a matter of fact but a *personal category*. Bible, doctrines and tradition describe the living truth, but are one step away from the real thing: that is, they are necessarily second-hand. But through prayerful reading the one who seeks truth is able to discover Jesus in and through what others have recorded. The discovery of truth lies in and through a lived relationship with God, which grows and changes.

Secondly, truth is to be obeyed,[90] and this gives it a practical dimension. Truth is not only to be thought, spoken and written but *done*: and that is not just putting something into practice as if truth was a theory to be acted upon. *The action is part of what truth is.* Indeed there is no way of knowing that it is truth until it is acted out.

If it remains theoretical only, it could be a fantasy or a game. Life is understood by living it. Theology cannot be understood with the mind alone: our knowledge of theology is also by participation in its truth. Lambourne described the way in which true knowledge is given:

> The general pattern in the Old Testament is that God reveals to his people what is truth, what is true knowledge about themselves, what is just, what is good, what is health, and what he is. But God always does this to a people in a particular place, at a particular time. So, having true knowledge for their day of what it is to be healthy, what it is to be man, what it is to be godly, is related to the obedience of the people at that particular time. True knowledge for tomorrow, God's recurrent self-revelation, is dependent on being obedient to what they know today. If they are not obedient to what they can already know, they become blinded to the truth for tomorrow.[91]

Thirdly, practical work is important because a Christian has a *task to be done* (mission) in the world for the kingdom of God. It is in relationship to this 'being' and 'doing' that personal growth in the Christian faith takes place. In order to grow towards maturity a Christian must give him/herself to some cause great enough to enable that losing of life which is essential for finding it. Without an all-demanding purpose in life, efforts to grow can end in a *cul de sac* of self-cultivation.

Some of the best courses in learning by living are run by the Outward Bound Schools. There is little doubt that the church has a great deal to learn from such education for maturity. Reliance on others, responsibility, sense of identity and the close relationship between head and heart, are best learnt when a group of men and women give themselves wholeheartedly to a project. Such an experience must push a person to the limits of their endurance, to discover that limits are not brick walls but horizons with unseen land beyond. Mathers[92] has described such courses as 'a wilderness experience'. They are a valuable way of training the will, and developing a sense of one's utter interdependence with others. Would that every pastor had the chance to be refined in such a fire!

I have frequently been using the words 'learning' and 'experience'. An important relationship exists between them. The way we experience things changes as we grow and change. How we experience life and what we learn from it is formed by our Christian spirituality. More and more we learn to experience things through the mind of Christ. *Our very ability to experience is open to Christianization* and the way we see things is continuously changed by our learning. In Christian discipleship we submit our senses and our understanding to purification and moulding by God (formation) so that we may 'see' and 'hear' (i.e. experience) clearly.

Experience by itself without time for reflection may be wasted. It is through reflection that past history is transformed into wisdom for present discernment and future action. It is in reflection upon experience that faith and life, the study of theology and everyday theology co-inhere. Pastoral studies have explored group apprenticeship and found it to be a good working model both for learning theology and learning to live the Christian way.

In the Old Testament the people of God do not speak of their experience but of the experience of their fathers: that is, they call to mind God's past acts in their tribal history, and the God of history who acted then is the God with whom they have to deal now. It is God who has chosen them as his people, a historical fact which helps them to deal with a present feeling of impotence: for the truth is that God is with them now and they must respond to him by hopeful action. *Present experience is fallible and changeable.* We not only need to grow individually in spiritual discernment but also to be rooted in the on-going history of the community of the people of God. Theology is a community production and learning theology is a community activity.

Discovering the everyday use of theological words

The Resurrection of Jesus is . . . a laugh freed for ever and ever (Patrick Kavanagh).

We have noted how theological words have lost their base in everyday conversation. This happens in all specialized work. For example, today in medicine specialists develop a language of their own. Medical jargon may not only be unintelligible to lay people but one specialist may even find the journal of another specialist difficult to understand.

However, because theology forms the basis for a way of life, it is serious if ordinary people cannot understand the specialists. The use of the word theology in political debate means irrelevance – surely a sign of disastrous loss of connectedness.

One can start with theological words (like Covenant, Resurrection, Creation or Healing) and try to establish connections in daily life (e.g. the relation between sin and sickness, or forgiveness and acceptance). Or one can start with everyday issues (like racism, pollution, sexuality or education) and try to link them with theological ideas. We will begin with a theological word: *Covenant*.

In a government agency such as social work the employees are paid, work to a time table, and have a considerable work load. The notion of 'contract' is an important one which takes the limitations and responsibilities of the situation into account. The employee, for example, works a certain number of hours because longer hours might damage health. On the other hand, the notion of covenant (God's limitless concern for human beings which cannot be broken from the human side because such concern comes from the heart of God) offers a very different pattern of long-term costly self-offering love for others. In the experimental general practice to which we have already referred, there is a lively sense of vocation to serve patients to the limit. Staff are exposed to the stress and demands of people who come for help. The doctor, however warm and human, is defended to a certain degree by professional style (a personal room, a clinical examination). So are the supporting staff who may be busy with records. But doctor and staff, in so far as they are prepared to be more available to help people, are vulnerable to stress. This has been a real problem. The conflicting duties of a covenant relationship (without limit) and a contract relationship (from 9 a.m. to 5 p.m.) are a constant concern for a Christian. The receptionists are particularly exposed and the pressures can be beyond human endurance if they live in the area and are liable to be 'consulted' in the street or over the phone at home. This is what professional defences are all about, to save the carers from breakdown, burn-out or personal involvement which can destroy integrity. There are no tidy answers to it but the reply of a hospital chaplain[93] is as near as one may get. His top priority, he said, was 'to keep himself on an even keel otherwise he ceased to be able to help people'. This is one reason why Jesus withdrew from the demanding crowds to a desert place.

Wholehearted involvement is essential. Complete withdrawal is essential. *It is the balance between the two and the manner of its organization which is the nub of the matter.*

Michel Quoist[94] has written a prayer in which the one who prays finds him/herself overwhelmed by the ever-extending needs of suffering people. It is, however, the prayer of an idealist not a realist. You could not run a general practice like this and survive. Jesus himself withdrew from the crowds to renew his power and sense of direction from God. One must not naïvely try to say that covenant love *should* be practised instead of contract care. Human limitations require contracts. We recognize that in many ways contract care was born from and continues to draw strength from the understanding and practice of covenant love. It is through some such movement of the Spirit that the probation service grew out of the Police Court Mission, and a district nursing service out of the Ranyard Mission.

In these examples of difficult and highly professional work it is possible to recognize *agape* embodied in the gentle toughness of work with people in need. James Mathers once described *agape* as a 'certain quality of staying in relationship'. The Greek word *agape* is simply translated in the English versions of the New Testament as 'love' or 'charity': but this does not convey sufficiently the meaning of *suffering* love. The theological word covenant is therefore important today because it both illuminates and judges the work of the caring professions.

I have written elsewhere[95] of ways in which *Resurrection* may be understood not only as a unique historical event at one time and in one place, but also as a continuing built-in feature of life today. It could be expected that the world created by a dying-rising God should reflect patterns of life-through-death in its texture.

The theological word resurrection (life-through-death) can describe a pattern in life (like the dawn of day, the renewal of spring, the recovery from grief, the experience of forgiveness, and the discovery of new life after retirement from work) which gives us delicious foretastes here and now of the ultimate victory of life over death. Harry Williams[96] has described some vivid examples of contemporary resurrection. I remember well the astonishment on the face of a teenager who had left home for the first time to go to college and was suffering from homesickness, when it was suggested that this was a normal period of grief as she had to 'die' to her childhood and rise to new life as an independent person. Suddenly her faith connected and she knew how to cope. Such theological insight encourages us to trust the power of life and to look for its emergence in even the most desperate situations of destruction.

If we begin with an everyday word or situation, and ask whether it has any connection with Christian doctrine, theological word or biblical example, then we may find that everyday words enrich our theological imagery. Technology might appear to be refractory material for theological insight, but Pirsig writes:

> . . . Technology is – not an exploitation of nature, but a fusion of nature and the human spirit into a new kind of creation that transcends both.[97]

A new kind of creation . . . indeed human beings have taken the centre of the stage and often unwittingly taken responsibility for this new kind of 'making'. By what values is humanity guided in this activity? As *co-creators*, responsible to God, we can affirm science and technology as possible contributors to, rather than destroyers of, human community. It is essential to keep science and technology as servants of human society, rather than as dictators of its values.

In my own lifetime, many people have been gripped by the sight of our earth from the moon; and the myth of *Planet Earth* has been born with all its implications for the care of nature and a common life of peace and shared resources for all nations. Many young people today have a poster of Planet Earth stuck on the wall of their room – this vision like 'new wine in old wineskins' is bursting wide open our theological images of creation.

It was Bonhoeffer[98] who brought together the words *holy* and *worldliness* in such a way that faith and life are interwoven. Davies[99] has followed this insight and rescued the word holy from an over-emphasis on transcendence given to it by Otto. He finds the holy amid the homely.

The rending of the veil of the temple has been given new content by the modern building of an *Iron Curtain* down the middle of a nation to separate two power blocks based on different ideologies. The word of God within the situation is that God would not be contained in a Holy of Holies but was, at the moment of the rending of the veil, to be seen in a man dying a cursed death in an unclean place outside the walls of the holy city. Even the darkest corners of the world must be taken seriously as places of God's indwelling. All human beings are offered the gift of *shalom*.

Neve Shalom[100] (Hebrew for oasis of peace) is a cooperative village in Israel where a dedicated group of Jewish and Arab (Christian and Muslim) families and individuals live together in harmony. They demonstrate that their two peoples can coexist in peace, given the will to do so. More than six thousand teenagers alone have shared in their programmes, and carried back to their villages what they have learned from the school of peace. This is an everyday way to live out the creative word spoken in the rending of the veil.

The global spread of television makes people more visual than verbal. This means that the contribution of Two-Thirds world theology may become even more important than Western rational theology in the spread of the gospel. Literacy is being overtaken by receptivity to visual images.

People both fashion and are fashioned by myths, symbols and images. We can respond to God as creators made in the divine image by assuming responsibility for the renewal of our thoughts, words and deeds, both theological and practical. Our human destiny is continually being put by God into our own hands. Fr Andrew said:

> The world is not shaped by sermons but by sentences got by great men in their silences.[101]

9 The Unity of Personal Care and Political Action[102]

One of the ways in which I can love my enemies is to destroy the system which makes them my enemies (Archbishop Tutu).

In a society structurally unjust – as is ours – good deeds may in the end only support injustice (Edward Bond).

I have described a division between the work of personal care for individuals in need, and the work of politics in society. We saw this as a particular problem in Western society which has resulted in a failure to turn private tragedies into public issues, both in church and society. The example of unemployment was given; and in worship, a prayer for Mr X who has been admitted to psychiatric hospital for depression (due to unemployment) is more likely to engage our attention than prayer for political measures to create jobs.

I recorded previously the apt comment of a woman on her experience of vandalism on a new housing estate: 'Can't we do something more radical – prevent it? I mean these are just symptoms of a deeper social malaise aren't they?' Pastoral care and political action are as closely related to one another as coping with symptoms and preventing disease. If that is true, how short-sighted to treat the cough but leave the tuberculosis in the lung alone. This, of course, is a modern view because we have only recently acquired sufficient knowledge to prevent disease. Today, therefore, personal care, if carried out in isolation, falls under the judgment of Edward Bond's sentence at the head of this chapter.

The founders of the first hospitals and early medical missionaries concentrated with real compassion on the relief of individual suffering: there was no more to be done. In medicine it is still hospital treatment of individuals which commands greater funding than community health. But in the world at large the church has taken the initiative in preventive work: such as the leprosy work in the villages of Nigeria, and the influence of the Christian Medical Commission on the World Health Organization's policy of Primary Health Care. But in pastoral care more generally we still have to make this *metanoia* – this change of mind – from concentrating on problems to promoting healthy ways of living. Pastoral care at present tends to be impoverished by the amputation of a social dimension.

Halmos[103] describes an oscillation between personal and political attitudes as desirable: by which he means that each can act as critic and inspiration of the other without confusion of the two. Campbell, much influenced by his visit to South Africa, has spoken of the politicization of pastoral care.[104] He has developed the theme of ministry to structures (like the National Health and Educational Services) which calls for prophetic insight in regard to the values and social functions which they perform, as well as personal care of the people involved.

I propose now to describe an actual example of a Christian congregation which achieved not merely an oscillation but a synthesis of personal and political elements in its mission.

I was brought up in the Potteries in the 1920s and 30s when my father was vicar of Sneyd Church, Burslem. He was a member of Conrad Noel's Catholic Crusade,[105] and was generally Anglo-Catholic and Left Wing. There is a direct connection between the Catholic Crusade and the Parish and People Movement of recent years.

The social situation was the great hunger and unemployment of the years between the two Great Wars. I remember the general strike of 1926 and the economic collapse of 1929. When I was five I sat in the C. of E. primary school next to children barefoot through the winter. At the age of fourteen, in school holidays I often sold 'Daily Workers' to the dole queue, and saw girls with the green anaemia of malnutrition.

The church, black with soot, was next to Doulton's pottery. On one occasion the keystone of the chancel arch fell out due to mining subsidence. The cross behind the lectern was flanked on one side by the flag of St George, and on the other by the Red Flag of the martyrs (the Union Jack was not displayed[106] because it was regarded as a symbol of brutal conquest of minority peoples). In the vestry there was a stirring poster depicting Lenin leading the people. — where ?

The mission of the church was founded on the kingdom theology of F.D. Maurice.[107] In the oppressive situation in which the church found itself, with a mostly working class congregation, there developed an everyday liberation theology. People understood it because they hammered it out in the weekly Parish Meeting,[108] and it formed a sensible reason for their activities. In those meetings, pastoral needs of families were recognized and political actions decided: for example, the care of a penniless evicted family whose bedding was soaked in the rain; a demonstration against the evils of landlordism; or the public protest by vicar and churchwardens at the A.G.M. of the Church Commissioners (about 1930) over church investments in the manufacture of armaments. Considerable attention was given in the Parish Meeting to preparation for forthcoming public meetings so that a speaker from the Government (for example) could be thoroughly questioned by an informed audience, and the meeting made more useful. Politics, it was said, was far too important to leave to the politicians.

Amongst his papers, my father had a letter from a collier whose wife was in hospital. Please could he borrow a suit in which to visit her? The only clothes he had were his work clothes. The miner would have known 'the red vicar' because he would have seen him on the back of the same lorry when Arthur Cook the miner's leader had visited the North Staffs coalfield. Pastoral care for a miner demanded the public witness against injustice.

The congregation was committed to its task for the kingdom of God in Burslem, and its worship – the Parish Mass – was made as beautiful as possible because in it we saw a foretaste of the kingdom to come. Perhaps the centrality of worship would be a distinctive thing in making any comparison with the much later (and now more academically developed) liberation theology of South America. The sharing of funds with the poor and political activities for justice were simply related to the Mass: if you shared the eucharistic bread equally inside church, then you shared bread outside the church also. That is a political matter and at this level the word of God is explosive.

I can best illustrate the facets of this case study by some quotations[109] from what are mostly confirmation instructions for new church members, bearing in mind that the purpose of this case study is to show that personal and political approaches were actually *unified* within the mission of a particular parish church – in the Potteries of the 1920s. After the quotations, I will discuss their implications for our study.

Worship and Justice[110]

Unless bread and wine and all they symbolise are produced and used in the right way there will be no Kingdom of God on earth, for the Kingdom includes at least these material blessings. In the Mass a band of comrades produce bread and wine and divide it and share it as God wills, in the spirit of service for common use, and in fellowship and justice. In that bread and wine they see God, not hiding himself but manifest, expressing himself in the material creation, his very body and blood. In the Mass they see the way to the Kingdom and the values of it. To win the world to such a way of life, and to change this present system means struggle and risk and danger. It means the breaking of our bodies and the shedding of our blood.

Service[111]

A worker who can win the respect of his or her mates and perhaps become one recognised as courageous enough to speak out against injustice, who is not afraid to voice grievances of others, who can keep calm, who consistently talks sense and puts forward a sensible line of action at a Trade Union meeting, and who is known to be a member of a church group which is active in a social way: such a worker is doing excellent work for the cause of Christ's Kingdom. He is acting as leaven in the world.

Care and Common Life[112]

As members get to know one another, and their different standards of living become apparent, the inequality of incomes may lead to some searching of hearts. Some may be led to consider the possibility of income sharing. A common purse for the group, to which those who can afford to contribute do so anonymously, and from which any communicant can draw when in need as a matter of justice, is a valuable help. Such a fund could probably provide help in time of sickness or unemployment and also holiday money for those members of the group who would otherwise have none.

Salvation and Justice[113]

But where people urge us to confine the Christian religion to the saving of souls, to personal salvation, and forbid us to mix religion with politics and economics, they are really the deadly enemies of personal salvation, for the soul can only become 'sound' or 'saved' when, forgetting self, it is merged in the love of God and the comradeship and service of its fellows, in the battle for that new world wherein dwelleth righteousness.

It would be folly to try and point in the passages above to personal or political 'bits'. We are in the presence of an overmastering theology which draws both together in faith and life. Certain themes, central to this book, run through this case study. They may be summarized under four headings as follows:

1. The centrality of worship

Both personal and political approaches are interwoven in worship. As a whole the parish mass tried to present a vision of God's social order – beauty, warmth and sharing – with an earthy sense of our worldly situation where sin, starvation and Empire stalked. Mass was followed by a common meal – parish breakfast, Such worship was an inspiration not an escape. And in the light of that vision the church's work, individually and corporately, was planned in the parish meeting and carried out in the drab world of the Potteries.

If intercessions (for example) are to be lively, then there has to be a free flow of information from the weekday situations of the members back into worship – the situations in schools, dole queue, agriculture, mines and transport, homes, and so on – giving both a personal and solidarity-in-politics flavour to the prayers. In worship they are one. Prayer and action are kept close together, thus helping to turn private suffering into public and political issues. Otherwise prayer for healing (for example) can get trapped at the level of Mrs Jones' bunions. It isn't that Mrs Jones' bunions are not important. She may not be able to walk on a demo, but she can sit by a bedside or address envelopes. Bunions or not, she has her task for the kingdom of God and his righteousness – a master purpose that unites both personal and political insights and action – which gives her dignity and puts her bunions in a wider context. Yes, and it will sustain her too even if she should be dying of cancer.

2. Mission in the world

To the poor man God does not appear except in the form of bread and the promise of work.

Here I am using the word 'mission' (as elsewhere in this book) to cover evangelism, service, healing, prophecy and suffering – all aspects of the work for the kingdom in the local situation. A sense of purpose in a group raises morale and helps to build a healthy community.

Although some mission involves extra effort (visiting the sick, public speaking, work in a Voluntary Society, attending a demo, or Trade Union work), the key to the situation was each member's understanding that their own place of work was where their mission and ministry lay. For some this could be mainly personal, for others mainly political, and for a few both. Perhaps one should point to a process of growing awareness and enlivening of conscience which flowed from worship and the theology of the kingdom of God. The Burslem congregation decisively rejected an individual pietism which they saw as a threat to their personal/political gospel.

It may well be that an unbalanced development of pastoral counselling in the West stems in part from a loss of political vision, and hence a sense of outgoing mission exciting enough to raise morale and outflank individual problems, which loom large when secular models of individual self-development predominate in society. Perhaps we can only achieve individual fulfillment when we are caught up in a corporate cause that is greater than our individual wholeness. Exploration and mountaineering have much to teach us.

3. *The body* (I Cor. 12)

> *Things will not go well in England till all things be held in common (John Ball, Essex Priest, c.1380).*

If we have difficulty in reconciling personal and political approaches, there may lie behind that the polarity between 'individuality' and 'corporateness' which we have already discussed. The word *membership* encompasses *both* individuality in all its uniqueness *and* belongingness together. It is a concept of a higher explanatory order which unites the two into one. For the Burslem group (as for the early church), membership was highly important, with its admission, apprenticeship, sharing and responsibilities.

4. *Gifts* (I Cor. 12)

> *God's gifts are free but we must slave to receive them.*

The aggression and insight necessary for prophecy, confrontation and politics are different gifts from the empathy and gentleness of the personal pastor. (Not that confrontation is absent from pastoral care, nor gentleness from politics.) But I do accept the weight of argument for the differences which Halmos has described (p.22). The different gifts, however, are unified within the body of the whole congregation. It is Western individualism that separates them. A strong doctrine of gifts seems essential to unite both personal and political involvement.

The list of gifts in I Corinthians 12 is only a sample, and God's gifts are related to the particular situation so that we look now for gifts appropriate to the twentieth-century urban milieu as well as timeless human attributes.

I do not distinguish between so-called *natural* gifts and *spiritual* gifts. All gifts, whether the gift of music or the gift of prayer, are compounded of biological and spiritual elements. I would distinguish whether a gift is used selfishly or for others; whether prostituted, exploited or developed; whether used for promoting relationships or not; for God's glory or not. These, I think, are valid distinctions: but *all* gifts come from God.

Paul's vision of gifts given in trust for the service of the whole Body reminds us of the priority of pastoral care to build a community: in I Corinthians the gifts mentioned in chapter 12 are given *for a community* whose quality of life is described in chapter 13.

This discovery of gifts in a community bound together by suffering love points to their origin as well as to their use as a resource for all the community's members. Gifts are not given by the Holy Spirit without recognition of the human work involved in their development. In the case of the catechuminate, the catechumens had to work extremely hard during their apprenticeship (including the unlearning of faulty ideas, attitudes and values taught by parents and peers). Baptism/confirmation set the seal on this co-creation through learning and change by Holy Spirit and human persons. The sacrament was not a substitute for an arduous apprenticeship, any more than Kathleen Ferrier,[114] having received the genetic gift of a contralto voice, could evade the hard work of an initial apprenticeship and a life-long discipline of training in music and singing. So, also, gifts in the Christian community are developed coinherently by Holy Spirit and the community *in the context of the needs of the community* (not just randomly) for its work of celebrating and furthering the kingdom.

Personal and political approaches become separated and polarized when we lack some higher understanding in which both are synthesized. I have suggested that a unifying concept may be found in an understanding of *membership of the Body of Christ engaged in a mission to bring God's kingdom into being in the world.* This particular theology can unite personal and political approaches, but there are other theologies which reject political involvement altogether. It depends how we understand God's relationship with the world – how spirit and matter are related in the body of Jesus of Nazareth, in the eucharistic bread, or in you and me.

10 · Towards a Wholeness of Theology

Our first task in approaching another people, another culture, another religion, is to take off our shoes, for the place we are approaching is holy. Else we may find ourselves treading on men's dreams. More serious still, we may forget God was here before our arrival (John V. Taylor).

Inter-cultural dialogue

Western theology is one-eyed. It relies heavily on a tradition of academic debate. Its perception of Christianity is strongly left-brained and influenced by its development in a literary culture. Western theology is therefore a partial view of Christianity and is in need of healing itself. Inter-cultural dialogue can provide a necessary infusion of different points of view to make up a more whole theology. Western academic theology and Two-Thirds world theology (which is a less verbal tradition) need one another.

Pastoral studies may provide such a wholing activity in four ways: 1) They integrate faith and life. 2) They take seriously the inter-wovenness of reason and emotion. 3) They attempt inter-cultural dialogue, and 4) they are studies undertaken with an emphasis on theology, both the study of theology and everyday theology, as a community production.

Pastoral studies thus have a wholing task both for academic theology on the one hand, and Christian faith and life on the other. It is to the third contribution – inter-cultural dialogue – that we now turn as a way towards a wholeness of theology.

The transmission of insight, experience and values from one generation to another, from one culture to another, involves the perilous process of translation. Translation involves so much more than the conversion of one form of words into another form of words, for the very meaning of words involves history, subtleties of context, local colour, variations of tone and non-verbal mannerisms.

Our language is a living changing creation, a medium through which our deepest interpersonal relationships find expression. One of the most obvious and brutal ways of conquest is when the oppressor imposes his own language upon the victims.

Traditionally, Christian theology has been a Western discipline. In the expansion of Christianity from Europe to Asia and Africa the gospel has been dressed in European culture and delivered from the position of centuries of theological debate and schisms. In training converts for the ministry, many Western churches have produced Westernized African and Asian pastors after their own image, for whom the medium of education has been a language foreign to the student. The method of communication – verbal instruction, all too often prescriptive, with a high value placed upon logical debate through argument and counter argument – has invaded the African and Asian spirit. Until very recently we have expected theological students from other cultures to do their studies on our own terms – in Western languages and Western thought forms, and on our own particular hiccups like transubstantiation or the natures of Christ. Often this has Westernized them away from the roots of their own people.

A black pastor from South Africa once remarked that if he had done practical field work while at his theological college in Africa in the same way that he did on his Pastoral Studies Course in Britain *he would not have become so Europeanized by his training.* His theological studies could have been earthed constantly in local African language and thought. Theology should have been based among the local people – democratized – and not learnt by being extracted from the community and processed by an academic system introduced from the West.

Practical work, which is an integral part of a Pastoral Studies Course, is a way of wholing theory and practice. It may also prove to be a way of communication between cultures – in a dialogue, say, between Western missionaries and local Christians theologizing the questions thrown up by everyday life, as both wrestle together for truth from their different cultural viewpoints.

It is at this point that inter-cultural translation takes place. In many parts of the world the communication of truth makes more use of rituals, songs, proverbs, stories, myths and parables than in the Western world of today. But one has only to mention Western communicators like Homer, Dante, Shakespeare and Blake to know that this has not always been so: and to visit Coventry cathedral to know that the artistic method of communication is still alive.

Christianity was nurtured in an oral culture and therefore memories of Jesus' own sayings were at first passed on by word of mouth. In that context gestures assume a much greater importance than words. Hans-Ruedi Weber,[115] from experience of Bible study with illiterates in the Far East, has described how vividly the Lord's gestures – hands receiving, blessing, breaking and sharing bread – are described in the New Testament and remembered in an oral culture.

Hollenweger[116] has written some studies in narrative theology which illustrate well the disciplined research that must underlie this method of communication. It is of particular interest as a method which has proven to be understandable to both professors of theology and illiterates in the same audience. An academic argument is like a chain, as I have suggested in the Preface: if you miss one link you have broken the whole thing. But a story is like a rope: if you miss one thread, other threads ensure continuity. Narrative theology therefore is a method of communication which can bridge the cultural gap between literary and oral cultures, and enable the dialogue which both traditions of theology need for their future wholeness.

In 1978 a Centre for Black and White Christian Partnership[117] was opened in an industrial city in the UK. Its educational programme includes a Certificate in Theology course run jointly by the Centre and the local university. It has brought together black and white ministers and lay people for joint study and to share different cultural, theological and pastoral traditions. Its aim has been to create mutual understanding and to build bridges between the traditions. The disastrous situation previously described (p.45), when a diocesan bishop did not know of the existence of local black churches, could therefore in the long run enrich both black and white peoples. They will share their traditions (dialogue) rather than immigrants simply being absorbed into the British pattern (conquest). Interaction and participation are the life blood of this way of education, as also of other integrating ventures in education like the Pastoral Studies Courses, the Danish Folk High Schools,[118] and the United World Colleges.[119] The centre has also aimed at creating informed leadership among peoples who work at the grassroots of church and society.

Christians, being a minority in the university, can do things differently from the institution. The ritual for the annual presentation of Certificates of Theology to the successful candidates of the Centre is therefore a celebration of stupendous joy and variety. It is set in a context of ecumenical worship in a hall in the university, and presents a kaleidoscope of events which may include formal intercession and free prayer, addresses both read (in the white manner) and spontaneous (in the black manner), sacred dance, and a eucharist concelebrated by black and white pastors (on one of the occasions when I was a guest I received the broken bread from a Quaker woman). The Presentation of University Certificates is opened and closed with great dignity. Each recipient is given a personal charge relevant to his or her ministry by the presenting professor. The whole occasion is spiced by songs of praise from two black Pentecostal choirs and afterwards is continued in fellowship downstairs with supper together prepared by friends, relatives and fellow church members.

The Centre has other international activities and work with local churches and theological colleges. It has succeeded in bringing

> British middle class academics to reason with working class black Pentecostals on matters of faith and politics. It has brought Africans, West Indians, Germans, Americans, Irish, Scots, Welsh and English at one and the same level to look at crucial issues affecting our world – theology, paternalism, discrimination and racism.[120]

I mentioned above the cultural invasion of worship in Africa by European styles. In the Anglican Communion, the Book of Common Prayer has preserved a wide similarity between worship events from culture to culture. There is virtue in shared rituals. Yet it is in worship that one looks for the riches of a culture to be offered in music, ritual, dance, costume, style of preaching, prayer, church architecture and furniture. There is also virtue in difference.

Worship is a very whole method of communication because it contains a great variety of different modes. One can learn a great deal from a people by sharing their worship. One learns, for example, what kind of God they believe in and what their priorities in life may be, by listening to the way they make their intercessions: or simply by joining them in their rituals (which act like wordless scriptures – containers for beliefs and perceptions).

The different styles of pastoral care based on different cultural theologies need to be explored side by side in the urban milieu where cultures encounter one another all over the world. In my own experience with an inter-cultural group of students, there are at least five important insights which black theology (and the pastoral care based upon it) have to contribute to white theology (and the pastoral care based upon it). These are: indigenous methods of counselling, imaginative rituals, a capacity for suffering together, a corporate view of humanity and a political awareness.

A fascinating account of a Western missionary bringing the gospel to the Masai of East Africa is described by Donovan.[121] Considerable time and freedom were given to a local village community to discuss each session among themselves, to digest its message into their own culture, and to produce their own indigenous patterns of worship, evangelism and pastoral care.

These four examples of exploration into inter-cultural dialogue – the Centre for Black and White Christian Partnership, the DPS course, shared worship, and evangelism with the Masai – are all creative of a more whole theology than either Western or Two-Thirds world traditions on their own.

In our plurality of cultures in a city we may bring together our partial glimpses of what it means to be fully human in the image of God.[122] We can think and act together in the study of theology and in theologizing the issues common to our lives. In that dialogue, our very understanding of God is open to change in the encounter with my sister and brother of another faith. That is the risk of freedom in dialogue between cultures. The stranger may convince me: s-he will certainly change me. The end result of such mutual inter-change is well summed up in a Chinese proverb:

> Not until the dust settles will you know whether you are riding a horse or an ass.

PART FOUR
Living Faith

The love of God has the power of uniting things: it reduces human affections from many to one. Love of self, on the other hand, divides up human affections and diversifies them.

In the first three parts, I have described some ways in which human life together is changing world-wide. I have discussed a loss of wholeness in Western culture, with special regard to the separation between theory and practice, private and public life, and the treatment of persons as objects. Christian faith and theology are being influenced by secular/scientific values so that a system of beliefs, rather than a way of life, is on display.

On p.109 I write of a revolution in outlook which changed the emphasis in medicine from curative treatment towards preventive work and community development – in other words, to a concern for the quality of people's common life. In the church we have still to accomplish this revolution and change the emphasis in pastoral care towards building healthy community life. In Part Four I have tried to follow this new direction.

There is, therefore, a shift of attention from lack of wholeness and the need for integration to a description of the Christian way of life. It is a shift of attention from defects and their remedies to the creation of a way of life based upon belief in God who draws all to one centre. Our attention turns from the immediacy of rescue to the long-term creation of a pattern of relatedness, meaning and reverence: from a remedial process to the promotion of health, hope and fullness of life.

Pastoral Care, Pastoral Theology and Pastoral Studies hold a special place in the wholeness of society's thoughts, words and deeds (ch. 11).

The first task of the church is to grow community (ch. 12) where suffering love is nurtured, acts of mutual care encouraged, Christian values learnt and practised, and theology and ministry democratized (chs. 17–18). The heart of living faith is explored through a study of responsibility (ch. 14), God's response (ch. 15), and friendship (ch. 13). Further discussion of a life-long apprenticeship explores a way to become a member of the Christian community and grow towards maturity (ch. 17).

Although this Part is, therefore, concerned first with creation, there is a constant movement to and fro between the Christian vision and the everyday world, which involves an exploration of some ways of being a Christian in the modern world shaped by the values of science and technology (chs. 18 and 19). Inevitably this means facing conflict (ch. 21). Although matters of saving, healing and integration weave in and out of the argument, they are always within the context of health and creation.

This Part is not primarily concerned with skills or methods, but I have discussed counselling (ch. 16) because it has become a typical profession of the Western world and needs transformation from individual rescue work to a valuable place in the growth and commissioning of a Christian community for its task in the world. In the living faith of Christianity, neither freedom, wellness nor a high IQ are essential, inter-relatedness is.

11 Pastoral Care

Why pastoral care?

> *Every idea, intuitive or intellectual, can be imaged and translated in terms of the body, its flesh, skin, blood, sinews, veins, glands, organs, cells or senses (Dylan Thomas).*

We have traced the divisive effects of secular humanism on our ways of thought and behaviour in Western culture; especially the division between theory and practice and the effects of treating people as things. In theology we have seen a possible way of thought which brings belief in God, his purpose for the cosmos and our everyday human life into a coherent whole of thought, word and deed: although our Western theological vision may in itself be partial and therefore need wholing by contributions from other cultures.

In this struggle to hold together divided areas of life there is one critical area with great potential for wholeness – the area of human care. It is in normal human community, whether a family, a team, a group, or a tribe, that an innate urge to love and be loved finds ways of expression. People learn to care for one another, whether in health or in trouble – nurturing children, healing the sick, feeding the hungry, tending the old, being a friend or neighbour. People are then holding together in a natural way knowledge, human warmth and technical skill. To be a good mother, a woman needs scientific knowledge (however simple), skill and tenderness. To be a good teacher, knowledge, skill and a care for children are necessary. It is in works of care, in theologizing them and in study of the related sciences, that we have a critical area for living faith.

It is particularly important to note that I have first spoken of human care in terms of *life together*, that is, in terms of normality. Out of this foundation in the common life there may grow acts of human care for those members of society who fall into any kind of adversity. When the latter acts of care are given priority then they tend to become specialized and to be given at arm's length. *A caring society* is composed of good neighbours first. But in Western society the phrase more often refers to casualty care (which, of course, is included in a wider good-neighbourliness).

In all everyday caring work, and in the caring professions (like teaching, medicine, nursing and social work) knowledge, faith, scientific expertise and human compassion must be held together. Therefore the whole area of human care in community – parenting, neighbourly and professional – is in our society critical for the future wholeness of theology, faith and life.

In Christian thought and practice this area of human caring is generally called *Pastoral Care*. Already secular influences are at work dividing theory and practice, and resulting in arm's length care for people. Already pastoral care is the victim of false professionalism and divisive specialism in concentrating on casualty care rather than growing community. Already normal parenting is being invaded by statutory services which can be so specialized as to undermine the confidence of parents.

Pastoral care may be said to be a crisis area for the Christian faith and for theology in that Christian and secular values have immediately contrasting effects in the ways people are treated, in the ways technology and science are used, and in the consequences for human relatedness. It is in the area of pastoral care that the study of theology on the one hand, and everyday theology on the other hand, are having to face the present division between theory and practice. This is particularly so in the ways theology is *conceived* (an exploratory discipline), in the way it is *learnt* (apprenticeship), in its own *wholing* (through inter-cultural dialogue), in the way it is *embodied* (practised) and in its *democratization* (every Christian using everyday theology).

The crisis/opportunity/judgment of which I write is one part of the wider encounter between Christianity and secular/scientific materialism. But I believe pastoral care, pastoral theology and pastoral studies to be in the eye of the hurricane because of the special way in which an act of care by one human being for another must hold together the depth of our humanity and our modern scientific knowledge. This applies equally to the mother and her baby, or to the heart surgeon. To care pastorally one must be truly human and truly of the twentieth century.

What is pastoral care?

'It must be something like that' (pointing to a flock of geese which were flying overhead in a V formation). He then went on to explain that the V formation enables each bird, except the leader, to find an uplift in the air-stream created by the bird ahead of it. The lead bird changes from time to time when the flock alters its flight direction. In this formation the flock can fly longer hours and further distance on the same energy reserves than a single bird alone. If, for any reason, one of the birds must descend to the ground, another will accompany it in order to help and support it.[123]

Pastoral care may be an entirely secular activity. If I go into a bookshop and take down from a shelf at random a book on Pastoral Care, I may not know until I open it whether it is a book dealing with pastoral care in a religious or an educational context. Today pastoral care is an accepted description of part of the task of education. Religious definitions of pastoral care such as that of Clebsch and Jaekle (see p.11) therefore no longer describe the activities which people normally mean when they speak of pastoral care today.

Popular usage of the term pastoral care is almost synonymous with caring for the casualties in life. A local church publishes a monthly newsletter which presents a lively account of its activities under various headings – minister's message, baptisms, weddings, membership, appointments, congratulations, welcomes and farewells, thanks, various meetings and appeals, a wide range of social and personal concerns, and items from 'composting' to the 'rights of the child'. The width of interests is very great. There used to be one regular section entitled 'Pastoral Notes'. In 1980 during three months this section covered the following items: Deaths 14, Obituaries 4, Admissions/Operations/Falls (in hospital) 18, Sundry Diseases/Unwell/Falls (not in hospital) 22, Convalescents 12, Thanksgiving for progress 2, Keeping well 1.

The word pastoral is here being used in a sense which covers human problems and crises – almost all sorrows. It assumes that pastoral care means a ministry to men and women in trouble – a ministry to casualties. This is a common enough usage of the term but only gives a partial picture. Of course pastoral care *includes* work of rescue for those in crisis or distress. I am simply pointing to a common *limitation* of the term pastoral care to casualty care. This is probably due to the strong influence of medical modes of thought in our society: the term has become 'medicalized'.[124] Because popular ideas of pastoral care centre around tragedies, they inevitably exclude the need for challenge to normal people which the love of God contains. Both care and confrontation exist in tension in pastoral care: a pastor can be both comforting and disturbing.

When I was making a survey of the work which hospital chaplains do in hospitals, one of the questions which I asked them was: 'What problems do patients most commonly ask you about?' I was composing an impressive list[125] which covered a wide range of human problems from anxiety to loss of a loved one. But then I interviewed a chaplain in a maternity hospital. He replied quite simply: 'No problems at all. Just hundreds of happy mums feeding their babies.' I was brought up sharply to realize how easily we weep with those who weep and forget to rejoice with those who rejoice. Of course this chaplain had to comfort some couples and their families when a baby was stillborn or handicapped, but *he put abnormality firmly in the context of normality.* I think his hold on the richness of life made him a better comforter (strengthener) of those facing tragedy.

We noted previously that one of the favourite images of care in the Bible is the shepherd and his sheep – hence our use of the word pastoral. But I argued that the image no longer fires the imagination of urban people. However, by retaining the adjective pastoral, even in secular contexts, I hope to retain the meaning of *personal* (in contrast to 'arm's length caring'), and of *corporateness* (in contrast to Western individualism), and of *openness* to the dimension of the kingdom of God whence resources become available beyond our own resources. I do *not* wish to suggest an overtly religious or church connection by using the word pastoral because those who fed the hungry, clothed the naked, visited the sick and the prisoner, just did those things because they cared. They had no idea that they were already citizens of the kingdom of God[126] – *that*, they may have thought, required some sort of 'religious' behaviour.

Much professional and public assistance work (of nurses, teachers and civil servants, for example) as well as work such as that of homemakers, supervisors in shops and guards on trains, could be understood as pastoral care: also the community-growing work of the probation service and home help service which promote health and social well-being. There is an enormous amount of unobtrusive good neighbourliness which goes on in society and the motives for it are mixed and usually undeclared. A woman from Kenya described how most of the pastoral care for fellow villagers in need was done by the women. Such care both proceeds from and builds up the bonds of a village community. This is pastoral care based in the common life.

By using the adjective pastoral, however, I do not mean to imply that the care of Christians and secular carers in society are necessarily identical in the *values* which undergird their work, in the *resources* available (such as prayer), or in the *long-term aims* of world transformation. Indeed, on closer inspection there may be decisive differences of motivation, self-giving, and mutuality.

It is partly true to say that

> Christian pastoral care is not about one person helping another, rather it is a way of changing the whole fellowship.[127]

It is *both*. It *is* about one person helping another and that receives the highest recognition as help done to Christ himself.[128] But it is *also* a matter of seeing that act of help wholely. Of seeing it also at a person-in-relationship level, as one representative person (representing humanity by being human; or representing the care of society through the Social Services and the National Health Service; or representing God's care in and through all who care) helping another representative human being who suffers in their person a symptom of the general malaise of their whole society (of all humanity). Any member of the family or neighbourhood who witnesses the help given may themselves be helped too, and become sharers in the rescue (as helper or helped) not just spectators. In this way the whole fellowship or community is changed and grows together.

At a deeper level still the act of help may be seen as part of God's continuing work of creation – of the transformation of the whole world.

An act seen and carried out in this way is an act of *pastoral care*. But whether the act of help is *spoken about* in this way or not, or God recognized publicly to be at work, will depend on the local situation, the nature of the beliefs of the society, its culture, and the readiness of people to hear. In a church context there may be open rejoicing in thanks to God and renewal of hope. In a secular context the full nature of the helping action is more likely to remain hidden. It can be seen but not 'seen'.

There is often not much point in using the adjective pastoral of such acts of care in a secular context, except that this is how Christians may see their care for others when they are seeing it whole. The word pastoral then distinguishes their inner understanding of what they are doing; including the motives, prayer, clear-sightedness and values on which fully human action is based. But it does not necessarily distinguish the outward actions which may often appear the same as those done by people of other faiths or none, who have come to the same point by a different route. *'By their fruits you shall know them.'*

I seriously considered using the word *'share'* rather than 'care' in writing of pastoral care because it points to the fact of *mutuality* in full human encounter. The word care tends to be patronizing. We have become anaesthetized to its meaning and nowadays even Securicor cares! Indeed it was the attempted one-sidedness of professional caring (arm's length caring) which we criticized earlier: it was a general criticism of Western ways of personal relationship by African students. One of the distinctive things about African culture is mutuality: they therefore found our excessive functionalism shocking and inhuman.

Pastoral care has two distinct styles in two distinct areas. *Firstly, within the congregation* pastoral care is overtly Christian, making use of worship, prayer, counselling, healing, forgiveness and theological language to build a congregation whose members are equipped to carry out the Christian mission in the world. *Secondly, when the congregation is scattered in the world*, Christians, like anyone else who may be a humanist, Muslim or Marxist, are called to share with others in building local community life through families, blocks of flats, neighbourhood, local school or politics. Although Christians may need to reflect on these situations in terms of their faith (especially where two or three are gathered together), their words and actions will most usually need to be secular. The merciful Samaritan, foreigner though he was and a man of alien faith, acted with such commendable skill and compassion that he has become a model of Christian care for all time.

Pastoral care has two thrusts in relationship to both these areas, namely to the Christian congregation and to the common life of society. *The first thrust* is promoting health, a struggle for excellence in the quality of community life together. Within this context of health promotion, *a second thrust* is that of caring (rescue, healing or reconciliation, etc.) for those who are sick, handicapped or broken. These two aspects of pastoral care are rooted respectively in the processes of creation (making) and salvation (rescue). They are not alternatives but complementary to one another. As creation is the context within which salvation makes sense, so the promotion of health is the context within which caring for the sick makes sense.

The curative approach to disease through hospital medicine failed to build up the health of local communities in the Two-Thirds world, until a revolution in outlook (about 1960) changed the medical emphasis towards preventive and community development work – in other words to a concern for the quality of people's common life. In the church we have still to accomplish this revolution in outlook and change the emphasis in pastoral care towards building healthy community life.

The pastoral care described in this Part is traditional in the sense that it is based in the local church and in the common life of the local community. It is an attempt to welcome with discernment the insights that come from recent thought in medicine, psychology, social studies and group dynamics. Thus to describe pastoral care as primarily concerned with 'the science and art of building groups of normal people' for their particular task (whether in the church or the world or both) is to recover the Old Testament vision of *shalom* and to root pastoral care in the New Testament promise of the kingdom of God.

Christians take this common life of the world very seriously for several reasons:

Firstly, it is a fact that most of our life is spent outside church premises living, working and playing. We are infrequently, by comparison, gathered together in church or as 'the church'. Nevertheless, wherever we are and whatever we are doing we do represent the church. Bonhoeffer wrote: 'Everything the disciple does is part of the common life of the Church of which he is a member.'[129]

This way of understanding the life of the church however is all too infrequent. Church members who do not volunteer for some extra church-related activity may be described as 'doing nothing for the church', although they may be bringing up a family twenty-five hours a day. This does not mean that home-making needs to become 'churchy'. It means that through membership of the church a mother and a father find strength and wisdom to grow a family which is sensitive to God's indwelling. Christian parents in bringing up their children do lots of things which all parents do. But the context of their parental or pastoral care is their membership of the church, and therefore they do some things differently because their values and long-term aims are related to the purpose of God. At the heart of the unity of faith and daily life is a rhythm of gathering the members of the church for worship and scattering them in the world. Gathering and scattering form a rhythm of the church's life: they are interdependent. 'When I open my fingers, where is my fist?'

Secondly, the fact that Jesus embodied the spirit of God in a human life gives everything human special value – as he valued everything from lilies and sparrows to friends, feasts and good conversation.

Thirdly, that God created the world and has a purpose for it. In Genesis[130] it is recorded that humankind was given dominion over all living creatures. This dominion was at first interpreted as being given power 'to lord it over' nature. In the New Testament, however, lordship has the very different idea of *service*.[131] Humanity has no licence to rule and exploit nature, but is given responsibility for service of the natural world based upon reverence for it as God's creation and as a place of divine in-dwelling. Modern movements of conservation grope after the implications of this heavy responsibility for all the living creatures of planet earth. Part of the task of pastoral care is this stewardship of the earth's creatures and resources: an ecological responsibility.

Fourthly, Christians take seriously the common life of the world because our own bodies are built out of the very stuff of which the world is made, and our own ancestry is rooted in the animal kingdom. Human beings are enfleshed in the world from birth to death and are made in the image of God. We live *in* the world, not just *on* it.

Fifthly, human life-together (giving and receiving love) is the milieu where God's love is and will be expressed. Both *shalom* (in the O.T.) and the kingdom of God (in the N.T.) are corporate models for the building of a common life in this world and the world to come. The purpose of religion is to enable all life to become what it truly is – communion with God.

I have made the assumption that pastoral care is situational; that is, it varies from place to place, culture to culture and age to age. There is no blueprint of pastoral care anywhere that can be applied to all situations. The situation which I have chosen to consider is the life of people in cities all over the world as they develop in the last twelve years of the twentieth century – the situation (or context) which has been discussed in the opening chapter of this book. Pastoral care is influenced by the long-term questions which shape its context, such as 'What kind of world do we hope for? What kind of society do we want to be in this country?'

In the general mission of the church, all its members are scattered during the week to home and work situations. Every member is called to be like light, leaven and salt in their particular place. The particularity of a local church's work must not, however, blind it to its global membership. Wider tasks, such as the sharing of resources between rich and poor countries, also require tackling.

The task of care is therefore very varied. Sylvia Talbot, speaking at the World Council of Churches assembly in Vancouver (1983) on the issue of 'Healing and Sharing Life in the Community', said:

> In its broadest sense, healing can be understood as anything which contributes to the health and wholeness of the individual and the society. It can be effective only when, as in Jesus' ministry, it responds to the needs of the whole person. Because health is about our interconnectedness – God, self, neighbour, environment – it is precisely in those acts which preserve or re-establish our interconnectedness that we experience healing.
>
> Thus, the scope of the healing task extends beyond insuring that our body functions properly. Unemployment, being sexually abused, living under a repressive Government, being constantly excluded from participation in your congregation and having a spouse who is an alcoholic become as much health concerns as diabetes and gastro-enteritis. In this context also, such disparate concerns as land reform, nuclear disarmament, equitable distribution of medical care, national economic policy, can be recognized as health concerns.[132]

Therefore members of the church minister to all people, including the institutions and organizations which shape and are shaped by them. This means working for the transformation of society both by building local community, reconciling divided groups and by rescuing those who are victims of oppression, hunger, or disease. The spiritual and material, personal and political, individual and social tasks are one whole task for the kingdom of God.

To put the growing of healthy community life first is not to deny that people and their relationships are often sick, sinful and broken, and that healing, confrontation and forgiveness are required. But it *is* to resist the take-over of values, language and patterns of work which secular humanism and professional expertise have already stamped upon the giving of care in the modern world. 'Set your hearts on his kingdom first, and on his righteousness, and all these things will be given you as well.'[133] The priority is growing community.

12 Growing Community

God does not call isolated individuals, he creates a community (Suzanne de Dietrich).

He who loves his dream of a community more than the Christian community itself becomes a destroyer of the latter, even though his personal intentions may be ever so honest and earnest and sacrificial (Bonhoeffer).

We have described the first priority of pastoral care to be its contribution to the growth of healthy community life. This at once brings a conflict of values with the individualism and competitiveness of Western society. For example, confrontation tactics between employers and workers is deeply rooted in manufacturing and service industries. Competitiveness, which stems from loss of a common sense of purpose, is promoted as a social value beginning in education.

The growth of community enables human care for one another to find expression through mutuality. This is a primal urge in every human being which is strengthened or warped by the nature of our childhood mothering. In community humankind realizes its corporate nature and holds in unity people of varied gifts, realist and idealist, politician and pastor, amateur and professional. We have described theology as a community production: let the community be rich with a diversity of perceptions and cultures!

People form communities for many different reasons. They vary in size, purpose, membership, behaviour and length of life. They may take the form of a family, tribe, country, group, congregation, sisterhood, village, orchestra, expedition or team. Their membership may be homogeneous or very mixed in terms of sex, marital status, age, profession, race or religion. The word is often used generally to mean a loosely-knit collection of people or more specifically a close geographical unit such as a village.

Clark points out that the Basic Christian Community movement tends towards a community of *common concern* rather than a shared place of living. In fact such a community may be scattered widely in terms of residence, and its coherence depends on personal choice. In a place where the congregation is made up of people who live in one place, work in another place and worship in a third place, the church may not be able to form a close community but its members will be more loosely associated together. The church building may be a centre for worship together but otherwise little used.

On the other hand, in a village or other more compact community the church may be a centre for many social gatherings of both members and non-members in addition to worship. In city centres a modern type of church is the 'Church Centre', which serves both congregation and local community with facilities to meet for diverse activities from worship and Bible study to badminton, Muslim school and clubs for young or elderly people. The word community may also be used for a closer-knit group of people who know one another well (face-to-face group). Or the word may point to how the members of a group *feel* about their relationship: they may speak of their fellowship or solidarity with one another or of their sense of worth.

I mentioned above that in Britain we tend to regard people as related to one another like 'marbles in a box'. People are seen as separate individuals: they may form a tenants' association or a Parochial Church Council in which people come together and are related because of proximity and common task. But they are still viewed as a collection of individuals although in the same box – the same room, block of flats or club.

The Christian view of community, of the way people are related to one another, is much more personal and corporate than the view generally held in Western society. In the tradition of English spirituality there has been harmony between the uniqueness of every individual and their corporate belonging to one another.[128] *Membership* (of the Christian body) is the word that holds together *both* our individual uniqueness *and* our belongingness to one another. The members of a body are different with different functions: their unique individuality is not lost but rather enhanced by membership. The Xhosas say 'A man is a man by reason of other men.' The African sense of community is summed up in words of Winnie Mandela: 'I have ceased a long time ago to exist as an individual . . .

Whatever they do to me, they do to the people in this country.'[134] It is this deep sense of relatedness which is common to African and Christian community.

An important task in encouraging the growth of community is therefore a re-discovery of how human beings are created in relation to one another. The word neighbourhood means several different things. A neighbourhood may mean a geographical area, our street, our housing estate or our village (although perhaps built up with other villages into a modern city). But neighbourhood also means 'the state of being a neighbour', just as motherhood and childhood are the states of being a mother and a child.[135] This gives neighbourhood a personal meaning. The parable of the Merciful Samaritan is about *being* a neighbour to someone. In a block of flats one can *have* neighbours, but may not know any of them: we have described this loss of community as alienation. So when it comes to neighbourhood, we can speak of having a neighbour, being a neighbour, and in between is a process of becoming a neighbour.

These distinctions intimate that community means more than a mere collection of people. 'Community spirit' indicates a quality of 'being together' which stems from personal knowledge of one another, common interests, some degree of common life and loyalty; and most cohesive of all is the personal choice to belong to this group of people with a common sense of purpose or task. The church is such a *personal* community.

The pattern of pastoral care described in this section is based on the growth of community. It would also be true to say community is *given* (as among geese and other social creatures). But certain things can be done which make growth of community possible. The word '*growth*' is used to describe the coming of the kingdom of God.[136] Growth (as in gardening) is a word which includes both the given, and the work of cooperation: passive (cabbages grow) and active (the gardener grows cabbages).

Good human relationships grow in groups of people who communicate with one another face to face. This takes time, which is why I use the word 'grow'. There is therefore a limit to the size of a community — not more than somewhere between 500 and 1000 people. Below this limit we get to know people by name. Above this limit we begin to group people as members of a class, age group or other feature which inevitably depersonalizes them. In the Parish and People movement it used to be said that the limit for a parish communion was about 150 people. At this size people can become well bonded and learn to trust one another and find a common aim. Above this limit the congregation begins to become anonymous to one another, a collective rather than a community.

The church may be thought of as a community which embodies in its own life the life of Christ. This quality of life may be described as 'resurrection life', 'the life of the new age', 'a foretaste of the kingdom of God', '*shalom*' (peace), 'fullness of life', or simply as 'the truth that sets us free to be fully human'.

How may this quality of life be expressed in the gathered church, whether there is a large congregation or only two or three? J.G. Davies has described it as follows:

> The Gospel is a Gospel of *shalom* (Eph. 6.15), and the God proclaimed in the Gospel can often be called the God of *shalom*. *Shalom* is not something that can be objectified and set apart. It is not the plus which the haves can distribute to the have-nots, nor is it an internal condition (peace of mind) that can be enjoyed in isolation. *Shalom* is a social happening, an event in interpersonal relations. It can therefore never be reduced to a simple formula: it has to be found and worked out in actual situations. The goal towards which God is working i.e. the ultimate end of mission, is the establishment of *shalom*, and this involves the realization of the full potentialities of all creation and its ultimate reconciliation and unity in Christ.[137]

It is the work of the people of God through pastoral care to build the church into such a personal community: and to build the world into such a community of nations. These two tasks are inderdependent. If the church does not show forth in its own common life the same quality of life which it is seeking to build in the world then its message is unbelievable. I remember an African in Ghana making the comment: 'If the church cannot reconcile a Roman Catholic and an Anglican, how can you expect it to reconcile an Ewe with an Ashanti?' (two tribes in Ghana).

In the same way if the church is building its own community life but is not concerned about the quality of community in its own town, country or internationally, then it becomes an inward-looking church, cut off from the rest of humanity, and without any sense of its mission for the kingdom of God. The inward and the outward tasks of the church go hand in hand and develop interdependently.

Indeed the effectiveness of a church's work could be judged by the quality of the life in the society which it serves. *The essential gospel language is the action-in-fellowship which gives spoken words point.*

Palmer[138] describes various mistaken ideals about community which mislead those who try to *build* it. First in importance is the mistaken expectation that community is comfortable where like-minded people can agree. In fact a Christian community is shocking: it is not a group where we choose our companions but where the members are *given*. Consequently *'community is that place where the person we least want to live with always lives.'* Diversity and conflict are usual – and indeed vital in order to disturb our own partial viewpoints and shake us loose from our need to build the world in our own image.

Community spirit evades those who aim directly at it. Community is held together by the spirit of God and it is truly a by-product of commitment and struggle, for example to right a wrong, heal a hurt, give a service. Community is rather like being in a crucible where the collision of individual egos is hotted up: and we do not always get our own way but may find 'The Way'. One of the tasks of pastoral care in growing a Christian community is to enable it to become a place where forbidden subjects may be faced. In this regard the church has some achievements in the field of settlements for those with leprosy and hospices for the dying.

In the experimental general practice (see Appendix 1 pp.221–222) the staff have tried to make the surgery a place of community-growing. Patients-in-the-inner-city (to write it like that emphasises their relatedness) tend to come as individuals to a doctor. But in this medical centre they are seen as a mini-community *together with the staff*. This means that the community spirit is not broken up but actually enhanced by a visit to the doctor. Here relationships are being built. This place belongs to the local community. It is theirs not foreign territory.

The special approach of Christian pastoral care is illustrated well in the field of education. Pastoral care is often regarded as primarily remedial whereas it is in fact much wider than that. Remedial certainly, and much good personal work helps to resolve individual and family problems which may be destructive. But primarily it is preventive – better, creative – and concerned with community growth: that is, with developing a school community (which may also involve making smaller units such as a team or class) of high morale which makes learning possible and challenging. I have deliberately used the word 'learning' because that includes not only academic work but also the work of enabling growth of pupils towards maturity individually and corporately. The basic pastoral approach therefore is to build a healthy school. This is the context within which individual and family problems may properly be dealt with (or prevented) by staff.

Dr Lambourne often said that the Pastoral Studies course could not work unless the group was cohesive – a community rather than a collection of students. 'Unless we can trust one another we shall not do the sort of theology that really matters.' In reflecting theologically on the nature of this task we saw the group as having a vocation to study *together*. This had implications for the sharing of insight and experience as a special responsibility of being a student with other students. In no sense was the course competitive: it was cooperative. We saw the task of becoming a community called to study, share and grow together as work *Towards Shalom*. Most students did not simply 'attend the course'. They became part of a community committed to serious study with pastoral responsibility for enabling one another to carry that task through.

One can take certain steps which make the growth of community possible. I will set out some of the steps taken in our particular situation: that is not to suggest a method of universal application, but simply to illustrate how we tried to become a community ready for the task of theological apprenticeship to which God called us.

On the first day of arrival we had a party in our home to which students, their spouses and children all came. The following week was spent in orientation to life in the city, its history, peoples, industry, planning, health service, housing and a local church. The course therefore deliberately began with work in the city in order to emphasize the primacy of active exploration of the context for theology, and to avoid the all too common theoretical approach to theology as if it was only an academic subject. By the end of the week the group had begun to work together and were ready to separate to their individual places of practical work.

Each year, within the first month, a weekend was spent together with our families in a house or farmhouse in Wales. All the planning, catering, sleeping arrangements, cooking, programme and cleaning up was organized by the students and carried out by students, staff and families alike. Not only does a period of residence and holiday together increase our friendships, but being together on a Sunday morning faces the group with the question of worship together. It is much more effective to encounter the problems of interdenominational conflict in this practical way rather than first approaching them academically at arm's length. The way things are must be faced.

During the first term the group met one evening a week in a member's flat or digs. Simple food was provided, sometimes a national dish or sweetmeat. The evening belonged to the student (and his or her spouse) whose hospitality was being enjoyed in order to tell the group about his or her back-home situation. This might be biographical, an account of the home church, or the situation in their own country. Over the years we heard first hand accounts of life in Korea, the Philippines, South Africa, and many other parts of the world, most of which could be described as disturbed.

The purpose of the back-home sessions was to enable us to get to know one another, to widen our knowledge of the world church, and to explore our resources as a group in knowledge and experience. We could not discuss the nature of community in the presence of a man from Brunei, who had grown up in a Long House where numerous families lived under one roof, without referring to him for experience. Nor could we discuss ministry without listening to a priest from the Philippines, who was able to tell us of the dramatic changes in the style of his priesthood which Vatican II and the political turbulence had brought about.

On the two days each week when the students were in the university the tutor's room was used as their common room. The supply of coffee and tea was maintained by the students. I remember an occasion when a frustrated colleague put her head round the door and asked: 'When can I see you when you are not sitting round drinking coffee with a lot of students?' I am proud of this testimonial to my style of education. The Pastoral Studies course never did many miles to the gallon!

This brief account of everyday events (although unusual in a university course) will help to convince the reader that there is no sovereign way to grow a community. But year after year both students and staff gave considerable time to making a group whose common life subserved a common purpose. More comprehensive accounts of growing community are available for study, for example from L'Arche.[139]

Tragedy can be the raw material out of which human bonds are forged and community strengthened. Edward Wilson of the Antarctic wrote: 'It's not what happens to you that matters, it's what you make of it.' To emphasize the corporateness of this, we could say '. . . it's what *we* make of it.' The making of 'we-relationships' means the building of a common interest group (even if only of two or three members), who share each experience with its feelings of doubt and despair or of happiness and celebration, and forge human bonds out of adversity or triumph. Mathers explored the importance of this approach in a child's identity formation[140] if it is to grow in consciousness of its human membership.

When a Maori dies the family hold a *tangi* for which relatives and friends gather from far and near to support the bereaved ones. Through the tragedy, which is the cause of the gathering (to which high priority is given), Maoris build their family bonds stronger. They are an excellent example of care for the bereaved in the corporate context of building a community.

The attempt to solve problems in solitude, or to use counselling, parenting, educational or therapeutic relationship in such a way that the helper, parent, teacher or counsellor solves the client's or child's problem means that the opportunity to form human bonds (even at personal cost) may be lost. Perhaps a minister who puts too much faith in one-to-one counselling can actually rob his congregation of opportunities for building the strength of their bonds one with another.

It is a continuing feature of Christian pastoral care in the UK that it is based in the local church. Kean[141] stresses that it is a *'continuing ministry to life's normality'*, and so any help for those in distress arises from an everyday relationship already established. A doctor or a social worker only makes a relationship with people on the basis of need. A minister has a relationship with people when there are no pressing problems. This is even more true of lay people and neighbours in whom the church is *present* throughout society.

Pastoral care is therefore untidy and open-ended because it is not structured around crises (as clinical medicine is) or buildings (as education is) or professions (as social work is), but based in the local church of living bricks – people scattered all over the place.

The great variety of gathered church meetings will be familiar to most readers. In the Methodist church there is a structured system of regular class meetings to one of which every member belongs. The Methodist class (first pioneered in the Anglican Church by John

Wesley) enables members to grow together in the Christian faith by sharing fellowship, by study and mutual support. Members are in the pastoral care of a class leader and all members care for one another. These classes are potential apprenticeship groups.

Southcott[142] pioneered house churches in the Anglican Church which were initially gathered on a street basis for a weekday eucharist. In the Catholic Crusade,[143] and later in the Parish and People Movement, a regular parish meeting[144] was held each week at which the congregation were able to discuss matters both pastoral and political related to their local task. Influenced by both these more informal and sharing patterns of work, there have been, increasingly since the nineteen sixties, people from different denominations meeting in ecumenical groups, often in members' own homes. Such groups may study the Bible or celebrate an *agape* together. This is a ritual of shared bread and wine, which is both rooted in the tradition of the early church[145] and does not infringe denominational disciplines which make inter-communion difficult. Traditionally in Methodism the Love Feast was celebrated with cakes and water.

This raises the question discussed by Reed[146] in relation to the purpose of worship. How far are the multiplicity of church-related meetings on weekdays the result of a failed act of worship on Sunday? Is worship failing to give us an internalized trust in God which can carry us through the week's secular involvement with courage and independence? To what extent are these weekday meetings an opportunity for Christians and others to equip themselves for common action, and for the complexities of everyday Christianity?

The relationship to worship is crucial: as Orchard[147] points out, without groups, worship can get detached from the local and particular mission of the church; without worship, groups may share a lively sense of common purpose but lack resources and a sense of direction from beyond themselves.

Before his retirement, Archbishop Ramsay said:

> Looking at the whole stream of Christian history, is it true that Christianity in the world in general is now passing into a post-establishment phase? I believe that it is so passing, and that we need to be seeing the picture in terms of our own involvement with our fellow-Christians in every part of the world, and not only in national terms, because I believe Christian history is passing into a new phase.

I believe that another perhaps more important issue is appearing on the scene, not the contrast between State Churches and non-State Churches, but the contrast between institutional Christianity, as we have known it in highly organised Church structures, and what may be called experimental Christianity. Christian people of real conviction, finding conviction, worship, fellowship, not in a superficial way but in real depth, yet rather loosely related to the old institutional structures.[148]

In 1980 a Community Congress was held which demonstrated the growth of a 'Basic Christian Community' movement in the United Kingdom. A National Centre for Christian Communities and Networks was founded in 1981 as a fruit of the work of David Clark, who has coordinated the varied activities of hundreds of communities through his writings[149] and travels. The journal *Community*[150] has provided a forum of information and interchange between communities. In 1987 the Centre has become an association more representative of its members. Such a movement is in fact world-wide and particularly strong in South America where it has all the appearance of Ramsay's *experimental Church*.

Because it *is* experimental its identity and future potential are hard to grasp. We need many experiments in the shape of the church because it is still not clear in this 'post-institutional phase' what work the Spirit will bless and take into the future.

Clark's book *The Liberation of the Church*[151] explores the variety, nature, theology, and mission of the Basic Christian Communities. He sees their growth as springing from several roots. *Firstly*, a desire to grow in a living faith and lifestyle based on alternatives to the secular values of modern society. *Secondly*, an attempt to give power and choice – responsible membership – to lay people as an alternative to clerical domination. *Thirdly*, the discovery of a common area of personal and public concern as a basis for community rather than a shared neighbourhood. *Fourthly*, an endeavour to encounter one another as persons not being content with superficial meeting. And *fifthly*, a desire for ecumenical fellowship as an alternative to the limited horizons of denominational Christianity.

To what extent these communities can renew the life of the mainline churches is a vital question; or are such communities the new church of the future restructured for mission in a technological society? Time, perhaps a long and testing time, will show.

In growing community at least three elements are important: authority, morale and leadership. Each is worth separate discussion although all three are interwoven. By discussing the pastoral care needed for the growth of community I am putting forward a way to wholeness of life which treats faith and life as complementary; confirms people in responsible membership; and gives them an overmastering purpose in both private and public life.

Authority

Authority is that personal quality or status which enables someone to attract or exact service from another person or a group of persons. It is also a quality possessed by one who gives service to another.

Mathers in a paper on 'The Authority of the Pastor'[152] points out that most definitions of authority seem to equate authority and power, but he convincingly points out their difference, and the person-centred quality of authority. Many other writers[153] have also explored the nature of authority in pastoral care. It is no exaggeration to say that the right use or abuse of authority in any situation can build up or destroy people's cooperation.

Windass distinguished[154] between two kinds of human authority-figures under the terms *dux* (one who leads) and *rex* (one who rules). The one who rules does so by virtue of an office to which appointment (with authority) is made. So the centurion[155] was able to say to his servant 'Go' and he went; and to another 'Come' and he came. Clearly in the army it is necessary that orders shall be obeyed (whether through fear or love). When anyone 'signs on', they give authority to those appointed over them to direct them. This type of authority is impersonal, authoritarian and depends upon rank. But the best officers do *not* rely purely upon rank: they earn the trust of those under them so that their authority becomes personal.

In many other human situations such as a surgical operation, rescue of a man down a crevasse, a fire, a motorway pile-up or a boat race, an authoritative style of leadership is appropriate. These tend to be situations of crisis and an authoritative structure renders the situation safe. In these situations a more flexible and democratic style of authority may make people anxious and uncertain. In a crisis people look to someone – a person whom they can trust – to take charge. Here again I have used the word authoritative to denote the element of trust which those who follow give to someone who is recognized as leader because of knowledge, skill and personal charisma. That leader may be ranked as 'rex' or may not be; but in either case will not keep authority by virtue of rank only (authoritarian) unless in a position to enforce obedience through power.

For the same reasons various institutions tend towards a hierarchical system of relationships (e.g. hospitals and prisons) which gives them relative stability in work involving stress and anxiety. There is however a cost to be paid in keeping anxiety down to tolerable levels by imposing an authoritarian regime of power: patients, prisoners and staff suffer some dehumanization due to the loss in quality of personal relationship between them.

The second type of authority figure, the one who leads, does so because his or her knowledge, experience or charisma enables them to give hope and vision to other people. S-he tends to be a prophetic figure, more flexible in approach. The one who leads may hold no rank or office but is able to inspire others to give him/her authority in their shared crisis, to lead them in thought, word or deed; whereas a ruler's authority may rest in the holder's rank or office. The 'leader' may in fact be disowned, imprisoned or crucified by the statutory rulers of the day; because s-he has no power, only the authority which is received from, and can be taken back by others.

Another factor in this is the personalities of the followers. Some people by reason of upbringing need an authority-figure over them and feel very insecure without direction. This has widespread implications for both society and the church, both in matters of political or ecclesiastical dictatorship, and in the type of authority that is given to God, church, leaders, scripture and doctrine.

The official type of authority was widely challenged in Western society especially during the nineteen sixties and seventies. The roles of both clergyman and medical doctor for example have gradually diminished in public esteem. Authority can therefore be withheld as well as given. That authority which I possess in my self I can give to others (e.g. when I consented to obey others in my years in the army); I may also receive authority from others (e.g. from patients when I worked as a doctor in a hospital). By coming for help someone in trouble authorizes a counsellor to make interpretations of the situation as s-he sees it. These may include not only observations on the situation as it is but also on how it could be: and such interpretations may be painful, even unwelcome, and alter the situation by changing the client's awareness or perceptions. The authority to do this can be withdrawn by the client breaking off the relationship.

Authority to lead in a group may move from person to person as a situation changes and new insight or new action is required. Like geese flying in V formation, a change of direction may bring a change of leader.

Some years ago I was chairing an Open Forum after preaching the evening sermon at St Martin-in-the-Fields. Because there were a number of strangers present I began the session by saying that it might be important to know who was present and something of their experience. For example, I continued, suppose we were to discuss the Vietnam war (a random example: I had not mentioned this situation in my sermon) it would be useful to know if anyone present had any knowledge of the Far Eastern situation.

For some reason the group then elected to discuss the Vietnam war (perhaps it offered a more interesting alternative to my sermon) but without first discovering who was present in the room. It was not until we had debated a number of issues that we discovered sitting in the back row a man who had been for many years a political adviser to the Prime Minister in Saigon. Having declared himself he soon (quite humbly) put our ignorance to shame. His knowledge of Vietnam was clearly authoritative.

This was an illustration of the point I had made at the beginning of the session which was so telling that many people thought I knew of his presence beforehand! In fact I had been making a simple point about authority and was as shattered as everyone else.

Those attending the Open Forum always expected the preacher to sit at the head of the group and answer questions. He was given authority as clergyman and preacher. But consistently I tried to act as an enabler to free discussion. I sat in with the group not at its head (where a chair was always kept for me until they knew me better). The suggestion that we should get to know the members of the group was to enable any person with knowledge or experience of a subject being discussed to take their proper authority and lead us at that point. This open style of leadership is appropriate where one is seeking to develop people's maturity and initiative. However this open type of leadership may also become sub-personal if members of a group refuse the risks of assuming authority, and collude in designating one leader upon whom they depend in an immature way.

If an authoritarian style of teaching is used it may destroy relationships. A fourteen year old boy[156] described his encounter with an authoritarian school teacher. From a tender age he was a sensitive artist of unusual talent. Forced to draw rocket ships like the other boys, and to conform in dress and behaviour, his inner light was quenched, so that he died in spirit some years before he eventually expressed that death in suicide. The prescriptive method of teaching appeared to work for the other children but my own experience suggests that there is a long-term cost to be paid in loss of creativity. Uniformity quenches so many possibilities.

Obviously experts in certain situations are authoritative and not to follow their advice could be disastrous: for example in learning to drive a car. But authoritarian teaching may instill subjects into heads (with appropriate rewards) yet destroy people. There are no experts in how to become fully human.

In a group of Pastoral Studies students it was essential to know each member well because in many areas they were far more knowledgeable and experienced than the staff. It was with great difficulty when the tutor was present (the designated authority of the university) that some students (most notably from India) were persuaded to accept their own authority in the group, which was due to them because of their maturity and experience in the pastoral ministry. Sessions were regularly structured (tutor present!) to give each student an appropriate opportunity of leadership. Perhaps the tutor's true authority sprung more from his being a good participant member of the group than from his designated office.

It was recognized by Martin[157] and others that in a psychiatric hospital ward it is not only the comparatively short periods of individual or group therapy that influence a patient's recovery. *All* the inter-personal relationships between patients, between patients and staff, and between staff and staff, make for progress towards or regress from mental health.

The Therapeutic Community which Martin consequently pioneered has much to teach us about changes in the exercise of authority which are applicable both in medicine, in a local congregation and in pastoral care. In a ward meeting, staff and patients sit together and may discuss recent ward events, the daily running of the unit, patient/patient or patient/staff relationships. A psychiatrist could come under public criticism for moving patients from one ward to another without explanation.

Staff try to exercise less authority and to grant more authority to patients for making decisions about ward and treatment affairs. The change both for staff and for patients is painful: both have to suffer the insecurity of loss of definition in their roles. Staff feel vulnerable. Writing of his experience in piloting one of the first Therapeutic Communities in Britain, Martin wrote:

> It has been my particular experience to see healing issuing from a certain kind of community life. As a Christian I ask myself – should not the Church fellowship be a Therapeutic Community based upon the free-flow of Christian love? Should it not be providing the kind of atmosphere in which people are free to be themselves and to find healing in the redemptive nature of an accepting sacrificial love, the love of God, mediated by the members of the Church?[158]

Martin uses the words 'sacrificial love'. He himself suffered. So did his family. The way in which sacrificial love draws out hostility and hatred, where it can be faced and healed through suffering, cost him dearly.

Balbernie was appointed principal of a traditional borstal for delinquent boys. His appointment was made to initiate changes in the institution towards a Therapeutic Community. The changes of role and attitude required of staff and boys – including a more democratic distribution of authority – resulted in immense hostility towards the new principal and his family:

> The whole school seethed with resentment and hostility, all of it directed at one man, the principal. In facing all this venom, this hatred, he knew he had the full support of the Rainer Foundation. They were solidly and enthusiastically behind him. But they were far away, and within the community itself there were at this time only two or three at the most among his fifty or so colleagues whom he knew he could rely on as allies. Anyone who has lived with his family in a Community of this kind knows how hostility to a man can be reflected – often with exaggeration – among wives and families.[159]

The violence of feeling evoked in those who are threatened by a change of authority structure occurs as much within the church as in society, and no one should be unaware of the costs of leadership. This is a point to which I wish to return because it is crucial (literally) for those who exercise pastoral care in a time of change – learning and change are painful and costly: those who are vulnerable need support.

In a New Zealand psychiatric hospital which I visited there was a system of 'prime therapist' for each in-patient. That is, when someone was admitted, the staff would agree among themselves as to who would be the responsible person in charge of that patient's therapy. It could be the social worker (who perhaps knew the family well), or the ward sister (who perhaps had known the patient over a number of years). The other members of staff made their own contribution under the direction of the chosen 'prime therapist'. This is an example of a doctor who did not presume that he was always head of the team by virtue of his profession but delegated his authority to others. It is also a good model of how to use authority creatively in pastoral care.

Jesus gave authority to his disciples[160] when he sent them out to preach the kingdom of God and to heal the sick. When they returned he took them aside so that he could listen to what they had to tell him and use their experience for further learning. The disciples learnt about authority by being given it, exercising it and reflecting on their experience. They were trained as apprentices not as students by lecture and examination.

After washing his disciples' feet before the last supper[161] Jesus pointed out the significance of his acted parable. He who was rightly addressed as teacher and lord had at the same time acted as a slave. Luke, the chronicler for the Gentiles, records that following a dispute among the disciples at the last supper about who should be the greatest Jesus said:

> Among pagans it is the kings who lord it over them, and those who have authority over them are given the title Benefactor. This must not happen with you. No; the greatest among you must behave as if he were the youngest, the leader as if he were the one who serves. For who is the greater: the one at table or the one that serves? The one at table surely? Yet here am I among you as one who serves![162]

Nevertheless Jesus was able to act in a highly authoritarian manner in ousting the money changers with violence from the temple precincts – an event which caused the authorities to question him: 'What authority have you for acting like this? Or who gave you authority to do these things?'[163]

In the healing of the paralytic[164] Jesus forgave the man's sins in a manner which was visibly authoritative to all present. His authority was seen to work. Likewise in pastoral care some people by temperament respond to confession of sin to a priest and an authoritative pronouncement of absolution. Others respond to a more open type of counselling where personal discussion may bring understanding and repentance. I remember an occasion of formal confession and absolution which was completely transformed for the penitent because the priest, instead of sitting in a chair and receiving the penitent kneeling, came and kneeled beside the penitent both facing the altar. This act of solidarity in sin found its mark in the penitent's heart. It declares authority to be truly personal.

In the parable of the Last Judgment[165] it is the so-called marginals of society – the sick, the immigrants and prisoners – who are given their full worth as embodiments of Jesus himself: that is, he accords to them his full authority, which gives them priceless worth. Authority is an aspect of personal worth.

In human affairs both kinds of authority figures, the ruler and the leader, have their appropriate place. In pastoral care one key to growing rather than destroying inter-personal relationships lies in that word *appropriate*. These two styles of authority are both personal: but both are open to de-personalization. Perhaps it is only through participation in group work and hearing the interpretations of others that we can learn to know ourselves, what our natural bent is and therefore how we tend to use authority. Only through growth towards maturity as a person can we learn to use authority appropriately.

Mathers writes:

I have tried to draw a distinction between personal authority, which is accorded moment by moment by those who recognize it; and institutionalised authority – authoritarianism – which has behind it the sanction of impersonal power. I have suggested that the former makes for flexibility, adaptability, and newness of life, while the latter makes for rigidity and conservatism. The first is adventurous and fragile, the second is stable and apparently secure and safe; and mankind – both those who possess authority and those who live under it – share an apparently ineradicable tendency to allow the versatility and vitality and iridescence of the former to solidify into the dreary dullness of the latter. As

Christians, as pastors, we are called to cherish and foster the growth of the personal; for it is only in the personal that there is hope for the redemption of the institutional.[166]

Leadership

Leadership is of the spirit, compounded of personality and vision, its practice is an art (Field Marshal Sir William Slim).

The subjects of leadership and authority are closely interwoven so that the previous section on authority has already discussed some of the issues. For example, when we described the way in which different members of a group assumed authority at different times, someone was able to take the lead because the group gave them its authority. We mentioned knowledge and experience (of the situation in Vietnam) as reasons why someone becomes authoritative on a particular issue.

But there are also more personal factors involved. When working in a group with others most people have a natural gift that equips them to take the lead when the task is suitable. When a group silently consents to fight an issue through there will be someone whose natural bent equips them to become a 'fight leader'. The group mind unerringly seeks them out and authorizes them to take the lead. Or a group may similarly decide (unconsciously) to back away from an issue. I once belonged to a committee in a parish: I always got forewarning that the committee was not going to face an issue because there was a certain member who always rose to his feet and left the room. He was the group's 'flight leader'.

Then there is also the dependable 'let me be your father' type of leader who will have an answer for all doubts and questions. With such a leader many people feel secure, but of course all leaders are fallible and sooner or later fail to protect their sheep from the wolves in the hard world outside. On one occasion in a group of doctors, medical students, nurses and clergy, whenever the conflicts generated too much heat there was a hospital chaplain who always assumed leadership at that point and poured oil on troubled waters. Fearing his own inner aggressive potential he was able to appeal to the insecure members of the group sufficiently to lead everyone into calm waters. Under his leadership conflict would not be permitted and creative debate was impossible.

There are two inter-related factors in all those situations. The individual's personal bent for a particular type of leadership in a group; and the corporate mind of the group tending to follow a particular course of action. Both factors operate together. The group chooses its leader; its leader represents the group. This is part of what membership of a group means – to be a member of a body which uses the most suitable member (hand, eye or foot) to pursue its aims.

It is possible however for a person who is aware of the unconscious behaviour of human groups to refuse to represent the group's intention, to offer a different line of action, and to try and influence the group to follow such a lead. This is likely to be very painful for everyone involved and the group may accept or reject the new initiative. A group can be very cruel to someone who disappoints their expectations. Or alternatively if the group is immature and dependent they may follow the leader like sheep.

Both gifts, experience and the mind of the group equip people to take the lead. It is not therefore always that *a* leader needs to be appointed but that the person best suited for the job in hand may be permitted to assume leadership:

> . . . . all men will lead, some of the time – even the meanest of 'em. It is their nature. And some are gifted different, whether it is for shootin' the wicks of candles or divinin' water, or catchin' rats. You'll be well advised to let 'em 'ave their glory, take it from me.[167]

I have described the struggle which some leaders in society have had to introduce a different style of being a doctor or an educator appropriate to the situation in which they found themselves. Another example comes from Dr Berhorst in Guatemala, who has described his work of community development in an Amerindian village.[168] His preliminary survey was not primarily an objective study of medical needs but was inter-personal, that is to say the villagers themselves talked about their own life and what their objectives were; he listened. Two comments were made: (*a*) all our chickens have died, and (*b*) we want to grow apples here as a cash crop. This was where help began, although medical eyes had already detected a range of treatable conditions, and Berhorst had to fight his own professional identity as one who had been trained to treat disease. Tuberculosis was later found to occur among the landless peasants, who had to migrate to the coastal towns for work where they became infected. Such money as was available was therefore spent on a land distribution scheme, not on the importation of anti-biotics for treatment. When a peasant receives land he may say: 'Now I am a man again.' In this way medicine finds a more humble place in the whole context of human and social development.

Dr Sibley, a surgeon trained in the U.S.A., found himself on an island off the South coast of Korea called Kodje Do.[169] It was with all the shock and denial of a first stage of bereavement that he came to realize that the style of medicine in which he had been trained did not fit the needs of the rural people whom he was called to serve. Sibley has described the painful stages through which his Western style of medicine had to be adapted to the local situation.

First came the stage of *recognition* (by himself as a surgeon) of the inadequacy of institutionalized medicine. This is difficult. As the proverb says: 'To every mouth its own spittle tastes sweet.'

Realization of need for change may be followed by a *willingness to change*, a response which involves uncertainty and changes in attitudes and medical practice. This leads into the phase Sibley describes as *trial and tribulation*. Authority and security are lost. The final stage he calls *denouement*, when some of the new patterns begin to work (or perhaps not). Not until then is there any assurance of right decisions having been made.

These leaders whom I have mentioned are members of the church scattered in the world, carrying out their ministry. They are discerningly involved in the world as agents of change. They are very busy people who cannot volunteer for extra so-called 'church work' and special training. Each doctor has taken up his cross in his own work and suffered for the sake of the kingdom. How do we nurture and support Christian lay people of this calibre who are scattered as light, leaven and salt in the world?

Of course some leadership is appropriately in accord with the expectations of its followers, but a major task for pastors is the care of leaders who suffer not only from external opposition but also from the inner anguish of changes of attitude, beliefs and values (true *metanoia*). Leaders tend to feel isolated, and the support and pastoral care of a group (even a group of two) is almost essential if they are to continue their work without breakdown. This also means that the pastoral care of the husbands or wives of leaders is a high priority.

Changes in a leader also call for changes in their followers. I mentioned this above in relation to two men, Martin and Galbernie, who pioneered Therapeutic Communities, and suffered because they worked to share their authority with those who preferred them to keep it. This is a situation in the church also where many people prefer to remain dependent on their ordained ministers, and many ministers prefer to have it that way. Change in such a situation is threatening and painful for all concerned.

Leadership is best learned through apprenticeship, being given opportunities for leadership with a chance to discuss the experience afterwards. Leaders need vision if they are to inspire confidence in their followers that they know in which direction they are going. Vision means that the leader both has an immediate task in mind and also sees that immediate task in a long-term context. For a Christian leader the long-term objective is the furtherance of the coming of God's kingdom, which makes it possible to move hopefully into the future even when human tragedies seem overwhelming. Without that long vision the leader's grasp of any immediate task could lack wholeness and seem to lurch from problem to problem (like so much 'progress' in Western society). A leader's hopefulness is part of a personal spirituality which is rooted in the worship and mission of the church.

The leader needs to be perceived as reliable, not necessarily liked. Indeed people may positively dislike a leader who brings them into necessary suffering, and no one likes a leader who can bring them into a knowledge of themselves. But it is the ability to give others a sense of purpose, and to inspire people to give themselves to a cause which is greater than themselves which raises the followers' morale.

Morale

The morale of a group of people may be high or low: it is relatively easy to recognize but not easy to define. We may speak of the morale of small groups like a football team, or large groups like a nation. In either case a lot is known about the conditions which make for good or bad morale. The building of a community whose morale is high is a basic task of pastoral care. In the building of a church congregation, a scout troop, a family, a class of pupils, a hospital kitchen, or the staff of a superstore, there are common factors to which attention must be paid if morale is to be good.

The section above on *leadership* has already dealt with one of the key issues. The quality of leadership (in an army unit, for example) affects morale. The style of *authority* being exercised is important: and although it is possible to give commands and expect obedience in an authoritarian manner, in fact the best-disciplined units often have a highly participatory style of authority (as was clear in the Falkland's war). It is important that members of a unit understand their task and its place in the overall strategy and that they trust their officers. General Montgomery had an absolute flair for getting the support of his troops, and the Eighth Army's high morale in North Africa (1942) was notable. He took great trouble to get around the units and to communicate well with the men. By doing this he was able to give them a sense of common purpose which each person understood, and to which all felt committed. This meant that each soldier had a sense of his own place in the battle: each had a knowledge of his own worth and responsibility.

A sense of purpose is vital for high morale. Each person must be able to see what the next objective is. Following the bombing of a church in Manchester, the congregation set about rebuilding it. This was a task to which they committed themselves with enthusiasm: in the meantime Sunday worship was held in the neighbouring church school. With such a common purpose to unite them morale was high, and this gave their worship a united and lively spirit. However as soon as they had achieved their objective and the new church was opened morale began to fall. Within a very few weeks the young people, previously integrated in the worship in the school building, began to sit at the back and become noisy.

It has been flippantly said that to keep a group's morale high it should never achieve its aim! In practice it is important to identify a series of tactical aims within the overall strategy for the kingdom of God. A common interest can hold people together in comradeship more often than a shared street or town.

There is another reason why the kingdom is to be given first priority. It is the basis of spirituality to be wholeheartedly committed to the immediate work of God's kingdom, whether that work be in teaching, homemaking, commerce or industry. Human growth and development towards maturity, the realization of an individual's potential, takes place through that commitment with others. In scientific humanism, on the other hand, the growth of human potential is often given first priority instead of commitment to a cause. But he who seeks to save his life will lose it. And in any case, *God can raise up mature, integrated, autonomous human beings from these stones.*[170] It is through work for the cause of God's kingdom that personal growth comes: but not personal growth as the world understands. The very criteria of human greatness are different.

One of the reasons for 'good work' which Schumacher[171] gives is the challenge which work offers to cooperate with others in an enterprise that produces something which other people need. This kind of self-giving saves people from egocentricity and enhances their common humanity.

A common sense of purpose can be fostered by nurturing the common life of the group. Some groups of course may live together anyway. But others, drawn together for a particular purpose, may need to grow together through sharing meals, celebrations, play, parties, rehearsals, reading weekends or worship. There are many things which can be done to make the growth of group cohesiveness possible, and I described earlier (p. 118) how this was done with a group in a university. It is significant that one of the most exciting patterns of education at this time, the United World Colleges,[172] makes specific educational use of the opportunities which arise when students from different countries live and study together. In Lester Pearson College, Canada, both British and Argentinian students were resident together at the time of the Falkland's war. Student representatives of both nations had to present their country's case for debate before the whole college assembly. But learning at a deeper level took place as they lived and worked with one another day by day. A similar crisis of living and learning came for Egyptian, Israeli and Arab boys and girls when Sadat was assassinated. Such education is only possible in a community of high morale. Their commitment to the peace-making ideals of the college transcended the narrower limits of patriotism.

If morale is to be high some basic attention to a team's physical needs is clearly part of the task of a leader, and of the team's care for one another. Maslow's hierarchy of human needs[173] gives us a guideline: everyone has bodily needs for enough food, water, clothing and shelter. In addition to these material needs there is a desire for security. Clearly a lot of adventures are dangerous, but if morale is high people are prepared to suffer and to make sacrifices for a cause that they believe in. In war it could be enough to assure troops that if anything happens to them, their loved ones would be cared for: and that if they were wounded the medical services were well equipped and ready to care. In other words although good morale does not remove the fear of death and hurt, it does enable ordinary people to cope with their fear.

We have already mentioned that people have social needs – a need for affection and a sense of personal worth. Good leaders are able to promote these feelings.

The pinnacle of Maslow's list of human needs is that of self-actualization. Here is the nub of both leadership and good morale – to help someone discover that *it is in giving oneself to a cause that is greater than oneself that one realizes oneself*. It is not by developing the self in isolation that humanity flowers, but through belonging-ness to others in a cause that takes us 'out of ourselves'. '*A man can have no greater love than to lay down his life for his friends.*'[174] A unit, team, family or nation of high morale is not only prepared to make sacrifices for the common good but is able to withstand more stress. In units of low morale the threshold of stress is lowered and the sickness rate rises. Revans has published research in nurse training schools [175] and coal mines[176] in which the sickness and accident rates were correlated with the level of morale. In particular he related morale to good and bad communication between management and students or workers. In a university it is also noticeable how sickness rates and 'examination nerves' vary from one department to another: in the case of a high incidence, it is the staff one would wish to scrutinize before the students.

In Western society it can be difficult to build a church congrega-tion of high morale because social factors may constrain their meeting together. Laity have the similar task of building community where they live or work. An individual has high morale only as a member of a group. *Morale, authority and leadership* are all inter-personal ideas related to people living and working in groups: they are ideas which invite us to take seriously the self-realization of an individual through personal relationships cemented by a common life and purpose.

13 Service and Friendship

When one man can open his heart to another, that is true friendship; nothing is worse than a liar and no true friend tells you only what you want to hear (Lay of Loddfafnir).

I am just going outside and may be some time (Capt. L.E.G. Oates, Scott's Last Expedition, 1912).

We are what we share.

A great deal has been written about the church as a servant in the world.[177] There are powerful images in the New Testament which point to the Christian duty of service – for example the parable of the merciful Samaritan,[178] Jesus washing his disciples feet,[179] Jesus as the suffering servant of Isaiah,[180] the parable of service to the Great King[181] and the shepherd leaving his ninety-nine sheep in the wilderness to go to the rescue of the lost one.[182] The Greek word in the New Testament (*diakonos*) which we translate as 'minister', 'deacon', or 'servant' means a 'waiter at table'. Christians are called to wait on one another.

In his book on the Blood Transfusion Service Titmuss[183] has shown how important *anonymous giving* is for the cohesion of society. In recent years in our neighbourhood the practice has developed of *paying* baby-sitters. This service always used to be voluntary and free. When someone has come to baby-sit for an evening, if you pay them you feel you have discharged your obligation. If you do not pay them you are under an obligation (a clumsy way to put it) to give a service in return, perhaps to someone else in a different way. Payment may thus undermine the community building contribution of simple neighbourly service. Paying a wage kills altruism.

It is written that it is more blessed to give than to receive. This implies that receiving is blessed: a giver can only be more blessed if s-he finds a willing receiver. In a mature person there is a harmony between giving and receiving. One who becomes a habitual giver may learn to receive the hard way – by sickness, accident or old age. Indeed the grace of receiving may come violently.

One who gives at arm's length treats the one in need as an object, and I have seen people with leprosy gradually robbed of their independence and initiative by the generosity of Christian givers. Giving made beggars of them: professional receivers.

Simon Weil writes:

We have invented the distinction between justice and charity. It is easy to understand why. Our notion of justice dispenses him who possesses from the obligation of giving. If he gives all the same, he thinks he has a right to be pleased with himself. He thinks he has done a good work. As for him who receives, it depends on the way he interprets this notion whether he is dispensed from all gratitude, or whether it obliges him to offer servile thanks.[184]

Martin of Tours was a Roman soldier who cut his cloak in two and gave half to a naked beggar. That night he dreamt he saw Christ wearing half his cloak: 'This,' Christ said, 'was given to me by my servant Martin.' He did not throw his cloak with the lordly gesture of one who has a spare cloak at home; that can hurt. He shared it, thus meeting the beggar's need not only for covering but also for a brother. In doing a service he also shared himself.

In tracing the decline of the Bushman in South Africa, Jane Taylor[185] points out that their exposure to the cash economy of surrounding peoples has eroded their traditional value of sharing everything, from material goods to spiritual gifts. Western culture has destroyed their innate mutuality.

Gifts can be a sacrament of self-giving. We referred to this in relation to the giving of a prescription or an injection in ways which enhance or prevent a personal relationship between giver and receiver. The sharing of material things like bread and wine point to the central significance of sharing both our bodily needs and also the gift of God's presence in our common life. The giving of the self to another in words is at the heart of intimate relationships. But words can also defend us against 'giving ourselves away', as much as they can be the messengers of love. The culmination point of the whole creation is self-sacrifice: that is the acid test of 'self-realization'.

I believe that the 'arm's length' separateness of professional styles is a defence against self-involvement. The first step towards mutuality is deliberate human contact. It has been observed for example that nurses often do not speak to their patients unless they have some procedure to carry out. I have myself watched nurses sitting outside a ward reading magazines when there were patients lying alone in the ward worried about what was to happen when they went for an operation next day. It is simple but costly to take the first step, to be 'present' to people, giving them creative attention. 'Talking *with people*' not 'talking about patients'. In a recent instance when a patient was likely to die, the chart was marked 'Not for resuscitation'. The nurse proposed that if the patient collapsed she 'would not telephone for help, but turn her back and walk away'. It came as a surprise when the chaplain suggested that she should *stay with* the patient and support her by her presence. I empathize with that nurse. After being a doctor for many years, when I first visited sick patients as a priest I just didn't know what to do with my hands!

There used to be a consultant in London who not only did his medical rounds but also returned in the evening when the ward was quiet, without his retinue or his white coat. He sat on people's beds (he was nicknamed 'the bedsitter') and listened and answered those questions which people wanted to ask him. Such behaviour is generally foreign to the culture of hospital medicine. It takes a courageous initiative to act like this. More usually physicians complain that they have less and less time to practise medicine in a communicative way. The deeds are done but the words that give them meaning and which build relatedness are missing. Reverence is missing.

Dewey writes:

Our growth in dialogue moves through several stages as we expand what it is we mean when we say 'we'. At the first stage, it might be 'we' Christians talking about a 'they', the Buddhists, for example. The Edinburgh Conference on World Mission of 1910 was in the mode of 'we' and 'they' discourse.

A next step is taken when 'we' talk *to* 'you'. Much of the language of proclamation and witness is still shaped by this one-way language.

If there is real listening and mutuality, 'we' talk *with* 'you', and this is the beginning of dialogue.

A further step is when 'all of us' talk with 'one another' about 'us'. At this point, dialogue is not merely an event or project which enhances our mutual understanding. It becomes the foundation for a new kind of community.[186]

We need to utter ('outer') our joys and sorrows and make them real. Another human being with whom we share them can help to diminish the unreal and enhance the real of our inner experiences. This was perhaps part of the suffering of Gethsemane that Jesus could not share his suffering with his disciples. They escaped that responsibility into sleep.[187]

By pointing to God in matters of curing disease or providing bags of wheat for the starving we are pointing to the meaning of life as interpersonal. The scientific approach is leading to our treatment of people as things. We tend to cure the sick and feed the hungry without building personal bonds between giver and receiver. Ultimately this can only increase distance between human beings, which is hell.

Good community depends on mutual service. Thomas Chalmers (1780–1847) was one of the pioneers whose parish scheme of mutual service among poor people in Glasgow influenced the aims and methods of social work in the nineteenth century and up to the modern era.[188] It was Chalmers's experience of the indignities and humiliation inflicted on his destitute parishioners in Roxburgh by the English Poor Law Guardians that determined his future work.

Before his experiment was started in 1819, he undertook the visitation of all families in the Tron parish of Glasgow, about 11,000 people, noting their circumstances. Two-thirds of them lived hand to mouth on Poor Relief. Many were destitute, malnourished and isolated from family or friends.

He divided the parish into twenty five units, each under the care of a deacon who thus looked after about fifty families, or 400 people; and had the task of encouraging an *esprit de corps* among them so that they helped one another. Chalmers chose his deacons carefully. They met as a 'deacons court' to share experience, discuss and advise on people in distress, and exercise discipline.

His work with those in need was aimed primarily at character building through Christian education, and to promote neighbourly charity. This was carried out through the 'Four Fountains': first was the principle of '*Self Help*' to which every effort was bent. If that was insufficient to rescue a family from destitution, then the second line of defence was '*Help of Relatives*' whose family kinship was stimulated and affirmed. Thirdly, the system of help might have to draw more widely on neighbours in '*The Help of the Poor for Each Other*'. The building of community and responsibility for one another was a basic task of the deacons in their unit. Lastly, '*Help from the Rich*' was based on a fund built up from the collections at evening service: the significance of this fund was that *local people* attended evening service (whereas the richer people from afar – whose charity was not sought – tended to come to service on Sunday mornings). Financial help was given to encourage self-help and to build responsibility. In his day and age Chalmers was sensitive to the corruption and loss of incentive which too often followed help from the legal system.

Chalmers was in Glasgow for four years, but this well planned scheme of service lasted after he left for another fourteen years. Rimmer[189] has pointed out how Chalmers' creation of small units in the city has similarities to modern work based on a City Settlement, where a village-in-the-city scheme has been organized in an inner city.

The work of Chalmers among the poor compares and contrasts with the work of Wilson (pp. 89–95). Chalmers organized his work to reach every family in the parish. Wilson's work in the Potteries (100 years later) comes nearer to our own situation. Because society had become more secular people would have resisted such interference and organization of personal and family affairs by a church. Wilson therefore built a community of interdependent and discerning people who not only shared with one another and others in need, but were educated to theologize the local situation and to take the lead in wider issues of politics, justice and the redistribution of wealth through the State. Both men were concerned for the worth of human beings living in the degradation of poverty. Both, in different social contexts, acted pastorally for rehabilitation through building community and personal development; also for social change.

Voluntary societies can contribute to the quality of everyday service by taking the turn-over of volunteers as seriously as they do their recruitment. When someone has done a few years with the Samaritans or the Marriage Guidance Council they often find it necessary to leave for one reason or another. They then need to be trained how to use their valuable experience for society, family and friends: not just in helping work, but in building community life and educating children for human growth and social development. In this way the Voluntary Societies could be feeding back into society the lessons of the symptoms with which they have been coping.

The division created between giver and receiver by arm's length giving is a secular corruption of service, and may be an outward compensation for an inner fear of giving oneself. Pastoral care requires mutuality, the promotion of inter-dependence not dependence. Apart from other considerations, certain things like hope and a sense of human worth cannot be conveyed by a giving/receiving relationship but are communicated by a sharing relationship such as friendship, colleagueship or companionship.

The church has accomplished a great deal of service, but the image of the servant has been a dominant one for Christians at the expense of other approaches. Service may appear to be an easy option (which raises no protests or persecution) compared to the tougher tasks of prophecy and political involvement. However the model of the suffering servant of Isaiah[190] gives us pause for remembering the cost of suffering love in every corner of the work of the kingdom. Jesus was not crucified for healing the sick (although the writer of Matthew's gospel indicates the inner cost of healing[191]). It was the challenge to authority involved in healing (on the sabbath or by the forgiveness of sins) which drew the hostility of the authorized establishment.

Additional models for Christian behaviour need to be given attention as well as the servant. Love is not primarily concerned to serve, but to enjoy people. Friendship is a more freely chosen relationship than service and calls us to enter into the enjoyment of our relationship with God.

John Macmurray addressed some students in 1943 on the topic 'Ye are my Friends'.[192] He said:

The world-revolution of the Christians came when Jesus discovered the true centre of human life. 'Not servants but friends' is the proclamation of the revolution. The key word of the Christian gospel is not service but friendship. Of late, I believe, we have been thinking too much in terms of service – service of God and of the world. There is nothing distinctively Christian about that. It is the natural way of religious thought when it becomes practical. Socrates called himself the servant of Apollo. Christ's revolution consisted, like that of Copernicus, precisely in denying the 'Natural' point of view and substituting friendship for service.

In scripture both Abraham[193] and Moses[194] were called the 'friend of God': to the latter, God spoke face to face. Jesus was taunted as a 'friend of publicans and sinners',[195] but that is what he was, in eating with them. It is in John's gospel that the warmest words are spoken by Jesus of his friendship with the disciples, 'Ye are my friends', and further he specifically replaces a servant relationship with that of friendship:

> I shall not call you servants any more, because a servant does not know his master's business; I call you friends because I have made known to you everything I have learnt from my Father.[196]

In pastoral care 'befriending' is loosely used as a description of the relationship between helper and the one in need. A probation officer would claim to befriend a delinquent, although the notion of friendship under constraint from the law appears strange and denies the aspect of free choice which is characteristic of friendship. In practice, the hand of friendship is often accepted and mutuality established. Similarly the Samaritans befriend those in despair although the relationship may be confined to a telephone (but then 'pen friends' exist through the post). It would seem that the boundaries of friendship can genuinely extend to patients, clients, counsellors and others under the constraints of need or crisis as a temporary and healing life-line. But friendliness is different from friendship. A walk in the country or a day on the beach with one's counsellor, doctor or probation officer could be a crashing bore even to contemplate. Clearly we are struggling for words. The merciful Samaritan was not described as a 'friend' but a 'neighbour'.

Friendship belongs to the normality of human community. This is the basis. Service grows out of that human care which bonds humanity into one family. Service (sometimes highly technological) is a consequence of that care but can never be a *substitute* for it. If the basis is lost (at its deepest a reverence for Christ in others[197]), service will become arm's length.

A friendship freely chosen between different but equal partners is a treasured human relationship which the Bible uses as a model for the relationship between God and human beings. The word friend however is being muddied in the confused waters of helping relationships (service), and for better or for worse is part of our pastoral language. Campbell[198] has suggested *'skilled companionship'* as best describing the temporary helping relationship between nurses and patients. It could however mislead us if we try to read back our present concern with counselling and healing into the New Testament idea of friendship with God. The relationship with God is primarily healthy, freely chosen, growing and long-term – 'for God himself and not his gifts' – and that *is* healing, reconciling, and saving, rich with gifts. It is in this sense that friendship is used by Easter[199] as the key to his pastoral ministry with mentally handicapped adults. In that situation friendship is sought with Jesus for its own sake and therefore bears fruit. The change from service to friendship also does something else. It introduces the possibility of a good laugh. Service can become too serious, and friendship enjoys a joke.

In most cities of the Western world there is a tradition of social service, neighbourly, voluntary and statutory. The members of the church will continue to serve alongside others in a common human endeavour. But their richest pattern of relationship is friendship. This is something from which a deeper kind of service may flow – a mutuality which is proof against treating others as objects, holding people at arm's length, and dividing people into haves and have-nots. There is a mutual sharing of God's gift of presence when both those who give and those who receive represent Christ to one another.

14 Responsibility

Thinking and speaking of God today in terms of categories of causality is the main source of atheism (Gabriel Marcel).

There is no Why in the beginning, only a Thus. If we are faithful to the Thus, we may arrive at some glimmering of the Why (Van der Post).

Responsibility is really response-ability, the ability to choose one's reactions (F. S. Perls).

Faced with some human tragedy the question which is frequently asked is 'Why?' Why did this happen to me? Why did God let this happen? Why has this happened to my husband, he was always such a good man? 'Why?' Often enough these are rhetorical questions which do not need an answer. They are cries of anguish. They might better be followed by exclamation marks rather than question marks. 'Why did this happen to me!'

Or the question 'Why?' may assume the existence of God and be expressing a sense of outrage at the injustice of what has happened. More practically the question 'Why?' *looks back for the cause.* Scientists are concerned to probe the question 'Why?' and gain control of the situation. Reasons can often be found as to why certain things have happened. We know that this child was born deaf because its mother got German measles during pregnancy. This child has died of diarrhoea because flies contaminated its food. This car crash occurred because the driver had a stroke or went to sleep at the wheel. And so on.

This question 'Why?' is important in African thought,[200] which is not content with physical reasons only. Interpersonal and supernatural reasons are taken into account as well as the relationship with ancestors. The African 'Why?' is a searching one, but the aim, like that of science, is in order to *gain control* and restore harmony. If an offence has been committed restitution must be made to put things right. A mother whose child has enteritis is not satisfied by knowing that flies carry germs: all her children ate the same food and only this one is ill. There must be a reason.

In general the Bible does not answer the question 'Why?' in the terms in which we would like the answer; that is to say with knowledge about causes and effects. Ultimately, if we press the question further, 'Why?' is a question about the nature of God which can only be answered through faith and obedience, leading to knowledge of God through relationship. Some people may be satisfied with the scientific answer as far as it goes – it may enable us to put right what has gone wrong, to prevent or cure a disease. But the deeper question remains. Why disease at all? Why is the world the way it is? Why make a world like this anyway? The answers to these questions lie in the mystery of God, and answers are hardly to be found by intellectual wrestling with questions.

The Bible suggests we stop looking back, face the future, and looking forward work out the consequences of what has happened to the glory of God. Not 'Why?' but, given this situation how do we respond to it? The answer is therefore *not a theory but practical*: what is to be done? 'It's not what happens to us that matters, but what we make of it.'

Rabbi Kushner[201] in a book *When Bad Things Happen to Good People*, written out of a situation of great personal anguish, describes well this complete turn around from looking backwards for causes to looking forward and coping with the present and future. We can redeem tragedies from senselessness by making them meaningful. Not where does the tragedy come from but where does it lead?

The attitude which must probe the past for causes asking Why? may be connected (in the unconscious) with a 'disastrous' interpretation of the 'Fall of Humankind' as something to be undone to get back to normal. Whereas the attitude here described sees the Fall as a disobedience which made *possible* a more mature independence for humankind; a more meaningful obedience because of a more freely chosen relationship to God. The Fall is a great step from childish dependence to the awful risks of adult response-ability.

It is important to be clear that there is here a decisive difference between the values which underlie the Christian way of coping with tragedy, and the secular way. The hope of secular society lies in scientific methods of searching for causes to establish control and to restore normality. The Christian hope lies in God, present and at work in the situation, and in responding to God's will. *This does not exclude scientific research* and trying to control or prevent a tragedy; but whether for joy or for sorrow, for success or for failure, for life or for death, the Christian looks forward in hope to the End, believing that any situation can be woven into God's long-term purpose for creation. Because that hope underpins pastoral care, *what I am writing now is tempered by a forward looking spirit.* In the Christian life there needs to be a shift in emphasis from our understanding of God's creative activity based on the *Fall* towards an understanding based on the *Fulfillment* of God's purpose.

In the gospel of John[202] Jesus encounters a man born blind. The disciples ask 'Why?' 'Who sinned, this man or his parents, for him to have been born blind?' (The cultural assumption among the Jews was that disease was due to sin.) Jesus replies that neither the man nor his parents sinned. But 'so that the works of God might be displayed in him' he turns to the blind man and cures him. Jesus turns the backward-looking 'Why?' into the practical matter of *what to do here and now*, how to do his Father's work in this situation. We might say that Jesus is less interested in the causes of evil than in its transformation.

On the other hand, we remember that Jesus himself asked the question 'Why?' on the Cross – 'Why hast thou forsaken me?' – perhaps a cry of dereliction rather than a question. Sydney Carter's folk song 'Friday Morning'[203] is a sharp comment on this 'Why?' but points out in a footnote that 'what is sung . . . is only half the song. The silent part is where the action really is.' And that is where Mary's work was being done – in silence at the foot of the cross. We must not use the Bible's practical approach as an excuse for just being busy. There is work to be done in stillness.

The word responsibility is commonly used in two different ways: looking backwards in moral accountability for one's actions (meaning blameworthiness), or looking forwards to a quality of character which develops with maturity (a most responsible person). It is this latter sense that includes the 'ability to respond' which I want to describe.

To be held responsible for one's actions is important for our human dignity. In secular society there is a drift towards explaining (even explaining away) human sinfulness by factors outside our control – such as inheritance, upbringing, natural and social environment. Blame for doing wrong is therefore diminished. There is truth in that insight. However in order to help people *towards responsibility* it is important to treat them as responsible. Responsibility is forward looking. We may help someone towards responsibility by trying to face up to the whole situation, both that which is outside our control (fated), and also the freedom to respond. Thus someone may say 'Yes I did this terrible thing. I know this runs in the family; I've had a rotten upbringing; life has been against me. But I am who I am, and I'll pay the consequences and hopefully make something out of the mess.' Ideal, perhaps: but a climb to be attempted – with help.

The argument has been presented in individual terms but responsibility is also a corporate term. We neither sin nor respond as if isolated. We belong in solidarity with all human beings in health and sickness, in sin and salvation: individual responsibility is matured by membership of a community.

Pastoral care is concerned with the kind of response we make and help others to make to any situation: with answering the question 'What are we going to do about it?' Scripture is full of examples of a wide variety of human situations and the kind of responsible actions that may be tried. No single response, however, is appropriate in all situations: and in some situations more than one response may be needed.

Repentance

The Genesis account of the fall of Adam and Eve suggests the view that suffering is an individual's own fault. Even if in a particular case it is not possible to trace the sin which is the cause of the suffering (as with the man born blind mentioned above), the general explanation for suffering in the world is said to be man's disobedience not God's intention. Retribution follows sin.

But the writer of Genesis knows very well from his own experience that the good are not always healthy and the wicked are not always sick. (The book of Job takes up this point.[204]) So the writer is describing the way things are between God and humankind, not trying to explain the cause; therefore he introduces into the garden a snake who is subtle. There is no explanation of his subtlety or his presence, but Adam and Eve are shown to be caught up in a situation that existed before their arrival. It is therefore only partly true to say that man is to be blamed for his own suffering in the world. The idea of human blameworthiness gives us true insight into some situations – greed, violence and self-seeking – but it is a backward-looking attitude which tries to identify the cause of trouble, and is not a truth that explains everything. Nevertheless in many situations it is right to repent, to make confession of our sins and to commit ourselves to God anew.

In a secular society the word 'sin' is hardly used in common speech. But Fung[205] points out that people today are more often aware of 'being sinned against', of being victimized or violated. Awareness of how others treat us may bring us to reflect upon our own treatment of others. Hence repentance is a response which we may be called to make when we find that one of our attitudes or values is at fault: we might then recognize the need for a painful change of outlook. Defensiveness, resistance to change, was seen to be the cause of much suffering to others in the development of the Cotswold Community (p.127) from one kind of authority structure to another. A change of heart (as we might call it) is at the basis of reconciliation between two parties in conflict.

If in a given situation the response of repentance is not helpful, there are other kinds of possible response.

Hope

The aim of the volunteers called 'The Samaritans' is to give hope to those in despair. The gift of hope may save life. But hope may be either true or false. For example, when someone has a terminal illness it may be said by hospital staff that they must not be told the truth because that would destroy their hope. Granted the need for hope in such a situation, but is the hope that they are not so ill after all, and will live, anything but a false hope that inevitably crumbles as day after day they find themselves weaker? And in what does one put one's hope in old age?

If our faith is a world-denying faith, then we may be able to kindle hope by turning our attention from this world into a future world where injustice will be put right. However the hope of a future life in the Christian tradition is not meant to cut the nerve of our present determination; rather to kindle it. The idea of a future life first appears in the Bible at the time of the Maccabean revolt[206] when the Jews were very hard pressed. It was a future hope which strengthened them to resist hopefully then and there, not to seek escape.

Hope, then, is one of the responses to a bleak situation. It is certainly one of the greatest contributions which Christians have to make to a secular culture which has lost a sense of purpose. The English tradition has always been hopeful: Mother Julian's *Revelations of Divine Love*[207] is an outstanding example. Faith, hope and love are inextricably linked in a Christian response to a God who is consistently reliable, purposeful and loving.

In pastoral care an important question is 'How can you give hope to someone in despair: and in what should they hope?'

There is no special technique for giving hope to the hopeless. I know no way of conveying hope to someone except by being hopeful. Our prayers shape us in hopefulness. All the preparation through worship and prayer is put to the test at the moment of crisis. It is in being such a person, such a church, that pastors help most, because our hope is real: our hope is in God, not in any particular divine gifts or blessings. 'I hold and am held.'

Learning

We have mentioned before the possibility of learning the lesson of the illness. Hunter[208] described the hospital as a 'living, learning arena' where patients encounter pain and suffering through which they are changed. The hospital is like a school of life. One of the conclusions of my research project was: 'That the primary task of the hospital in society is to enable patients, their families and staff, to learn from the experience of illness and death how to build a healthy society.'[209]

In the book of Job it is suggested that God teaches us through suffering: 'Who is a teacher like unto Him?'[210] Experience does show that suffering can be ennobling. We might think of a man like F. D. Roosevelt who was tempered by his disability into a strong leader. But this is not universally true and some situations are crushing. What does the starved mother in the Ethiopian famine, clutching a dead baby to her dried up breasts, learn from the experience? Most people were crushed by the experience of Belsen or the Gulag Archipelago (with notable exceptions[211]). In pastoral care we need to discern the learning possibility of a tragic situation (such as a car accident) and enable a person or a family to come through it wiser and stronger. But once again this is only one among many possible responses to life situations.

Rescue

This response means that a situation, whether it is prison, disease, slavery or oppression, is changed. Rescue is healing. Rescue is liberation. Rescue is amnesty. Rescue is feeding the hungry, welcoming the immigrant, providing a 'possum'.[212] Jesus' works of healing rescued human beings who were captive to disease. Healing was part of his commission to the twelve and the seventy disciples.

Much has been written on healing,[213] and nothing was more relevant to a rural community of his day, or more symbolic of the power of God to overcome the power of evil. It was an age, too, of intense interest in the miraculous. Jesus' works of healing (like all works of rescue from many sorts of captivity) were short-term answers to immediate problems. At a deeper level than this Jesus' works could also bring healing to those bystanders who recognized the signs of the kingdom of God and responded to them. At another level they, as fellow creatures in solidarity with those healed, were part of God's re-creative work of the whole cosmos.

The Old Testament model of rescue was the Exodus. Israel was constantly reminded of this historical event. 'Liberation' is a constant theme today in raising hope of freedom for oppressed peoples in South Africa and South America. They too are constantly reminded that the God whom they worship rescued Israel from slavery: but are less often reminded that God rescued Israel *for the sake of others*.

Rescue from slavery in Egypt and the building of a new nation were no guarantee against future slavery in Babylon. Healing, saving from oppression, rescue from prison or any other adversity is always a creative event; but the individual, family or nation then moves on to the next crisis. To be saved from death by coronary thrombosis in middle age gives new hope, but may mean perhaps that one lives on to suffer loneliness and feebleness in old age.

Short-term rescue from tragedy is one pattern of God's working. In healing the sick it appears to be a method of dealing with the symptoms of evil rather than solving the problem of evil. The cure of an individual with leprosy by Jesus was a sign of the presence of the kingdom of God, but leprosy is still a major problem of human disease and disfigurement in the world 2,000 years later. On the other hand, whereas Jesus cured a handful of blind persons, today doctors acting as his hands cure tens of thousands in the cataract camps of Asia. Short-term rescue from tragic situations is always a cause for joy and thanksgiving: but it can also be seen as one part of a much more radical long-term transformation of the world which forges good out of evil through suffering. The difficulty is to 'see deep'. Because 'blindness' is one of humanity's handicaps 'seeing' is in itself a sign of rescue – in other words, one way of describing salvation might be 'the birth and growth of Christian discernment'.

It is not enough to point to the fact that God, as known in Jesus, is one who rescues. The reality is that sin and sickness are continuing conditions in this imperfect world. Some of the toughest times in pastoral care are coming to terms with the fact that a given situation is stubborn, and rescue is not being given. But being well is not fundamental to being human, whereas relationships are: and God is still transforming the cosmos and working towards its final fulfillment.

Confrontation

God forbid you peace and give you glory (Unamuno).

Some situations are recognized to be wrong and therefore we must stand firm and refuse to be ensnared in them. More than that: some situations make us angry, they must be denounced and resisted. It is often quoted from the sermon on the mount that a Christian, if struck on the cheek, should 'turn the other cheek'. At his trial before Annas, however, Jesus objected strongly when he was struck on the cheek because it was unjust.[214] His followers are not called to be doormats.

Bonhoeffer could have remained in the USA with honour, but he chose deliberately to return to Germany and take part in the resistance of his church against the Nazis. This deliberate challenge cost him his life.

The cross is an instance of one who actively challenged the power of evil. Jesus did not compromise when he confronted the authorities of his day. In St John's gospel we are given examples when time and again Jesus evaded his enemies. He clearly recognized that the right time would come for a critical confrontation:[215] and a day did come when he set his face deliberately to go to Jerusalem and his disciples fell back afraid.

The cross is often trivialized by forgetting this deliberation. When we are urged to take up our cross daily this does not mean putting up with a contentious mother-in-law (I heard this interpretation suggested by a university missioner on one occasion), nor does it mean bearing one's disability. It means taking on something voluntarily, at cost, despite one's disability.

Contentious relatives, disability, poverty, apartheid, disease, or, alternatively, positive things like wealth, good health and loving friends, are the conditions which make it easier or more difficult to take up our cross, but they do not constitute it. The woman with rheumatoid arthritis goes up to Golgotha in a wheel chair. The choice whether to risk Golgotha or not is hers. The journey is taken by those who confront injustice or evil in themselves or others: it may involve anger, rebellion, protest, demonstration, even suffering unto death.

Examples of 'martyrdom through blood' present themselves as a sharp crisis when all that we are and have become is put to the test and even the saying of yes or no has dire consequences. 'Martyrdom through patience' spells out the deliberate taking up of a cross day after day. It is the continuing effort to express love, to be truthful, to communicate, to be vulnerable (like the bedsitter), even when the situation is hostile to such behaviour. Residential care is an area of social work which calls for martyrdom through patience (less and less are such conditions of service acceptable to social workers in a secular society).

I remember the mother of a family dying of cancer who would sit up in bed in the morning after a sleepless night and write letters to her nephews and nieces and godchildren. She deliberately set her face to reach out to them in love in the only way left to her. She chose to take up her cross daily when in fact she had every excuse to lie back and do nothing. How rich she was in her relatedness!

A man from Zimbabwe described how prisoners in jail during the struggle for independence created 'a community of freedom' within the prison itself. Their spirit never bowed down to captivity. They confronted it. Freedom is not basic to being fully human, but community relationships are.

Confrontation is a possible response to some situations but in pastoral care it calls for mature judgment to know when to confront and when to accept. In counselling, confrontation is only creative if based on a firm relationship of mutual trust between client and counsellor which takes time to grow.

James Baxter wrote:

A certain man decided that life was too hard for him to bear. He did not commit suicide. Instead he bought a large corrugated iron tank, and furnished it simply with the necessities of life – a bed to sleep on, books to read, food to eat, electric light and heating, and even a large crucifix hung on the wall to remind him of God and help him to pray. There he lived a blameless life without interruption from the world. But there was one great hardship. Morning and evening, without fail, volleys of bullets would rip through the walls of his tank. He learnt to lie on the floor to avoid being shot. Nevertheless he did at times sustain wounds, and the iron walls were pierced with many holes that let in the wind and the daylight, and some water when the weather was bad. He plugged up the holes. He cursed the unknown marksman. But the police, when he appealed to them were unhelpful, and there was little he could do about it on his own.

By degrees be began to use the bullet holes for a positive purpose. He would gaze out through one hole or another, and watch the people passing, the children flying kites, the lovers making love, the clouds in the sky, the wind in the trees, and the birds that came to feed on heads of grass. He would forget himself in observing these things.

The day came when the tank rusted and finally fell to pieces. He walked out of it with little regret. There was a man with a gun standing outside.

'I suppose you will kill me now' said the man who had come out of the tank. 'But before you do it, I would like to know one thing. Why have you been persecuting me? Why are you my enemy, when I have never done you any harm?'

The other man laid the gun down and smiled at him. 'I am not your enemy,' he said. And the man who had come out of the tank saw that there were scars on the other man's hands and feet, and these scars were shining like the sun.[216]

Involuntary suffering

We are partly fated partly free and the measure of our freedom is our capacity to relate to our fate (C. Jung).

No one would deliberately choose to suffer cancer. It is one of life's tragedies, like an accident or an earthquake, which comes upon us unexpectedly and leaves us vividly aware of the fragility of human life.

One must not separate voluntary and involuntary suffering, they are closely interwoven – how closely may be sensed in the agony in Gethsemane. But it is possible to distinguish, for example, between the anguish endured by a physician who voluntarily chooses to practise a different kind of medicine to that in which he has been trained, [217] and the involuntary anguish of a family whose child is born with a life-shortening disease like cystic fibrosis. I am privileged to know a priest in whose family this sorrow was woven with joy. It is this 'making something out of it' which gives us a taste of transformation, a foretaste of the kingdom to come. After a serious car crash recently, one of my earliest memories was the overwhelming support and love shown by family, friends and church. In discussing the growing of community I pointed to this truth – that tragedy can be the raw material out of which human bonds are forged.

If I have so far stressed the corporate side of this, one must not underestimate the individual struggle. It is not always easy to share one's deepest feelings – even if one could articulate them. The struggle may be one for survival. Survival against the constant downpull of illness, the limitations, the prejudices against handicapped people, the self-centering pain and dependence, the times of sheer frustration. Or the struggle against time: when the first determination, so bravely made, begins to wane as weeks drift into months and years. There is a universe of loneliness in stubborn situations, and to prevent its closing in on the human spirit like a mist at dawn means a struggle against withdrawal and running away. Ecclestone in his book on prayer writes:

> But the 'Yes' of such moments will never be made apart from the persistent plodding determination to use every scrap of its uneventfulness. [218]

There are many situations which must simply be endured and it seems that nothing can be made out of them. Vanstone [219] has described how the dignity of being human is expressed not only in our activities but also in passivity when things just happen to us and we endure them. He points out how the gospel writers emphasize that the glory of God is seen in Jesus at the time of his being handed over into the hands of men.[220]

I recognize people whom I would call the pain-bearers of society. I think they have an important part to play in building a community. In a family or a group of colleagues, certain people may be scapegoated by the other members. For example, one member of a family may have to bear not only their own anxiety but also that of the other family members who project their anxiety on to the scapegoat. Such a person may break down altogether. It may be very difficult to bring enlightenment into such a situation because the healing of the scapegoat (perhaps their discharge from psychiatric hospital) involves the other members taking back (as it were) their anxiety and bearing it themselves. The false stability of the situation is threatened by family therapy because members of the family are invited to save the scapegoated member by sharing the suffering themselves voluntarily – they can refuse and run away from it if they so choose. It is a painful way through group healing into a new harmony.

Scapegoating is basically an unhealthy aspect of group behaviour. But such situations are often locked; and someone, made to suffer by others in this way, may consent and suffer creatively for the group. In a similar way, someone like a ward sister or a probation officer, who is exposed to criticism or blame often unjustly, may refuse to pass on the feelings or complaints thrown at them, and may suffer them. These are the pain bearers. It is part of the burden of good leadership to bear hostile feelings on behalf of others. Both these voluntary ways of bearing pain are examples of 'martyrdom through patience' and are creative, in contrast to scapegoating which is defensive at cost to others.

We are responsible for bearing together the painful consequences of evil in our midst. It is running away from that pain and responsibility to project it on to another member of the family, another race (the Jews or the blacks), or some representative figure (such as a dictator who is supposed to mastermind all the terrorism of Europe).

We have discussed previously how we may understand God to be suffering in and with his children, helping to bear the unbearable. Those who suffer long may be destroyed, embittered or hardened by the experience. They may however grow in human stature and be quickened in sympathy for the many sufferers in similar or different situations; their contribution to intercessory prayer will be the more valuable.

Celebration

There are some situations where joy, thanksgiving, remembering and celebration are the right response. When the children of Israel had been rescued from pursuit by the army of Egypt and were safely across the Red Sea, Miriam led the women in a song and dance of triumph and thanksgiving. The Exodus from slavery is remembered every year by the Jews at the Feast of the Passover with symbolism that recalls and expresses the manner of God's mighty acts.

Christians from earliest days have always celebrated joyfully the resurrection of Jesus with the symbolism of the Last Supper, and the cup of wine is known as the cup of thanksgiving. The liturgy for the Holy Communion in the 1662 Book of Common Prayer has rightly been criticized for too much emphasis on the confession of sin. Too often this has had the effect of making the eucharist morbid and giving the participants a sense of failure rather than of celebration. There are important attitudes which underlie the tone of worship and these have important implications for pastoral care. In this city for sheer warmth and joy it would be hard to beat the weekly eucharist for mentally handicapped adults in their hospital church of St Francis. Here is an uninhibited gathering of the people of God to celebrate their friendship with Jesus and with one another. The mentally handicapped have a contribution to make to the whole church in the wholeheartedness of their worship.

Worship in the black churches also tends to be far more full of joy and spontaneity. This sometimes contrasts with the joyless stilted-ness of much worship in the main-line churches. In the early days of West Indian immigration into Britain, a Pentecostal Church found a home in the crypt of St Martin-in-the-Fields. They had been turned out of several meeting places because of complaints about noise! What came to be known as 'the clap hands' service illustrates very well the exuberance of feeling and physical expression which goes into the making of West Indian worship.

A number of biblical responses to different kinds of situation have now been described. No one response is applicable in every situation, so in helping others we need first to discover all we can about them and what response they are making or need to make. We must be gentle if we wish to suggest a change of response, for we must recognize how much we can hurt people by pressing on them our own ready-made solutions. Indeed those who try to help others must first respond to them as people – that is, in relationship – and not approach them with some preferred skill. Every personal encounter is a new situation in which Christ may be recognized in the face of friend or stranger.

15 God's Response

Man depends on God for all things; God depends on man for one. Without Man's love, God does not exist as God, only as creator, and love is the one thing no one, not even God Himself, can command. It is a free gift or it is nothing (Rabbi H. S. Kushner).

Greater love has no man than this, that a man lay down his life for his friends (John 15.13).

I will be what I will be (Exodus 3.14; RSV margin).

If the responses discussed in the last chapter have appeared to depend too much upon human initiatives, then it is important to describe three major themes which describe God's response woven into every human attempt to respond to the hopes of being human. Once again we are trapped by our lack of an interactionist language. Everyone dances or duels with their neighbour, and all dance or duel with God. Responsibility is co-responsibility.

Life-through-death

In the resurrection of Jesus, God affirmed not only the power of life over death, and good over evil, but also the life that comes through death. The seed which falls into the earth and dies bears much fruit.[221]

In Christianity this truth stands as the door through which we enter the kingdom of God. Baptism deliberately re-enacts this new life that is coming through death to the old life. The early church enriched baptism with symbolism that brings this meaning home to the heart – the stripping naked in a dark room before being plunged under the water three times (dying with Christ under the water to rise with him in newness of life[222]) and arising with helping hands of fellowship to be given clean white robes, a lighted candle, and the first Easter Communion with fellow church members. They were then free to serve God in the world by serving their fellow human beings.

One of the criteria of this new life is love of the brethren for one another: 'We have passed out of death and into life, and of this we can be sure because we love our brothers'.[223] Of a selfless warden of Edward Wilson House in London, Leslie Stabler, it was said at his memorial service that he was a man who 'had done his essential dying a long time ago'.

There is a hint here of an important approach in pastoral care to some kinds of sin. Resistance to sin, some bad habit for example, is not always fruitful. The injunction of the Sermon on the Mount 'Offer the wicked man no resistance', may seem surprising: but it is a matter of attention. We grow like the things to which we give our attention. If then we withdraw thought and attention from something that troubles us – even banning it from prayer – we let it die and wither from lack of attention. By looking in a different direction we allow newness of life to take its place. It is not possible just to *stop* hating someone: we can only transform hatred by the strength of our loving.

The whole pattern of grief following loss is another example of the same principle of life-through-death. The most obvious loss, bereavement, is only one particularly sharp cause of grief. Other losses have similar effect, such as retirement and redundancy, leaving home (culture shock among overseas students), menopause, and growing old. In each loss we have to let go the old pattern of life, to let it die, and await with hope the gift of new life. This is what grief means. It is like practising dying. If we are faithful in and through these little deaths of every day, then maybe we can approach our own last death as a well-recognized way of loss that we have travelled before – and trust that no death can have the last word because we have already tasted the reliability of God's presence and power of life to come through death. We die as we live. The dying and rising of Jesus gives us a key to understanding the way God has made us mortal human beings: life-through-death creatures made in the image of a life-through-death God.

Creation

Creation is universal talk about salvation (Daniel Hardy).

All our operations are co-operations (Athanasius).

I have quoted before the valuable guideline in pastoral care: 'It's not what happens to us that matters, it's what we make of it.' In this making we realize ourselves as makers in the image of our Maker – we are co-creators in an unfolding creation. A similar remark was made by Finnian to Columba: 'What happens to a man matters little: what happens in him matters much.' We are here dealing with long-term processes of growth and change.

A new balance between ideas related to *creation* and ideas related to *salvation* needs to be established. In the section on rescue I suggested that salvation is concerned with immediate correction of particular deviance. Creation is a long-term process going on in the whole of God's world of which human beings are one part.

Human beings are rooted in earlier forms of life from which we have evolved. We are still in solidarity with the ecosystem which is the whole canvas of God's creation. In both Colossians and Ephesians[224] the close relationship between creation and salvation is described. Elsewhere there are hints in the New Testament that salvation extends into the creation, for example 'When anyone is united to Christ there is a new world'[225] (New English Bible translation; and the margin reads 'a new act of creation'); and 'The whole creation is eagerly waiting for God to reveal his sons.'[226]

God's acts of rescue may be seen as one part of his continuing re-creation of the world. Human release is part of a greater cosmic liberation.

Salvation has a violent aspect. The scenes of the cross and passion are violent and masculine. Woman deliberately takes a waiting role at the foot of the cross, sharing the pain creatively. Creation is a more feminine process. In Genesis the Holy Spirit is depicted as brooding upon the face of the waters. I have suggested that the feminine gift of care in nursing provides the context for medicine. Such a view depends on this relationship between creation and salvation – on seeing salvation (short-term and masculine) within the context of the long-term feminine brooding of creation. I believe this restores the harmony between feminine and masculine elements in creation and salvation.

Pastoral care, certainly in modern times, has often been based upon a theology of the healing works of Jesus. This may explain why several British writers in this field (Lambourne, Lake, Mathers, Bird, Trowell and myself) have all been medical doctor/theologians. In the UK much of the interest in healing has passed into the counselling movement since the nineteen sixties. But pastoral care is not primarily concerned with healing or counselling as I have tried to argue in this book. Not only are the responses to tragedy in the Bible varied but the building of a healthy community is first creative and then saving.

Pastoral care of which healing is one aspect is founded on the long-term creative activity of God as well as the short-term salvation of God. I suggest that rescue (salvation) is creation made present and visible in one place at one time: compacted from a long period of time and much space into one moment in one place. Salvation is like a bit of creation accelerated and localized to the point of visibility – an outward visible sign of an inward continuing process. At the head of this section I quoted the following sentence: *Creation is universal talk about salvation.* Perhaps we may make a parallel sentence to it: *Salvation is here and now talk about creation.*

Creation and salvation, both ways of God's working, are essentially the same quality of event in terms of history, biology, physiology and social change. But the fact of visibility in time and place should not blind us to the cosmic contribution of even the simplest change. Israel was rescued from Egypt to become 'the light of the nations'.[227] In healing the sick Jesus was healing the world. Pastoral work is done by people involved in cooperation with God in both short-term and long-term work, in both healing and transforming, saving and creating. The smallest act of compassion vibrates through the cosmos.

I can only hint at a relationship between signs of the kingdom as short term acts of rescue, and the long-term process of transformation towards the final fulfillment of God's purpose, through a parable from chemistry:

When you titrate some acid solution with an alkali using phenolphthalein as an indicator, every time a drop of alkali splashes into the solution there is a pink flash where the change takes place: but it quickly disperses into the rest of the solution which remains clear. There is however a slow, invisible, long-term change going on in the clear solution. Every tiny pink flash is a promise of what is to come. Then the end point is reached: quite suddenly one drop of alkali does the trick: the whole solution goes pink. That slow build up of change, invisible to the naked eye – except for promising pink flashes – has reached the point of visible completion.

Emmanuel (God with us)

And now here is my secret, a very simple secret: it is only with the heart that one can see rightly: what is essential is invisible to the eye (St Exupery).

God himself will milk the cows through him whose vocation that is.

That God is always present is a matter of trust. In one of his last sermons Bishop John Robinson (who knew he had only a short time to live) said:

> When two years ago I spoke at the funeral of a 16 year old girl who died in our dale, I said that God was to be found in the cancer as much as in the sunset. That I firmly believed, but it was an intellectual statement. Now I have had to ask if I can say it of myself, which is a much greater test . . . By saying that God was in the cancer I did not mean that God was in it by intending it or sending it. That would make him a very devil. God is to be found in the cancer as in everything else. If he is not, then he is not the God of the Psalmist who said 'If I go down to Hell, thou art there also' . . .[228]

There may be long periods of wilderness experience when we seem to be alone and can only hold to God in trust. The traditional prayer 'I hold, and am held' is a simple affirmation of trust in God in periods of darkness – whether that darkness is due to the outward conditions of life (in bereavement, accident, war or failure) or inward conditions of the heart (depression, rebellion, loneliness, or apathy).

For anyone involved in pastoral care, trust in the presence of God – relatedness – needs to be in the marrow of our bones. 'It is in Him that we live and move and exist.'[229] We need to be able to enter into or live in a situation which seems to deny, or is an outrage to, the whole idea of God as present, 'held and holding'. But our sense of outrage cannot be greater than God's. It may be that our understanding of God is at fault: that our expectations are more idealistic than real. Those who help others may feel the presence of God more personally as companionship; especially this may be experienced in friendship with the living Jesus, who 'gives God a human face'. They act for him as his hands, his eyes, his feet. But if they are tempted to identify the presence of God's spirit in the helper only, then the parable of the Great King[230] presents another side of the equation. This parable completely upsets the battle of the powers. We are so used to basing our healing work on the image of Christ as healer that

we are shocked by the revelation of Christ as sick. For it is the king –
in the parable – who is sick. Poised to heal in the name of Christ we
suddenly find Christ in the wrong place. Poised to lay hands upon the
sick in the name of Christ we suddenly find the king kneeling to
receive the laying on of hands. Poised in our position of strength to
visit a helpless sufferer we are faced by the king, and ourselves
rendered helpless.

> There is a completely different pattern of power at work.
> Contrasted with a sick King and a crucified Christ, the cleansing of
> a leper and the stilling of a storm are quite different power
> structures. Beside the familiar picture of God as the one who
> intervenes to heal, set the picture of God in the place of the patient.
> Beside the familiar picture of the Good Samaritan as our Christian
> pattern, set the picture of God as the man in the ditch, naked and
> wounded.[231]

It may be easier to see signs of God acting in the everyday because
we believe Jesus gives us glimpses into the work of God: Jesus was
transparent to the will of God and therefore is able to speak
repeatedly of 'being about my Father's business'. There is no room
for any separation between God and the world, or faith and life.
Vanstone[232] has described how Jesus showed forth the values of the
kingdom, the dignity of being human and the glory of God, not only
when he was actively changing situations, but also when he was the
victim of a situation and was passively enduring what others did to
him. If we speak of learning to discern 'God at work in the world', it
is easy to become too triumphalist. Vanstone's book helps us to
become aware of God suffering in the world. There are some sharp
examples of this in the writing of Soelle[233] where she theologizes the
industrial conditions of slavery in some factories; and in her
reflections on an incident in a Nazi concentration camp at Belsen,
when God was perceived by a bystander as present, hanging on the
gallows in the body of a tortured Jewish lad.

> In so far as you did this to one of the least of these brothers of mine
> you did it to me.[234]

On several occasions Lambourne[235] commented on his understanding of Jesus' encounter with the Syrophoenician woman[236] who
pleads for help for her sick daughter 'Lord, have pity on me'. Jesus
ignores her. Silence is a powerful message. But she persists in

following him around until the disciples can stand it no longer and urge Jesus to 'Give her what she wants'. Jesus replies that his work is with the Jews. And again when she herself, a Gentile, knelt before him with 'Lord, help me' he replies 'It is not fair to take the children's food and throw it to the house-dogs'. Usually we try to soften what appears to be a brutal rejection. We may suggest that Jesus was testing her faith; that Jesus was seeking a hiding place from his enemies and did not wish to be recognized by some public act of healing. Are we defending Jesus against something we feel to be out of character?

But supposing the account quite simply means what it says? He did reject her. Jesus was a Jew of his day, brought up as a member of a race with a strong nationalist prejudice against the Gentiles. This encounter was typical of Jew/Gentile relationships; the Jews rejected Gentiles.

But the woman refuses a relationship on the basis of race or religion. She insists on being treated as a human being, as a mother in need. She throws his rejection back at him with a joke and forces Jesus to respond as a human being, as a man, with compassion. Jews and Gentiles cannot laugh together, men and women can.

At this point, we may say, Jesus' eyes are opened by a Gentile woman to the inhuman implications of the nationalism which was still part of his outlook. Nationalism, we must remember, had been a vital element in the creation of Israel. Without intense nationalism the Jews would not have survived as a race in the turbulent Middle East. National pride was their life-blood and it was handed on to each generation as a source of their identity and morale. But what is good and enlarging for one generation can become a straight jacket and a source of diminishment for the next. The good of one generation can become a bad for their children: a source of freedom for one, a prison for another. Jesus is suddenly made aware of the universality of his message, a purpose for all people including Gentiles not just his own race; and the Father uses a Gentile woman to teach him this. 'Oh woman' he bursts out in new understanding and gratitude, 'Woman, you have great faith!' and perhaps we could add 'You will never know what you have done for me.'[237]

This encounter is disturbing. It disturbed Jesus out of one of his received attitudes into new understanding. There is no reason to suppose that Jesus knew all the answers from the beginning. He was not spared the often painful business of new insights changing his current beliefs, of learning by experience and maturing in wisdom the human way. A word from God comes live to him through the red fleshy lips of a Gentile woman and Jesus 'hears' and responds at once.

Exactly the same kind of experience may strike any one of us in any of our human encounters. Are we open to discover that yesterday's good has become today's prison in our personal, professional, political and religious beliefs and values?

A woman once made a similar remark to me after we concluded a counselling session: she said 'If you come down our way, you would drop in for tea with the family, wouldn't you?' I was left speechless as I'd always thought of her as a rather difficult *patient*, but never as a member of a ꞌfamily with whom having tea might be fun. She disturbed the professional shell which I was wearing even though I was working as a priest. I experienced the judgment of God through her lips.

Theologizing life may involve such 'seeing' – the recognition of God at work in the everyday world: or such 'hearing' of a word from God in unexpected places. Any event at any time in any place may suddenly or continuously be seen as also occurring in God's realm. Religion is not a department of special events at special times and places, but the ability to 'see' ordinary daily life at this deep level. Religion thus discloses the true nature of life and enables it to be what God means it to be – continuous communion with God. Ian Ramsey described this recognition of God in the everyday as a *disclosure situation*. Some happening in the ordinary world is suddenly 'seen' as a happening in the kingdom of God also: it is recognized as a sign which points to God's presence and action. It is the secular happening itself which is the sign: it does not need to be an openly religious happening (though it may be) and the one who 'sees' it (in other words recognizes it as a sign of God) names God as the responsible agent and gives thanks.

The story of the young West Indian nurse from Billesley (p.43) is like the story of the Syrophoenician woman. She too refused to be treated as 'a black' and claimed her common humanity through humour. This also is a word from God. By writing 'like the Syrophoenician woman' I am suggesting a way of recognizing God's actions. Scripture is full of illustrative cases and situation studies of ways in which the tell-tale signs of God may be 'seen' and 'heard'. We can learn from these and recognize them in our own situations.

When Dr Lambourne was a general practitioner he wrote:

> Dragged out of bed in the middle of the night with nothing but resentment in my heart, it happened on several occasions, I rebuked my disinclination to give proper attention to some unattractive person and to make a thorough examination. I rebuked myself with the remembrance of Christ's word 'Ye did it unto me', and then it suddenly seemed that Christ was really and literally present under my hands in the form of the sick person. I saw him and I touched him.[238]

This illustrates a sense of the continuing incarnation which has been noted as characteristic of English spiritually.[239] It is the unity of the theological and the practical, of fact and feeling. This everyday experience evokes in the human spirit the recognition of a 'disclosure' of God's presence and reverence for God in the person in distress. An ethical response of thoroughness in the doctor's examination follows.

In the writing of Soelle and Vanstone[240] we are given deep insight, through the vision of God in Jesus, into God's suffering in our human tragedies. Only a God who suffers can command human love and trust. But somehow this still does not excuse God – humanly speaking – for the very terrible tragedies within the creation: a severely handicapped child, famine in Ethiopia, the Holocaust or Hiroshima. Our God may be too distant. It is in Jesus that the terrible mystery of suffering comes right beside us; we abandon the attempt to find a tidy explanation and meet a friend.

Professor Frances Young, New Testament scholar and mother of three boys, one of whom is mentally handicapped, has brought her knowledge of the Christian tradition of Atonement (tracing its development historically through the ages) to explore our contemporary human suffering. She writes:

> . . . atonement is no more and no less than the presence of God in the midst of all that denies him. I suggest that an important clue to this is to be found in the book of Job . . . In Job's speeches it is the *absence* of God which is most painfully felt. So perhaps the solution to the interpretative puzzle is this: that the fact of God's presence satisfies Job rather than what he says. When God himself appears no explanations are necessary. In his presence, anything and everything is bearable . . [241]

Jesus plumbed human helplessness to its very depths including our feeling of forsakenness by friends and God. Here is a descent into hell which pastors, following Jesus, may be called to endure with those they help, saying with their lips 'I hold and am held'. But there may be no light, no voice, no escape, no victory: only death. Just like the night of Good Friday afternoon.

16 Counselling

Creative and participative listening changes the dead letter of a person's tale to a living drama in which hope may be found (A. V. Campbell).

A man's greatness is to be measured by his capacity for communion with others (Quoist).

Counselling has great potential both for creating vision and kindling hope. I will therefore try to give a brief summary of the way it fits into the context of *nurturing a congregation for its task in the world*. After discussion I will attempt a Christian assessment of counselling.

Counselling is a conversation. Those who share in it affirm or challenge the values of the prevailing culture. In particular, faith in God, vision of God's future purpose for humanity (and the place of both counsellor and counsellee within it), the corporate and individual nature of personhood, the realization of judgment and forgiveness, the nature of professional help and mutuality, are all matters in which secular or Christian values may be controversial, and affirmed or denied. Counselling is not value-free.

Counselling has long existed in the tradition of Christian spirituality, but it has flowered in its modern form since the 1939/45 war. The work of Freud gave rise to a practice of psychotherapy upon which counselling is now generally based. There are many different belief systems, schools of training and ways of practice.[242] Both the British Association for Counselling[243] and the Association for Pastoral Care and Counselling[244] have published material which outlines the wide spectrum of approaches to counselling by their members.

In general one might say that conversation between two or more human beings is like a dance, each partner responding to the movements of the other; or like a duel as they argue to and fro. When they listen to one another, try to understand some issue more deeply, and share experience, the conversation partakes of the nature of counselling. Jacobs[245] has described the mutuality implicit in such listening. There is a continuum of *creative conversation* which begins at one end with friendship, moves through counselling in a more formal sense, and at the other end consists of psychotherapy and more specialized treatment. The partners in conversation may be equal in friendship, while in therapy they are equal in humanity but differ in knowledge and skill. But in *any* conversation the situation is always new and potentially creative or destructive for both partners. In my opinion it is undesirable to draw hard and fast lines between different types of conversation: mothers need to be as skilled as any professional in the conversations which they have when bringing up a family. Other people would not agree with me and would wish to define the boundaries of counselling more closely. I think counselling in this respect is like medicine in that you may need someone as professional as a heart surgeon; on the other hand everyone needs to be able to take a splinter out of someone's finger. However, both these examples refer to what Mathers calls 'non-personal skills'.[246] Counselling involves personal qualities which are basic to the helping professions.

The greatest amount of counselling is given one-to-one in a completely secular context. But pastoral counselling shares two areas with pastoral care: (*i*) work within the church in which prayer, sacraments, and Christian language form a natural part of the whole approach, and truth is sought through reference to scripture; (*ii*) a secular setting in which the work may form part of the congregation's out-going mission in the world for those in need. The kind of conversation is therefore influenced by the context in which counselling takes place: whether in a Mediation Centre,[247] a psychiatric out-patients, a Catholic confessional, a school or someone's own home.

The cultural context also has a marked effect on counselling. Lartey[248] has used African psychology and anthropology as a critique of Western types of counselling, to measure their usefulness or foreignness to African understanding of what it means to be a human being. In classical times people went for counsel to the Delphic Oracle. Today in Ghana people may go to the priests of the Ashanti shrines, where counselling methods are more intuitive than Western styles which depend on more articulate conversation. In Nigeria there are ancient and highly developed religious traditions of non-directive counselling[249] such as the Ife oracles.

Each setting has underlying values which influence – often tacitly – the counselling given there. For example, profession, agency, class, religion and national culture all tend to mould counselling with their values, which are usually taken for granted and not brought into the open for critical assessment. The First International Conference on Patient Counselling (Amsterdam 1974) virtually excluded any counsellors who worked in educational settings simply by the use of the word 'patient' in the conference title. The values of the conference were those of medicine and not education.

The same conference by its professional approach disregarded the *everyday* level of counselling which is the first level at which most people seek informal help – from untrained people who are available and speak the same language. For example, it is often the student nurse on night duty who gets asked the really heavy questions. Doctors especially tend to overlook the oppressive weight of their professional skills which may make it difficult to approach them for personal help:

> If as a result of the First International Congress on Patient Counselling, the international Press had reported that physicians were interested in counselling, there would be little celebration among ordinary people, who already find our professional style too remote and powerful. If, however, the international Press had reported that a significant body of physicians from many countries had determined to set aside time to talk with their patients, then this simple fact might have commanded instant attention among ordinary people.[250]

Lambourne thought that counselling should be held in higher regard and that it should be more central to pastoral care in the church. He was however highly critical of the ways in which counselling developed in both the USA and Britain. Styles of counselling based upon psychology and divorced from traditional resources of help such as prayer and sacraments have too often been adopted by the church without sufficient critical evaluation. In any case very little ecological evaluation[251] has been done more widely than on the individual effects of counselling – by study of the long-term effects on the family for example. Much counselling is still done with individuals when it would be more appropriate to work with his or her group through family counselling. I owe a personal debt to my 'Chief', Dr K. E. Harris, who plunged me into family counselling by suggesting that I should go round his patients on Visiting Afternoons – the very time when most junior physicians avoid the wards like the plague.

Lambourne[252] pointed to the effect of a counsellor's beliefs, attitudes and values on people coming for help. He spoke of counselling as 'ethical persuasion', and noted many of the effects of an apprenticeship on a learner – effects which were being caught, not taught in actual conversation. When it comes to accreditation of a counsellor, this aspect of the counsellor's quality is extremely difficult to assess (as also in candidates for ordination): rather it is the psychotherapy-based skill which is more easily evaluated. However the human quality of the counsellor's character has been shown to be significant for the outcome of counselling.

Lambourne also raised a number of objections[253] to the way counselling centres were being set up in Britain. He saw a need for counselling to develop in the community more widely than in centres manned by professionals. He saw the style of counselling which was needed as 'lay, corporate, variegated, adventurous and diffuse (where people meet)': in this way it would become part of the method by which every pastor could help others. An example might be the care of the bereaved. It seems ludicrous for someone who is distraught with grief to have to go to a centre to see a counsellor: it could normally be part of a congregation's care when a member visits the home. The pastoral work of the church is in some measure a general responsibility of all members.

Professional counselling is in any case becoming well established in Britain and the church needs to encourage a supplement and corrective to one-sided professional styles. Much counselling focuses on people's problems: this is in part due to the prevalence in British society of a medical and social work approach to distress. But only a minority of the church's acts for the distressed are concerned with individual problems or illness. It is important therefore that a minority of professionals, trained to help others in this way, do not shape the long-term strategy of the church, which is more concerned with promoting healthy ways of living together, and gives no credence to the problem-solving view of human progress. Without a lively sense of purpose in life, counselling can become trapped by the secular cult of individual self-development so common in Western society.

Considerable thought went into the establishment of a counselling centre at a church in the centre of a city [254] and it is worth reading the account of how they set out to staff the centre with teams of trained counsellors from the congregation – *mini-congregations*. This strong congregational responsibility meant that the centre remained a subject of thought, prayer and discussion within the church's compassion for lonely and troubled people in the city centre. Group membership also made it possible to share the suffering involved in counselling and to give one another support.

Oden[255] made a study of intimacy between human beings. In the course of his research he found that many of the factors in intimate human relations were also factors in counselling. Professional counselling is, he concluded, an intimate relationship; but of a special kind. It is intimate because the trust established in the relationship enables very private matters to be openly discussed and feelings both good and bad to be expressed. But it is also a relationship 'at arm's length' in the fact that the time and place are structured and the service may have to be paid for. It is a contract relationship; intermittent rather than continuous. Oden describes it as a relationship of 'surrogate intimacy'. This does not mean that it is unreal, but it describes the kind of relationship which it is – a therapeutic relationship.

How are we to understand a relationship that is therapeutic, if this is how counselling may be described? Truax and Carkhuff[256] have described a great deal of research into what has now become known as 'the therapeutic triad'. If a relationship is to be therapeutic three attitudes have been found to be necessary in the therapist: (1) *Accurate empathy* means the ability to sense correctly what someone else is feeling (but not necessarily expressing) – for example anger or anxiety. (2) *Non-possessive warmth* means a warm out-going feeling towards another with wholehearted acceptance of all they reveal themselves to be; free of condemnation and negative 'ifs' and 'buts' about what their story tells. (3) *Genuineness* means trustworthiness, openness, and a wholeness of character which is real and without professional facade.

These three characteristics of a therapeutic relationship might equally well apply (one would think) to the desirable qualities of a teacher who is a good educator (not merely a transmitter of subject matter), or of a parent bringing up children. However the description of this therapeutic triad, though helpful in selecting and training counsellors (and teachers and Mums?), is a one-sided description of a therapist (i.e. one who heals another). It is by no means certain that we should speak of one person 'healing' another (transitive use of the verb), rather than of someone 'being healed' (intransitive use of the verb).

One person does not do something to another in counselling; it is not like a surgeon operating on a patient. The process lacks an 'inter-actionist language' which could describe the mutuality of a relationship. We spoke above of a dance or duel between counsellor and counsellee. Research has not analyzed the qualities of the recipient of help with anything like the thoroughness of the giver (for whom training and professional ethics have to be described). Eysenck[257] was the first to point out that 'average' psychotherapy achieves no better results than leaving people to recover on their own. He also put forward the view, later supported by other observers, that psychotherapy may be harmful as often as helpful.

The results of research have constantly high-lighted the *quality* of the person helping those in need as vital to the outcome. This has appeared to be more important than the particular method of counselling or psychotherapy adopted. It is also true for a wide variety of illness and personal problems requiring help.[258]

There is an interesting study of an experiment[259] which confirmed these findings. Selected students were asked to befriend disturbed teenagers over a period of years. The qualities of the students and the responses of the teenagers (including parents' and teachers' reports) were recorded. The experiment was called 'Companionship Therapy'. Significant title! Companionship means literally 'one with whom I share bread' (see p.80 for the story of a professional counsellor who in desperation was forced to share bread with an unwilling teenager). It may strike the ordinary reader at this stage that to label companionship as therapeutic is to state the obvious.

Mathers[260] has described four levels at which counselling is given and learnt. As described above, there is the *every-day* level (for which people as amateurs are not trained but mature with experience of people and life). There is secondly a *basic level* at which counselling is an element in all caring for people by professionals such as nurses, teachers, clergy or social workers. Training would include study of human growth and development, and counselling would form part of the assessment for fitness to practise their profession. The third level of *competence* is a development of the basic care offered by professionals, and will be acquired through experience and course work as part of further professional education. The fourth level is that of *specialized* training, and here Mathers suggests that it is not those who work with clients who should be taught further, but that already competent counsellors should be taught to teach. In particular they need to learn the skill of a consulting rather than a supervisory role.

I am not sure that a Westerner like myself, in the midst of the situation, can see clearly enough what is the cause of a sickness in personal relationships, our loss of community spirit in the West, which has given rise to the growth of counselling as a remedy. 'Love' is popular, suffering love is not. If we hunger for intimacy, but our ability to sustain intimate relationships has declined, have we lost perhaps the ability to suffer pain as a complement to the joy of deep relationship? There seems to be a cluster of counselling concerns around various 'pain points' like death, divorce and bereavement, which might indicate such a change. Or perhaps counselling, which is age-long, has more recently been caught up in the professionalization rampant in the West: the work of Freud, Jung and others gave this impetus in the field of psychotherapy.

I have indicated in various parts of this book the processes of change which have resulted in 'things falling apart'. Basically I would agree with the proposition of the Duke of Edinburgh, previously quoted (p.12), that our culture is simply free-wheeling on our Christian inheritance. It could be an oversimplification to say that loss of faith in God is the root cause of the changes: but a principle of unity at the heart of our civilization has gone. There have been other periods when 'there was no open vision'. Fortunately the loss is not general among all peoples and Britain (including the churches) stands in great need of a transfusion of vision and faith from the Two-Thirds world.

I want now to attempt a partial Christian assessment of counselling as an important facet of pastoral care:

In the context of the church the aim of counselling is not primarily to sort out personal problems but *to clarify a purpose in life* to be undertaken with other people. This is not primarily *my* purpose in life but God's purpose for the whole world, into which I fit with a sense of individual and local purpose also. This could be described as catching a vision of the whole grand strategy of God for planet earth (and beyond), and being caught up in the whole enterprise with a wholeheartedness that begins to diminish personal problems and inspires a particular and local commitment to God's work. I would not deny that problems which hinder commitment, prevent forgiveness, make repentance impossible, and impair the capacity for relating to others in a joint enterprise, may require sorting out. But *counselling in a Christian context primarily serves the mission of the congregation for the kingdom of God in the everyday*: it is part of the process of equipping the people of God – as a Body – for their personal and public ministry. Personal development is a by-product rather than a prime objective of membership of a Christian community with a master purpose in life. There is a false personalism which has invaded pastoral care and counselling, and which has centred attention on individual 'spiritual' development. This can trap development into a self-centred enterprise. The Christian calling releases people from this by offering a public cause in which the self may find itself by losing itself. *Counselling in this way ensures that theory and practice, faith and life, personal development and public involvement are integrated*. And clients are always people not objects.

Counselling is to be understood more as an *educational venture* than a therapeutic relationship. 'It's not what happens to us that matters, it's what we make of it.' Problems are not solved in the way people hope: it is enough to receive light and understanding and to be given strength to cope. Out of our distress, human bonds can be created.

It would be difficult to draw the line between counselling someone in trouble and tutoring a post-graduate group in a university. Both are relationships of mutual learning. This leads to the interesting consideration that the better use of psychology and counselling may not be as a basis for therapy (Freud was a doctor and for worse rather than better gave the subject a medical context) but for learning how to grow up and live more fully. At present it forms part of a teacher's professional training, but why not a future parent's? *It should be a normal subject of everyone's education in how to become more human*. The significance of Marriage Guidance Counselling may lie not in the resolution of problems for marriages that have run on the rocks, so much as in the vast experience available for creating healthy marriages. Their educational work with schools may be more significant than their clinics. This is to make once again the point that we need, both in church and society as in medicine, to move our thoughts towards prevention and the development of healthy communities (creation) as well as tackling crises (salvation).

The practical context of being a Christian with others requires that we *grow in sensitivity* and our *capacity to relate to others*, both within the Christian group and in our secular calling. What Lambourne (following Mathers)[261] has called 'We-formation' is both the basis of working with others and also the expression of our full humanity in the life of the kingdom. Counselling is concerned to promote the capacity for *membership* of a Christian community of high morale by the development of cooperativeness, discernment, and compassion for others. It is also concerned to promote capacities for self-giving and sharing which may avoid the snares of arm's length giving and compulsive service.

This throws emphasis not so much on the therapeutic triad which is a description of the quality of an individual counsellor's character, but on *mutuality* between Christians who as amateurs (literally 'the one who loves') counsel one another. This is not to demote counselling: it is to raise the standard of what it means to be a Christian. The church's task is to produce sensitive and caring people – to kindle fire in an earthen vessel – not so much to provide structures (there are enough already) through which they can work.

Implicit in this whole discussion of counselling is the *value system* upon which it is based. We have noted that the values vary from one context to another. In the Christian context there is conflict with the secular values prevailing in Western societies, and the church must beware that it is not seduced by the obvious professional competence of counsellors into acceptance of values implicit in their practice.

The privatization of religion by secular society can be re-inforced by one-to-one counselling. Christianity, on the other hand, is concerned primarily with the public issues of God's purpose of building a just society locally and internationally.

Counselling, like worship, confirms the worth of each individual. But whereas acceptance is valued in counselling theory and practice, it is forgiveness that the gospel brings. Acceptance is a highly creative professional attitude which can be bought by the hour. Forgiveness cannot be bought, it is costly and free. If counselling is said to be non-judgmental, counselling in the Christian context *is* judgmental – but in a different sense to that commonly understood. It is non-judgmental in the sense of being *non-condemnatory*, but *is* judgmental in the sense that both counsellor and counsellee judge themselves against the revelation of God in Jesus, and both rejoice in the knowledge of God's continuous forgivingness for the dark side of our humanity.

Highly professional counselling is valuable, but in the Christian context everyday counselling is most prominent. Counselling too, like theology, needs democratization and rescue from the experts. Everyday counselling is the province of the amateur, and the insights of counselling belong to every mother bringing up her children in an apprenticeship to the way of God.

There needs to be a growing appreciation of *group and family* styles of counselling. Individual counselling will always have a place but on the other hand 'no man is an island entire of itself', and as the balance of our understanding of human nature moves towards such a realization of our solidarity with one another, group and family counselling will assume more importance than at present. It will become the norm, and individual counselling its accessory. This accords with a Christian understanding of the nature of our humanity and the use of groups as a testing ground for reality in theological exploration.

A possible archetype for a counsellor might be Kvasir in Norse mythology.[262] Wherever he went 'sewing and salting and scything and swordplay were laid aside; even children stopped chattering and listened to his words.' What was his secret?

It was as much in his manner as in his mine of understanding. Questions of fact he answered with simple facts. But to ask Kvasir for his opinion – What shall I say? What do you think? What shall I do? – did not always mean getting a direct answer. Sitting back in his ill-fitting clothes, as often as not with his eyes closed, he would listen to recitals of problems and sorrows with a kind, grave, blank face. He took in and set everything in a wider frame. He never intruded or insisted; rather, he suggested. Often enough he answered a question with another question. He made gods and men, giants and dwarfs feel they had been helped to answer their own questions.

Kvasir was created by the gods from the divine spittle of reconciliation. This living witness to friendship was brutally killed by two envious dwarfs. They mixed his blood with honey to make a sublime mead. Whoever drank it received the gift of wisdom or poetry.

By suggesting Kvasir as an archetype of counselling I not only have in mind his manner, but also the life-through-death gift of his charisma to others.

In the Odyssey[263] we have the less dramatic figure of Mentor, a friend of Odysseus, who chose him because of his wisdom as a counsellor to his son Telemachus. Hence the word 'mentor' has come to our language. Jane Abercrombie, in a university lecture has described an African sculpture of a 'Mentor and Child' whose heads are fused and who have a shared arm.

17 Christian Apprenticeship Today

Mature manhood, measured by nothing less than the full stature of Christ (Ephesians).

You do not train leaders, you recognise them (R. E. C. Browne).

We have previously (pp.74–83) discussed apprenticeship in relation to learning theology in a way that unites theory and practice. It has been assumed therefore that apprenticeship is appropriate for those who have developed the faculty of conceptual thought (above the age of about twelve years). However apprenticeship is one part of a long process of growing up from childhood towards maturity. We will now discuss apprenticeship in this wider context of living faith in the world from birth to death.

Prolonged inter-personal contact between a child and its parents (or parental figures in the case of an extended family as in Africa) is the required 'nest' for a child's growth in social and cultural abilities. This period of dependence, prolonged in the case of the human species, is marked by a plasticity in the child which enables imitation and acritical learning of speech, social behaviour, values, morals and even of the mannerisms of its parents. The child assimilates its parents' culture which includes their beliefs about God and their spirituality, whether Christian, Hindu or Humanist. We tend to forget that parents do communicate their religious experience consciously and tacitly to their children.

In addition to parental influence, membership of a family includes relationship to siblings (and later peer groups). They learn together, through cooperation and conflict in play, the lessons of being both an individual and a person-in-relationship.

During adolescence a young person may build on his/her early learning by hero-ine worship. Someone prominent in the family, society or history may be chosen by the child as a model for life and behaviour. This hero-ine becomes a significant influence in further shaping the young person's attitudes, beliefs, habits and values. At the same time membership of a peer group forms the context within which such adult models are tested out. Hero-ine worship does not influence a young person in isolation but enthuses him/her with attitudes and values which are shared with others and which bring a teenager either into conflict or common agreement with their group. Always the interplay between individual and corporate development shapes a person's growth towards maturity.

At any period during adult life a person may further choose a teacher under whom to learn some skill (such as carpentry); or more generally a charismatic leader, holy person or guru who is able to attract other adults to discipleship and inspire them – often at considerable self sacrifice – to grow in a faith by assimilating its tradition.

The way of acquiring skills such as medicine, music or art is through arduous apprenticeship to a teacher. Suzuki[264] has shown that under his 'parenting' even tone-deaf children can unlearn early patterns and acquire his musical talent. The artist David Shepherd[265] has given a vivid account of his apprenticeship in drawing and painting.

Apprenticeship has proved its worth in the transmission of skills and crafts. But the master craftsperson always knows more than s-he can tell. Hence the apprentice not only imitates every action, but seizes upon every word, every expression, every hint of the mysterious mastery which perhaps only time and experience can bring. Apprenticeship ensures the passing on of a tradition. But every mentor hopes that her pupil will stand on her shoulders and so not only gives him/her all she knows but encourages a pupil to stand on his/her own feet and to explore, thus ensuring that the tradition is continually renewed by new discoveries. It is in this way that science advances. It is in this way that the music of Mozart lives in a different age: everything – instruments, notation, musical appreciation – has changed except the score, which only awaits a musician to interpret. In the same way the scriptures have survived the changes of time – culture, language, ways of communication, all have changed – the text remains for modern Christians to interpret.

Such apprenticeship was the traditional way in which the Pharisees passed on their living faith: masters of torah trained their disciples. Jesus similarly apprenticed twelve disciples whom he chose. He was able powerfully to address their own religious aspirations which their Jewish upbringing had instilled into them, so that they left their work and families to room and roam with him. He formed a very mixed group whose shared life, conflicts and unity formed an integral part of their apprenticeship.

Milavec[266] has made a major study of apprenticeship and how Jesus the master trained and empowered his disciples. Milavec's understanding of how a tradition is learnt through apprenticeship is based on the work of Polanyi.[267] Milavec has recovered the original Jewish insight into the human responsibility which we carry for the painstaking transmission of religious knowledge, sensitivity and values. But I do not feel he has given enough weight to the way in which we *also* learn from one another in families and groups. It is both from parents and siblings that we learn; both hero-ines and peer group members; both skilled supervisors and our fellow disciples. The concrete discipline of church membership enables our fellow members to correct our fantasies and disturb our illusions. Every one teaches every one. I applaud Milavec's insight into the seriousness with which we should take the learning by apprenticeship from a master, but *also* wish to take peer learning with equal seriousness. I am describing a model of *group apprenticeship*.

In the early church, Tertullian (third century) coined the word 'catechumen' to describe an apprentice who enrolled in a pro- gramme of Christian initiation. This learning to become a Christian, at first undertaken during the weeks of Lent, involved an intensive character change, a re-formation of beliefs, attitudes, values, be- haviour and perception. The term apprenticeship is not usually used for a process of simple passing on of information. Apprenticeship involves the assimilation of a new way of life with its personal skills and values. The catechuminate involved a re-birth, a new life through the death of the old style of life, vividly symbolized in the baptism to which apprenticeship led. This was comparable in seriousness and ritual to the puberty ceremonies which in many countries mark the transition from childhood to adult responsibility.

When the catechuminate lapsed in the sixth century it was left to the prevailing culture to convey the Christian heritage. This reduced the depth of Christian discipleship except in special communities or orders. Today, with the secularization of Western society, *we are in a similar situation to the early church* because it is impossible for the Christian heritage to be passed down from one generation to the next except by the members of the Christian church. Crewdson[268] writes:

Today, less than ever are publicly accredited Christian standards woven into society and, in the absence of competent apprenticeship within the Church, any saintly wisdom or prophetic holiness which characterised the first generation of disciples is found only in isolated individuals, not throughout the general membership of the organised Church.

Why do so many young people opt out of the church soon after their confirmation as adult members? Part of the answer may lie in our discussion of apprenticeship above. Generally we may be trying to convey Christian faith by instruction in a belief system rather than by apprenticeship (in which instruction has its place) into a way of life.

If the general assumption which underlies this section of the book were to be described as the need for an apprenticeship to Jesus as the model and power for living, we must first answer the question put by the Greek enquirers to Philip: 'Sir, we would see Jesus.'[269] Where is Jesus to be found, to be known and followed?

After his death and resurrection Jesus bequeathed his charisma to the whole group of the disciples. He did not train and appoint one deputy who would take over to represent him: he trained a group of twelve, and Paul described an early Christian community as Christ's 'Body'. In addition to finding Jesus in the body of his followers he is also to be known through the eucharist, the word of Scripture, a word spoken to us by another human being, in simple acts of compassion such as feeding the hungry and visiting the sick, and in the needy themselves – the hungry and the prisoner. Varied patterns of apprenticeship and discipleship in the church today are aimed at discovering Jesus in these different ways and assimilating his lifestyle and power; in becoming his representative. Some of the more exploratory patterns of apprenticeship blend both individual and group learning from one another, as for example in Theological Education by Extension.[270]

I remember on one occasion the then vicar of St Martin-in-the-Fields remarking that in some ways the church should be like a university – 'learn and leave'. When people first become Christians they attend many church groups and grow in knowledge of the tradition and scriptures. But then after two or three years, as they become more secure in their faith, they move more into secular settings to attend political, professional or Trade Union meetings and so engage in work for the kingdom of God in the world;

consequently being seen less and less around the church premises except for family worship. To lay the foundations for and to maintain such an outward-looking vision of the church's mission in the world a basic lay training scheme was embodied in the church's programme.

A learning course for members of the congregation began with a residential weekend called a 'Parish Life' conference. From the outset the group learnt to think together as a church, not just as individual Christians; to discern the nature of the area where the church is placed; and to assess the present work of the church and how it should develop its local mission. Opportunities were also made for course members to visit, two by two, such places as hostels for discharged prisoners or psychiatric patients, homes for the elderly, and a church crypt where homeless people were fed. The purpose of such visits was to go into unfamiliar situations, to meet people hurt by life in a modern city, and to enable those who took part to learn ways of using theology and Christian faith for understanding situations and taking action in them.

In the sessions following the visits each encounter was shared with the rest of the group. Certain questions were explored. For example, 'How do you affirm the dignity of someone who has to come for food and shelter? Does your experience connect with any Christian doctrine, faith-statement or belief? Does theology help us to understand our mission as a church and what further action could we take?' Often the visits caused deep self-searching, new insight into the needs of the community, and changes in the church's work.

Members of the course were divided into small teams for various discussions: a course of thirty members would be divided into six teams (some of the teams being from other churches: thus the courses were ecumenical). Fellow members of their team would visit someone who had not turned up for a course session to see whether the absentee had flu or was suffering from stress because of course demands.

One of the discoveries during such training was the custom of taking problems to the vicar for counselling help. Problems raised by the lectures and practical work were often matters of personal relationships, disbelief, doubt, difficulties with prayer, understanding the Bible or the use of everyday theology, as well as anxiety and stress. Such matters are not problems to be solved but the bread and butter of growth in the Christian life: it became evident that by going outside the course to seek the vicar's help, much valuable learning material was being privatized out of the course. It was therefore agreed to tell members at the beginning of a new course that if they were in difficulty a particular member of staff was the person to go and see. This tutor's task was that of a long stop: when anyone came for help with a problem it was his task to see whether the matter could (if appropriate) be shared with the person's team. In this way some course members grew in stature by learning to support and help one another; and an attempt was made to wean people from over-dependence on clergy.

This parish course was staffed by consultants with experience in this kind of work.[271] The course had something in common with traditional apprenticeship, both in its serious and prolonged programme (three terms over a year), its combination of both theory and practice, and its initiation into attitudes, values and methods of living the Christian faith. Its aim was to initiate the habit of *thinking together as a church* about the local situation in the light of the Christian faith: and growth towards maturity in the Christian way. However it was unlike traditional apprenticeship in its emphasis on the value of the church members as resources for one another, and the less authoritarian role of the consultants whose task was to enable the group to learn from one another. It was a group apprenticeship rather than an individual teacher/learner relationship.

When discussing the effects of good morale in a team we noted that it raises the threshold of bearing stress. In training soldiers and policemen deliberate exposure to stress is part of learning the job. Similarly, for anyone who undertakes pastoral work it is essential to understand how one reacts to stressful situations (for example, visiting a mother whose small child has been diagnosed as having leukaemia, or meeting a group of sufferers from AIDS). The pastor has to be able to walk into situations which seem to deny the goodness of God, trusting in the presence and love of God. This presupposes considerable strength in bearing feelings of anxiety and despair which can overwhelm one at times like this: and also to bear the feelings of those involved who seek broad shoulders upon which to heap their guilt and grief. An old pastor wrote: 'You do not think you can help anybody? Hold fast to Christ, and *you* are the help they need.'[272]

It is not difficult to devise exposure to such stress for the purpose of training: but it often comes without seeking the experience. Whether sought or unsought it is important to have the loving support of a friend or a group with whom it is possible to speak of one's feelings, and by sharing the pain learn to bear it creatively. A pastor also learns to use these very occasions of stress for cementing personal and family relationships.

Learning about stress is not a matter of lectures although these may have a part to play. For example, it can be helpful to know the ways in which human beings defend themselves against suffering – by denial, by projecting one's feelings on to others instead of bearing them, by withdrawal into one's shell, and so on. But it is more a matter of learning from experience how each person reacts, what feelings feel like, and learning not to suppress one's feelings (when sooner or later a safety valve will blow) but to bear them and act sensibly. Heroes and cowards feel much the same: but they cope with their feelings differently. We need to learn to feel for ourselves even if we make mistakes.

Mistakes are good learning material. It is important to deal with them in a constructive way, because doing something wrong may be associated with bad feelings and guilt. Mistakes need to be transformed into enlightenment, humility and gratitude: they are valuable when used in an educational way to confirm a person's worth and build self-confidence and skill. But to achieve this often requires a painful *metanoia* in our attitude to badness.

When the church is scattered about its week-day business, many members will be at work on their own in home or industry. One of their priorities may well be to gather a group of two or three together in their own situation both for support and for discussion of what their Christian work might be where they are. A course of the kind described (like the Pastoral Studies course or the catechuminate) is only the beginning of a new way of maintaining everyday Christianity as a way of life, membership of a community, and constantly learning and growing. In this regard the church *is* like a university in so far as its teaching introduces students to a lifelong pattern of reading and researching their subjects: Christians, like good students, do not 'learn and leave' except in a physical sense, but the image set a useful aim for members of a congregation by directing their attention to mission in the world rather than membership of groups on church premises.

The heart of what is to be learnt both in parental training, Christian initiation and in lifelong practice is *everyday Christianity*. That is the art of relating Christian faith to daily life and work. This has been discussed throughout in relationship to pastoral care with our neighbours. What happens in the home, what happens at work, what happens in the town, what happens on the news and what happens in other countries: these are the situations which we strive to understand by thought, prayer and discussion, seeking what God calls us to do.

Preparation for church membership (e.g. for confirmation) has changed down the ages. Much can be learnt from the pattern of apprenticeship and the re-formation of character and lifestyle produced through the early catechuminate. Here the style of supervision was authoritarian and considerable commitment to the process was achieved by the catechumen's own desire to submit to re-birth. The supervisors of the catechuminate were themselves masters of the Christian tradition in thought, word and deed.

Adolescents in Western culture today are, however, far more sophisticated, and would expect their initiation to be more open and their own role more participative. Their whole approach to life tends to be more empirical, and it would be a tragedy if their education into Christian faith and life fell below the exploratory methods to which they are accustomed in school.

In Christian discipleship today, therefore, there is a gradation of supervision required. In the *upbringing* of children a long-standing apprenticeship is undertaken in socialization and the transmission of culture (including religious experience). In many ways the style of this learning is bound to be authoritarian in word and example.

As the child becomes *adolescent* the pattern of supervision needs to become less authoritarian and more mutual in character. Conceptual thought begins to dawn about the age of twelve and from then onwards adolescents may wish to understand and share reasons for belief, attitudes and values. By that age, however, a basic religious or non-religious stance has already been assimilated. To unlearn or re-learn that basis involves a painful change of re-birth.

An *adult's* initiation will be least authoritarian and the group learning from one another greatest. In Berne's language[273] there is a gradual development from an adult/child method of teaching to an adult/adult dialogue. But the words dialogue and development must not be allowed to mask the crises of self-knowledge, the repentance and the pain of life-through-death changes involved even in adults (or perhaps *more so* because adults grow more set in their ways).

As learning continues in *a life-long process* of growth and change, a 'spiritual director', 'soul-friend', 'confessor' or 'guru' may become a supervisor for a while: or (increasingly today) membership of a Basic Christian Community or local group may perform the same service. These represent different styles of teacher/learner relationship.

A *supervisor* (strictly) has a continuous long-term responsibility for a learner's work including attention to areas of weakness, and assessment of the standard reached (accreditation in professional work).

A *consultant* on the other hand has a short-term relationship with an individual or group and comes from outside the situation to help solve a problem or enable better performance of a task. The word consultant has changed its meaning due to changes in medical practice. Nowadays a patient is more likely to see a 'specialist' in the specialist's own place (hospital out-patients) and is taken over – even if temporarily – for investigation and treatment. A consultant however does not take over the work: his/her relationship is that of an equal with those seeking help except for the authority of his/her special knowledge. The consultant's task lies in helping an individual or group to increase *their own* expertise in solving a problem: and so to enable a group's activities that they become independent – that is, leadership now lies in the group. Enabling a group in this way is a more feminine style of help than supervision.

There are at least four aspects of what makes a good teacher in this context of Christian upbringing and learning. Firstly the *lifestyle* of the teacher – capacity for leadership, character, attitudes, values, moral behaviour and Christian practice in worship and prayer. Secondly the teacher's *knowledge* of the Christian tradition – scripture, worship and history. Thirdly the teacher's skill in *communication* and *education*. Those who teach church members all too often have no training in education. Fourthly the teacher's knowledge of and facility in the *building of group life* (family, class, congregation) and *enabling* the members of the group as a resource for one another in growth towards maturity.

Recognized teachers will be ripe in the personal qualities of the Christian life. Sometimes they will be ordained priests or ministers, sometimes lay persons, and often the work can be shared. It could be folly to give the supervision of an initiation class to a young ordained minister who had just left seminary, when there were ripe lay people with the requisite qualities in the congregation. But there is a tendency to give priority to knowledge about doctrine and scripture over the personal qualities of the Christian life which grow through suffering and love. *Both .... and .*

It is assumed in the West that educational objectives are measurable. However to take the measure of a person is a very different matter. An assessment of a standard reached is an explicit recognition by examiners who are encountered *face-to-face* (as it were). But a person who failed the exam might still be highly skilled in personal qualities which are best recognized by those who work with them *shoulder-to-shoulder* (as it were). If your wife died you would not necessarily turn to the examination-successful candidate for help but to the fellow learner whom you've rubbed along with over some time and *know* to be built on the rock. The same difficulties in assessment of personal and non-personal skills and the relationship between the two occur in the education and training of doctors, nurses, counsellors, clergy, social workers, police, foremen, many civil and public servants – not to mention mothers of families. It is a matter of *both* ripeness *and* knowledge.

In a culture where education is increasingly being usurped by training for work in a technological society, I use the word 'training' with caution. In matters of learning for leadership there is a process of growth in personal stature involved as well as the acquisition of 'hints and tips'. It is an education in sensitivity to group situations, moods and inner feelings, as well as in courage. If asked to carry this content, the word 'training' begins to burst at the seams. But every local church needs to be looking out for likely leaders and helping them to grow.

Group apprenticeship is a pattern for learning to live the Christian way. It is the very nature of apprenticeship to hold study and practice, faith and life, in unity. In the Christian context it is a life-long practice: living and learning go hand in hand. There is therefore also, in apprenticeship, a constant ebb and flow between worship and mission, gathering and scattering, individual and corporate being. Apprenticeship integrates individual and congregation for their ministry in the everyday.

18 Lay Ministry

In the New Testament, ministry belongs to Christ, and any service exercised in the world by the church is undertaken by members of the whole people of God (the body of Christ) who inherited Christ's ministry. The charisma of the Holy Spirit is given to every Christian for the task of the church in the world, and baptism/confirmation is every lay person's ordination for everyday ministry. A Church of England working party on the work of lay people produced a Common Statement which includes this vision:

> Because all human beings are made in the image of God, they are called to become the people of God, the Church, servants and ministers and citizens of the Kingdom, a new humanity in Jesus Christ . . . the call is there for all without exception.[274]

The idea that all lay people are called as members of the people of God to the ministry of the church in the world is contrary to the values of a Western society in which specialization and authorization are idolized. The call to lay people is therefore apt to be misinterpreted in one or more of the following ways:

It may be thought of in *institutional terms*, that is, as a call to duties related to the church itself, such as caring for property, reading lessons in church, membership of church committees, and so on. Laity who undertake massive responsibilities in daily life may be de-skilled in the church and given petty jobs to do. Of course an institution must be run effectively but the call to ministry (which means *waiting upon one another*) is not primarily institutional.

Or it may be visualized in *religious* terms. So many people who care for others are citizens of the kingdom of God, but are unaware of it because doing one's job does not appear to be anything to do with religion in the commonly understood sense. The church's task would seem to be to help those who care already to 'see' their care in its true light, not to produce an alternative religious way of caring for people.

Or the work is thought of in terms of *accreditation* – extra training by lectures and courses in order to acquire skills like counselling and recognition by the recognized. Lay ministry in the church is rapidly assuming an 'accredited' image. Rachel Moss[275] has pointed to the fact that the increase in training and accreditation of laity for parochial and diocesan work results in what she calls discredited laity going about their ordinary work situations. This pattern of accreditation and specialization is due to the pressures of professionalism in Western society: it is not founded on a theology of the ministry of the church which gives the amateur (literally the one who loves) prime place. The church needs to do things differently: there are plenty of courses for accreditation in society and the church needs to concentrate on nurturing human beings of spiritual depth to leaven the quality of everyday service. Because lay Christians are scattered in the world it is in their ordinary lives and work that ministry and service are normally carried out.

Or the work is thought of in terms of *voluntary service*, which is widely established today in most cities. It is an extra act of helping others over and above one's usual work. It is in terms of this additional time and effort which Christians give to voluntary service in society (such as the Samaritans, Cruse Club, or visiting the elderly) that most ministry or church service is often understood. Such work is of course excellent. But it is not the first call on a Christian's service.

A call to minister may be misunderstood as a call to the *ordained* ministry. That is a different matter. But a mixture of the above ideas – institutional, religious, extra commitment and accreditation – may tempt a layperson to ordination simply because a search for a deeper spirituality *as a lay person* may not receive the kind of enablement which leads to a fulfilled lay ministry.

Primarily a Christian is called to stay where s-he is. To be a minister of the people of God means to become a certain kind of person where we are. To let Christianization awaken us to what God wants us to be and do among our neighbours, in the family, at work, and in the local community. Much less often do Christians see their own daily work as ministry or pastoral care. Yet such work includes bringing up a family (homemaking), tending sick people (NHS or the elderly neighbour), counselling those in difficulty (the casual conversation over lunch) and education (at home, schools and university): as well as all the tasks of building community and the tough demands of personal relationships in marriage, commerce and industry.

Obviously service of others *may* require great skill, expertise and training. Counselling is an example where there is a range of work from the most expert (the counselling of people with sexual problems often requires special knowledge and experience) to straight befriending (such as many lonely people need). I am deliberately refusing to give a hard and fast definition of where counselling begins and ends. I am therefore refusing to de-skill ordinary people.

In many spheres of work such as mining, commerce, cleaning and transport, any person may be involved not only in matters related to standards at work (such as trustworthiness, punctuality, thoroughness, courtesy, or care of machinery), but also in ethical decisions related to work practices or strikes: and may further be involved in building team spirit through cooperation, or in crisis counselling and caring for someone in distress.

In the ministry of Jesus we see the centre of his concern has shifted from the religious to the secular. But in saying that I do not wish to imply that ordinary daily life is non-religious or profane. Such a distinction I believe to be false. Jesus showed us that God loves the world, and religion helps us to recognize God at work now as creator and healer.

There is a bias in selection for training. It is middle class articulate Christians who tend to opt for special training; they are favoured by the usual rather academic approach. Working class Christians who could respond to a more earthed apprenticeship type of training tend to be left with what should be normal for ministry – the work of the kingdom in their own place where they meet their fellows in street, pub or factory. This is a quite overwhelming task for which they get little training or support.

Many Christians are deterred from service because it often seems to require specialization. A lot has been written, for example, about bereavement counselling. Indeed it bids fair to becoming a specialist's job. One reads very little about the unobtrusive care given by those whom daily work or chance brings into contact with the bereaved. When my first wife died I remember with particular gratitude the very care-ful ministry of the clerk in the hospital who had the job of giving back to relatives the deceased's effects; and of my bank manager. Funeral directors of course may also exercise an important task of pastoral care for the bereaved and they are *there*. The Cruse Club for widows does a splendid job by disseminating knowledge among people of how to cope with grief in the everyday.

Hospital and other chaplains may unwittingly disable[276] their lay Christians by *seeming* to do the church's work for them. But even if there are no chaplains *the church is still present in its lay people.* Unless chaplains set out to encourage and enable lay people to think out and practise their ministry in their everyday work they will leave what appears to be the religious bit to the chaplains. The recovery of this perception of lay ministry in many areas is a high priority if the church is to be renewed. Archbishop Fisher of Canterbury[277] when he was in office wrote:

> When it comes to dying there is no distinction between doctor and chaplain – both are pastors and the faith of the doctor can often do far more than that of the chaplain, just because the doctor has been fighting the battle of life and death with the patients day by day more intimately than can often be the case for the chaplain.

Pattison[278] writing of the work of a hospital chaplain suggests a splendid variety of work which, however, would require a multiplicity of gifts rarely found in one individual. When viewed as a task to be tackled by the *whole people of God* in the hospital – the Christian doctors, nurses, social workers, cleaners and porters who are employed by the hospital – it becomes a possibility. I am not thinking of volunteer workers who come into the hospital from outside to visit on the wards as a chaplain's team, as described in a Bedford Hospital[279] – there may be a special place for such volunteers. I am thinking of Christians scattered in the everyday called to minister (to wait on one another in reverence) in their work situation.

Not all people have a gift for work of personal service. But there are many tasks (good neighbouring, parenting, politics, teaching, and homemaking) in the overall work of the church in the world, and a wide variety of gifts (administration, prophecy, public speaking, evangelism, teaching and understanding children) to further that work.

In the report of an Ecumenical Commission in a metropolitan diocese[280] the group concerned for 'Personal and Pastoral Needs' wrote:

> ... some Ministers are facing pastoral problems which are beyond their capacity to cope with. There was strong evidence of emotional disturbance and cries for help in situations where men

were facing the need for pastoral care or counselling support themselves . . . it is a serious need which is in danger of being neglected, 'Who cares for the carers?'

Most professional people today, whether doctor, nurse, social worker, teacher or minister, are exposed to stressful conditions of overwork, anxiety and rush. Whether these stresses are greater for the professional than for the housewife and mother or industrial worker is open to discussion, but the fact of stress is not in dispute. Consequently the group referred to above, in their survey of city churches, found evidence of strain amongst ministers and their wives, and commented that this did not surprise them.

An important piece of research[281] has outlined the strengths and weaknesses of 'The Helping Personality'. It shows how pastors, unless they face their own perfectionism, anxiety, or need for approval, may bring stress and strain not only to themselves but also to their spouses and families. A minister may need to be accountable to a 'supervisor' or 'soul friend' with whom s-he can share deep feelings and be helped to suffer and grow.

However *the primary responsibility for the pastoral care of ministers lies with their congregations*. Pastoral care includes the guardianship of a minister's style of life right from the first day of arrival, when a system of mutual care begins to operate between clergy and laity. For both this is a school of life in which deeper sharing is learnt so that the church may serve effectively in the world. Some churches are good at this: others do not see their ministry in this way but expect a one-way system of care for the congregation by a professionalized minister.

In what practical ways might mutual pastoral care between minister and congregation take place? *Firstly* I would regard it as the congregation's responsibility to see that their minister takes a day off every week. If ministers do not get one then their health is – in the long run – likely to suffer. So will their families who need some of their undivided attention if they are to fulfill the role of husband, wife, father or mother, and to present an image of healthy family life. It is the responsibility of the laity to see that the day off is kept and to accept responsibility for relief and finance as required. Some ministers are too weak, too obsessively active, or unable to sustain the feelings of guilt when leaving things undone, to take their full day off. Firmness in this regard is true care.

Holidays at Christmas, Easter, and in the summer are more generally regarded as necessary today. But the lay authority (PCC, deacons or church council meeting) should not hesitate to make extra holiday possible if a minister shows signs of strain.

Secondly it would probably be accepted widely that a minister needs time for proper study and reflection. Less widely thought about is his/her need for a refresher course. Laity should expect their ministers to do further study. It is essential for the vitality of their preaching and teaching. A church which has the same minister in charge for over five years may suffer from a dearth of new ideas. This is not an argument against long terms of office (there are other advantages of that), but it is an argument for asking at that point 'How can we arrange for our minister to take a refresher course?' A congregation often gets the kind of minister which it deserves. Unless a minister gets proper time for prayer, study and recreation – some of the very reasons why a minister is 'set aside' – then sooner or later s-he will cease to give what they are ordained for. The fate of many ministers is to be doing more and more at less and less depth, to become handicapped by anxiety or to break down.

These are simple examples of the way in which a congregation can begin to understand that pastoral care is mutual care: and the best pastoral care is to build up a healthy style of being-a-congregation-with-a-minister, to try and forestall some obvious points of weakness. At the moment ministers are often not seen as in need of pastoral care until something goes wrong – the casualty image. But pastoral care does not begin when something goes wrong: it is one aspect of the mutual care of every member of the whole people of God for one another in normality. Those who truly care for others rejoice in the care by others. And nowadays we *know* that the professional carers are high risk people. It is often a matter of changing the direction of one's gaze, and to look at, rather than just simply looking to the Minister.

I have described the pastoral care of an ordained minister by a congregation because such care is often unacceptable because of the gap between people and ordained minister caused by professionalism and clericalism. Before the kind of care which I have described is possible, there needs to be a change in the theological basis of ministry.

19 Discerning Involvement

It would be easy to be a saint if you hadn't to bother about being human (Marx).

Faith is not belief in spite of the evidence, but life in scorn of the consequences (Visser T'ooft).

To be a Christian does not mean to be religious in a particular way, to cultivate some particular sort of asceticism, but to be a man (Bonhoeffer).

Whether we think of home-making, industry or serving in a cafe, Christians are normally scattered in the world and committed to their tasks, to the needs of people at home or work, and to the aims of the many groups of people to which they belong. Since most of our lives are spent in the everyday, this chapter spells out a way of connecting theory and practice and living our faith in the everyday.

Although a Christian is a member of many different groups of people such as a family, congregation, work team, political party, Bible study group or football club, there are two memberships which are basic to all: to be a member of the human race by birth, and a member of the people of God by baptism.

Insight into the twofold nature of a Christian stance in the world I owe to the writings of R. K. Orchard, most recently in his *Servants of Life.*[282] Christians are both involved in the common life of humankind and at the same time open to the realm of God whence life of the quality of Christ's life is given to be shared by all.

Christians are therefore not only *involved* in the world as human beings but they are also called to stand back and to *discern their situation* with 'the mind of Christ': to see themselves and their institutions as all under the judgment of God. In this task theology provides a basis for standards, values and ethics by which to evaluate what is going on. The stance is one of 'prohetic incarnation': that is,

Christians are to be 'in the world but not of the world'.[283] This dual role is well illustrated by the prophet of the Old Testament.

The word prophecy has become narrowed in common speech to mean foretelling the future. In fact it is the prophet's insight into what is happening *now* in his own immediate situation which is significant. In the Old Testament this led to the prophet's often dramatic condemnation of king or nation. Or because he was on to something in the present, the prophet could foretell the future triumph or tragedy which he sensed was now present in embryo and ready to unfold. It is insight into the present situation which comes to a prophet with the force of a word from God.

There are two elements intertwined in this gift of prophecy. First the prophet is one of the common people, man or woman, deeply *involved* in their life, struggles, hopes and fears: no grandstand observer. Second the prophet through faith and prayer 'sees' the world through the eyes of God. This leads to *judgment* in the sense of 'sifting' right from wrong. Judgment is a neutral word. It is as much a judgment for a judge of horses to say 'That is a good horse' as it is to say 'That is a bad horse'. In the New Testament 'judgment' is the Greek word *crisis*, also meaning opportunity.

The prophet, then, discerns the issues of the day with – as far as humanly possible – the eyes of God. He calls for change of attitude and behaviour.

There is a sense in which all Christians scattered in the world about their business need, like the prophet, to be both involved in human affairs and also aware of another dimension of life, to see it related at the same time to God's activity. Christians are deeply involved in every corner of the nation's common life individually and together. The life of Jesus was notably involved – incarnate – in the life and work of a family, in a small country, in a race with a language and religion, at a specific time in history.

But Christians also have a common life and purpose which draws its inspiration from a centre in a wider and fuller realm – God's realm.[284] Therefore Christians have different attitudes and values, and need also to be discerning, that is, to take time to reflect on the situation in which they are. Christians bring, as it were, the mind of Christ to sift their situation. They compare the values underlying their situation with those of the realm of God. It is from this stance that the earlier chapters of this book were written, in which a Christian mind discerns the divisions between theory and practice, private and public issues, and the loss of long-term purpose which result from disbelief in God. In this way those who work (for example) in industry or in education will review their work. In industry human beings work together (do they?), both management and labour, to manufacture the things of God's earth to fulfill human needs for livelihood, health and enjoyment. Matters of ecology, quality, fair profits and rewards, team work, care of the disadvantaged, exploitation and greed are all matters which must concern those who make the wealth of a nation. In education parents need to discern the quality of their children's education: is this education for life, or just cramming for exams? Are my children learning competitiveness or cooperation?

Although discerning involvement is a way of being a Christian in the world, it is clearly most fruitful when two or three are gathered together in the same situation, particularly when conclusions are reached which may require practical action.

I have previously[285] used the description 'critically involved' for a Christian's way of relating to life: but in a *religious* context the word 'critical' can be mistaken to mean adopting a superior attitude to others, and even imputing blame. This however would be to misunderstand both the responsibility of the Christian way of life and also the nature of judgment. Christians who adopt a critical stance towards issues of the day or institutions in society must also be aware that they too are under the judgment of God. It is not that they try 'to play God'. In any case 'sifting' is *already* present where two or three are gathered together because one aspect of the presence of Jesus is that judgment happens.[286] In fact the gift of insight into their situation involves awesome responsibility: silence, in the eyes of God, is reprehensible.[287]

I therefore prefer to use the phrase *discerning involvement* which is less likely to be misunderstood. Even if criticism can come cheaply, discernment is always difficult, demanding and the product of Christian formation. In any case a group of Christians at work will recognize that their discernment is partial and they could be wrong: the strength of a group is that they can supplement one another's ideas. Ideas also have to be proved in action: and then they need one another's courage.

In an institution like a school or a hospital the two or three gathered together from time to time could form a Christian cell. They could arrange to lunch together occasionally as a deliberate meeting.

Sometimes they might need the help of a lay theologian or chaplain who would enable them (but not take over the leadership) to theologize their everyday situation and understand it more deeply.

Four doctors, a nurse and two social workers were lunching together when one of them, a GP, described how two of her patients had recently both had stillbirths, and been discharged from hospital without her knowledge of their tragedies. In one case she had actually rung up to hear 'the joyful news' (as she expected it). As a result of this lunchtime conversation the hospital chaplain subsequently organized a conference of midwives and theological students to discuss the care of the family when a stillbirth occurs. The conference was repeated with a larger group of professionals and led to the formation of a working party in the hospital which has changed the attitude of staff to the care of families in crisis. A counselling course for nurses has also been held to enable them to cope with such work as part of their professional and personal relationship with patients. Part of the function of a local church is to equip its members to work like this together in different fields – commerce, industry, transport, education, home and family.

Christians who are in the same or similar situations may need to gather separately for prayer, thought and support, to give their ministry the necessary depth. Careful thought is necessary as to how this is best done because it is important that Christian grouping should not erect an unnecessary barrier in a secular team (a conflict of values or a confrontation on some issue would be different). The cause of Christianity may often be advanced more by unassuming faithfulness to God in secret than by obvious Christian loyalty to somewhat exclusive groups.

The details of how an attempt was made to build a cohesive group of students for a particular task in a university has already been described (pp.118f.). The purpose of referring to the work of such Christian groups is not to put forward some structure which can be adopted as a missionary tactic: but to draw attention to the possibility of Christians meeting together *on the basis of their work or other common interest*.

It is already familiar that some Christians who work in the same institutions (such as probation service, business, nursing, or university) meet for fellowship, Bible study, conferences and meetings with a Christian speaker on some topic of concern. This pattern results to a great extent in a private spirituality with high moral standards,

'going the extra mile' and concern for personal respect in professional relationships. A pattern of one interesting talk after another
can become perpetual because the purpose of the group has become
social, and blindness ensues because no practical obedience follows
the talks.

The different pattern of work which I have in mind could be
described, but not exhaustively, as a 'ministry to structures' or as the
'politics of pastoral care'[288] – it is the very particular work situation
which brings Christians (and others) together. Their common
concern is for the public structures and institutions which shape the
way they have to go about their personal and public service.
Otherwise it is no exaggeration to say that many Christians – most
conscientiously and certainly without meaning it – are involved in
doing things which are de-humanizing to others.

This way of being a Christian in the world links together both
theology and life, thought and practice, spiritual and material,
idealism (as vision) and realism. In 1858 Mrs Ranyard's Bible
Mission[289] became a District Nursing Organisation, preserving its
Christian tradition. Each nurse was therefore both an individual
with her own visits and duties to perform: and also a Ranyard Nurse
belonging to a Christian body whence she drew strength and
support. In regular training days, conferences and worship, the
Ranyard nurses ensured that their salt kept its savour, their vocation
its clarity, and that their nursing standards were highly maintained.
Their badge was inscribed with '*Orare est laborare est . . .*' (To pray
is to work is . . .) in a continuous circle, thus linking both their
relationship to God and their daily pastoral care. Christians need
continuing support and access to theological resources if they are to
be *discerningly involved* in the modern world in a way which may
lead to pastoral care or political action.

Christians are 'new age human beings' indwelt by the Spirit of
God. The core of being a Christian in the world is thus their unity
with all people in a common humanity, not some search for the
security of being different. In a hospital ward there may be six or
more nurses only one of whom is a Christian. Perhaps God calls her
or him *for the sake of the other five nurses*, to be a receiver of love and
insight to be shared with them. This is one of God's ways of reaching
the 'deaf' and unbelieving. So far then from being in some way
superior, being a Christian in the world is 'being for others' and an
awesome responsibility. Christians receive life from the realm of

God which is to be *shared* with all in the common life. What fun! But how risky! It is dangerous to become a Christian disciple. The stories of the night of the Passion tell us of the cowardice and treachery which the chosen disciples showed. Great responsibilities involve risks of great corruption. But these are the men whose corruption was forgiven. These are the men whom he loved to the uttermost. These are the men through whom God loved the world.

There are three images which suggest ways in which Christians scattered in the world might see their work: light, yeast and salt. It makes a useful exercise to meditate on what these images have to teach us in our own lives: to compare our thoughts with others: and to use such reflection in a group or congregation for sharing ideas about style of life and mission strategy.

It is better for people to discuss their own understanding of these images rather than that I should try to generalize from my own life-situation. Three meditations on Light,[290] Yeast[291] and Salt[292] could begin by thinking what these things do: how do we use them? Then go on to explore our own situation (home, work, neighbour-hood, church, society, etc.) as thoroughly as possible. Next, what meaning have each of these three images of discipleship for each situation? Finally, what first steps can be taken? Action is possibly a key to the future, for one cannot help coming to the conclusion that we *already* know enough for the renewal of the church and society: it is obedience to what we already know that is lacking. In the service of God, theory and practice, words and deeds, are different aspects of one reality.

20 Conflict of Values

The cry comes principally from the young who before they can be anaesthetised and smothered by the urge to 'have', scream out their hunger to 'be' (A. V. Campbell).

To achieve real wholeness involves the difficult struggle to let go of perfection (Monica Furlong).

For Christians, fo live and work in Britain is to experience the constant undertow of the different value systems of a secular society. Social values were shaped in the past by Christianity, but now are rapidly changing under the influence of scientific secularism.

Politicians and clergy (among others) are constantly concerned with what motivates people to act. The unseen springs of conduct are rooted in values below the surface of reasoned argument. In a previous book[293] I have tried to unearth some of the values which underlie the British National Health Service. It is not easy to bring basic values to consciousness: they are normally assumed and acted upon unconsciously. A discussion of values may too easily become academic unless we are constantly reminded that it is the very sources of our actions and behaviour at which we are looking.

A student from East Africa recently went to a church reception one Sunday afternoon. In the course of conversation with a middle-aged lady he complimented her on some wise remark: 'You are growing old' he said. She didn't like it! In his culture old people are respected: soon they will pass through the door of the night and become ancestors. In Western culture that is not so. When my children say to me, 'Dad, you are growing old' it means that I'm forgetting things or not hearing so well: it is often a comment related to some deterioration. Yet deterioration in old age is quite natural.

The difference is not that Africans overlook the deterioration of old age but that *personal respect is more important*. What is right with someone is more important than what is wrong with them. The conversation described above was a personal meeting between two people from cultures based on different values. Both people represented in themselves beliefs, attitudes and values from their own countries/families/tribes which made them different. At their point of meeting there was a conflict of cultures and values. For them it was a crisis, a point where one or both could learn something new and change: or a point where one or both could refuse to learn and withdraw into their own position.

Of the two cultures which met on that Sunday afternoon the dominant culture at present is the Western one which devalues people. Van der Post has described the Bushman as being concerned with being human, in contrast to white civilization which is concerned with having possessions.

Economics dominate daily life and matters of value. The present Government gives top priority in the Health Service to cost-effectiveness. Everything has a price tag. (I even read recently an article in a weekly magazine which described starlings as 'cost-effective birds' because they do not build new nests, but repair old ones!) Much is being made of people's *rights* – the right to work, or the right to an abortion – and far less attention is given to people's *responsibilities*. The whole ethos of a consumer society and its passion for possessions is in stark contrast to the Christian aim – *to live simply, that others may simply live.*

Christian valuation of the individual (upon which the idol of individualism has been erected in our midst) reaches out in fact to the undervalued in society, the poor, the immigrant, the sinner and the sinned against, the handicapped and the lonely. In many cities of Europe today it is black people, women, the unemployed and the mentally handicapped who have special claims upon our value. But in secular society it is the *successful* individual who is held up for envy. Christian parents have difficulty in countering the competitiveness encouraged in the educational system. 'Get to the top' values have corrupted society.

Nelson[294] has suggested that in Western culture 'we are already well into fundamental long-term cultural transformation'. We may need to be developing a Christian strategy in response to this change. He also [295] points out the significance of a church report published in Canada, *Ethical Reflections on the Economic Crisis*,[296] which sets economic life in the context of human life *as if the latter has priority*. The report highlights a clash of values between the Catholic Church (economics were made for man not man for economics), and the secular State in Canada. In this way we need to recognize or to set up *signs of contradiction* in our own lives or in society: that is, actions which conflict with the accepted values around us. To do things differently.

In everyday Christianity we use theology as a critical tool for assessing social values. Killen[297] has written: 'Studied and disciplined theological reflection is a key to our churches putting into practice their values.' Elliott[298] describes how the coming of the kingdom of God brings a change in values, and Christian projects in a secular society may make visible a clash of value systems.

Jesus' healing works were spoken of as *signs* of the kingdom of God. Sometimes his healing works were a contradiction of the accepted order. He broke the law – by healing a man with a withered arm on the Sabbath; it was a test case which the religious authorities deliberately engineered to trap Jesus.[299] This was a sign of the kingdom coming not gradually but in sharp conflict. In conflict because he was acting upon a different value system – 'Doing His Father's will' – and rescue of a victim from illness took precedence over the law of the Sabbath as understood. On another occasion he healed a paralyzed man by forgiving his sins and it visibly worked – an outrageous contradiction of the accepted theology of Judaism. Jesus was crucified for openly challenging in such ways the doctrines of the religion in which he was brought up.

In Europe attitudes to death in hospital are fear-ful. A patient who dies may be virtually hidden: it can be one of those rare occasions when all the curtains round all the beds are drawn while the corpse is hurried away. When I visited Finland in 1975 I was told the story of three Finnish student nurses who decided that this behaviour was unseemly and contrary to the Christian dignity of the person. Accordingly when one of their patients died, they laid her out on the trolley, her arms folded with flowers on her chest; and wheeled her out through the ward in full view of the other patients. This was well accepted. A clash of values brought into the open may force society to choose one way or the other. To see a sign is to be brought to the point of choice – for better or for worse.

A widely known sign of contradiction is the Hospice Movement, which was developed by Dr Ciceley Saunders after working in St Joseph's Hospice, London. A hospice, which is devoted to the care of the dying, is founded on a different value system to that which exists in National Health Service hospitals, where the care of the dying is too often given low priority. The emphasis on clinical success, both in doctors' training and in patients' expectations, has almost led to a neglect of people with incurable illness. In a hospice the care of people is of value in itself, and does not have to be validated by clinical success. The worth of people as people is a value founded on respect for every human being as made in the image of God. The pioneer hospices were Christian Foundations: hospices have now proved their worth and are beginning to exist in the National Health Service.

Up until the 1939–45 war almost all the work amongst patients with leprosy was being done by missionary medical workers, and the foremost specialists in this disease were Christian. This too was a sign of the courage of Christians which enabled care to be given in the face of widespread fear of leprosy. The care of AIDS victims is a similar test of values in church and society.

The Pastoral Studies course could also be viewed as contradictory to some of the values of a Western university and therefore bound to be subversive to some extent. In its approach to educational matters the course integrates learning by practical experience as well as academic study. It also develops the feeling life as well as the intellect because pastors need to know about anxiety, stress and aggression, not only with their heads but also their hearts. The examination system was always a bone of contention because it is a test of individuals in isolation, whereas theology is a community production. The student group also vigorously protested at the high level of fees for overseas students, who were regarded as an asset who could help to make our theology more whole, not merely as course consumers.

In chapter 9 (pp. 88 ff.) there is described a parish in which the congregation's active involvement in politics during a time of great unemployment and hunger in Britain led them regularly into confrontation with the order of their day. This included a public protest by representatives of the parish against the investments of the Church Commissioners in armament manufacture. Today we would recognize the Peace and Green Movements as similar signs of a value system which conflicts with that of society.

Similarly, in the experimental health centre (see pp. 71–74 for examples) patients notice the style of health care and say 'It's different, why do you do it like this?' It is on the basis of *common experience* that people are drawn together into questioning and exploring together. A relationship is established out of which questions about God may, or may not arise.

Values are both 'caught' and 'taught' (from and by parents, teachers, counsellors and peers). Folk tales are a traditional way to teach values. Novels also provide valuable material for comparison of values in different societies and in different ages. Values are also transmitted in worship by hymns and preaching: they underlie public prayers. Growth in spirituality is based upon the internal formation of a value system in which God as known through Jesus is our 'highest value'.

Values are also studied in courses on ethics, and such study forms an important part of Christian apprenticeship. In the Youth Training Scheme of the YMCA values are taught through group methods: lively discussion can be initiated on hot moral issues such as sex and marriage, violence and stealing, nuclear arms, racism, and women's rights and responsibilities in society. I have facilitated such discussion among student nurses[300] and it is possible to begin to bring values into the open and recognize their importance in behaviour. A question-naire which always provokes discussion is one composed of a series of value-statements, such as:

1. Woman's place is in the home.
2. The unemployed could find work if they looked hard enough.
Each question is ticked off on a scale: Strongly Agree, Agree, Neutral, Disagree, Strongly Disagree.

Important as these discussions are among young people, their inner value system is already formed by their childhood parenting. It is then a matter of discovering what in fact their values are, and what the consequences might be for individuals and societies if such values are widely held: and exploring alternatives (which usually exist in any mixed group of youngsters anyway). A change of values is always slow and painful: we defend our inner value system tenaciously. A change involves both head and heart as we have described already in apprenticeship learning and the catechuminate. But membership of a group or community helps to forge that newness of inner value system which is so painful that only the word 're-birth' can bring together both the pain and joy of its achievement.

If 'deeds speak louder than words' then a local Christian com-munity always needs to be asking – given this situation 'How may the gospel be shown as well as spoken?' A faithful people will frequently find their Christian values in conflict with those of a secular society.

PART FIVE

Worship – the Consummation of Themes

Worship in the cathedral is an hour of sanity (Archbishop Tutu).

> *So make me to possess the Mystery*
> *That I may not desire to understand.*

Worship is a wholing activity because everyone and everything is centred upon God. Worship integrates theory and practice, faith and life, public and personal issues. In worship people are confirmed in their worth as individuals and as members of a community with a common purpose in life for the coming of God's kingdom in the everyday. In worship the Christian community is *formed* in its values and discernment, *empowered* for its task, and *scattered forth* for God's mission.

However this account of worship is bound to be partial because it serves the purpose of this book as a consummation of its themes. While setting out the way in which worship integrates the life of a community, it would be realistic, in passing, to point to ways in which worship is also corrupted by the values of scientific secularism because we ourselves are so corrupted.

Every loss of connection which we have noted in this book finds its echo in the worship of today in Western society. Here is a point of confrontation with God where the transformation of the world may begin with the transformation of the people of God.

21 Worship

Rituals reveal values at the deepest level (Monica Wilson).

Pavlova, after one of her performances, was approached by a young man who asked her to explain one of her dances. 'Do you think I would have danced it,' she replied, 'if I could have explained it?'

A work of Art with that alone which the artist puts into it is but a half of itself; it attains its full stature by what time and people make of it (Naum Gabo).

In worship members of the Christian community gather to celebrate the greatness of God. By paying attention to God the congregation sets the direction of their affection and will. The people of God open their hearts and minds to a realm within and beyond the everyday. It is as if the whole body of people turns like a compass needle towards an invisible source of attraction. As travellers take their direction from the steadily pointing compass, though the needle trembles, so the Body of Christ on earth constantly founds and refounds its vision, values and purpose in life upon God.

Worship grows community

In the minds and hearts of the members worship builds a commonality of outlook in beliefs, attitudes and values, which often conflict with those of society at large. In so doing it gives the Christian individual and community coherence, interdependence and courage. Worship empowers them for action in the everyday.

Hollenweger[301] has written and performed a eucharist for group celebration which addresses itself to the matter of conflict within the congregation. As part of the celebration the participants openly acknowledge the differences between themselves, while affirming their unity in celebrating the sacrament together. The differences between Christians today are as sharp as the differences present at the table of the Last Supper, or at a celebration in the church of Corinth. The kinds of difference which may have to be openly acknowledged in a congregation apply not only to Christian beliefs (both catholic and evangelical points of view may be represented, with quite different authority being given to the readings from scripture: modernist and traditionalist will have different beliefs about the virgin birth or resurrection); but also to conflicting actions such as membership of different political parties; and also to conflicting views on moral questions such as the death penalty, investment of money, abortion, CND, and homosexuality. Members of the congregation may be on strike and the community will have to accept them even if not in agreement. Divisions of wealth, class and race are often hardly looked at. Other members of the congregation – women, perhaps, or elderly people – may feel that their worth has been devalued by some attitude or remark endured from others. A space is made in which members may declare their differences as they see them, and the community responds with words affirming their common membership of the one eucharistic fellowship.

Here is the heart of what community is about. Not just acceptance between people; not just tolerance of one another; but a *mutual forgiveness* which includes both acceptance and tolerance, and also involves an attitude of mutual devotion that enables people to 'confirm' (that creative word of Martin Buber's[302]) one another – which means that members strengthen one another individually and as a group to realize their full possibilities of human life-together. Bonhoeffer wrote in a short note entitled 'Civil Courage?':

> Civil courage, however, can only grow out of the responsibility of free men. Only now are we Germans beginning to discover the meaning of free responsibility. It depends upon a God who demands bold action as the free response of faith, and who promises forgiveness and consolation to the man who becomes a sinner in the process.[303]

So in worship we recall our forgiveness and stand before God as the new people of his making. We do not imagine that the gospel makes sinlessness possible here and now; but because we carry with us the assurance of being forgiven, we can 'boldly' run the risks of sin in a world where perfection is an ideal not a reality.

In promoting community with a common sense of relatedness,

worship also rescues those who are victims of sin, illness or apartheid from purposelessness and alienation. In Christian eyes people are valued because they are people, children of God and loved by God. Human worth is intrinsic to being a human being made in the image of God. This is the basis of that reverence for God-in-people which keeps service for others human and godly. To give people their full worth is basic in pastoral care; and this assumes particular importance in care for the elderly, immigrants, and those devalued by society. It is in worship that we come to know our own and one another's worth in the eyes of God. Salvation consists more in seeking out and unfolding human possibilities for good – confirming worth – than in seeking out sins to cure. It is confirming worth which makes the context for repentance from sin. We stand the gospel (and pastoral care) on its head when we assume that worth comes through dealing with sin. On the contrary it is the glory of humanity (in the image of God) which makes sinfulness appear as inhuman behaviour, as a falling short of the glory of God. The early Christians expressed this sense of worth by *standing* to pray. That is, they stood before God in joyful recognition of the divine love for them, and of forgiveness for their constantly falling short of the responsibilities of being people of the new age. Heaven was in their midst.

In reality worship is often dogged by the individualism of a private faith which brings no sense of a Christian community engaged in work for God's kingdom coming on earth. The very word 'representative' – as one conceives each member on their own to be representative of the whole – has lost significance. Many still commonly speak of 'making my communion' – which is not wrong but falls short of the glory of 'we'. The conflicts of which we have spoken commonly divide the church into parties and denominations. But if the church cannot reconcile such differences, its words of reconciliation are denied by its deeds.

Worship commissions the Christian community for God's work in the world

Worship deepens our love for God and the purposes of the kingdom of Christ. It gives the community vision of what God's purpose means here and now in the city where the congregation is gathered to be scattered.

The link between faith and life is made clear in the words of dismissal to the congregation. At the end of the Latin Mass the ancient dismissal '*Ite missa est*' means (roughly) 'Go, you are sent'; or the more modern 'Go in peace in the power of the Spirit to live and work to God's praise and glory' (Methodist Service Book); or in the liturgy of St Mark's-in-the-Bowerie (New York) 'Go, serve the Lord, you are free.' In the Anglican tradition of a Parish Communion there has been a strong connection between worship and the scattering of the community to take part in God's renewal of society – a social and political renewal of the common life of the locality and nation.

Worship deepens the community's passion for justice, and the eucharistic sharing of bread and wine can lead to a greater sharing of wealth between North and South, and West and Two-Thirds worlds.

In a Lancashire parish many of the sick people prayed for regularly at the Parish Communion suffered from chronic bronchitis and heart failure due to breathing industrial smoke since childhood. What should we expect from prayer for them when they lived in a place where they continued to breathe smoke? In fact the parish worked for the establishment of a smokeless zone, and included in a parish exhibition, as an education for the public, a demonstration of the filthiness of the air we were breathing. The eventual establishment of a smokeless zone has affected the life expectancy and health of thousands of Lancashire children. This is another example of the kind of response in which those who pray for others may find themselves involved. It shows how to turn private distress into public issues, pastoral care into political concern.

The content of a church's prayer, especially intercession, reflects its understanding of the nature of God and his relationship to the world. Kierkegaard wrote:

> The immediate person thinks and imagines that when he prays, the important thing, the thing he must concentrate upon, is that God should hear what he is praying for. And yet in the true, eternal sense it is just the reverse: the true relation in prayer is not when God hears what is prayed for, but when the person praying continues to pray until he is the one who hears . . . who hears what God wills. The immediate person, therefore, makes demands in his prayer; the true man of prayer only attends.[304]

The distinction between prayer and action is here blurred: the relationship between God's action and our response inseparable. The epistle of James[305] is clear on this and a group who intercede will grow in understanding of their responsibility. Prayer opens the ears of the one who prays to God's word spoken in scripture, spoken by human need, spoken by human lips. Prayer brings consciousness of how God wills that we respond in a situation. And prayer is a well of courage into which we may dip deep, face change, and act.

Worship also makes clear that it is the whole people of God who are commissioned for evangelism, prophecy, pastoral care and political action in the world. Lay participation in taking worship can be a sign of the acceptance of that responsibility, but is not a substitute for it.

I think it was Archbishop William Temple who asked 'Why do we pray "Thy will be done" so often at funerals but so rarely at weddings?' Yet if we believe that God is as he is to be known through Jesus, then surely when God's will is done on earth as in heaven, that is the best thing that could possibly happen. We pray this prayer not in fear and resignation, but in hope and joy because God is as he is in Jesus. In fact the way in which we pray 'Thy will be done' reflects our attitude to God.

But we cannot be too romantic about God's will. In praying 'Thy will be done' there are risks. As soon as our understanding of divine purpose becomes settled, God may shatter us. Conflict and diversity prevent us making God in our own image.

However there is a long-standing and decisive division in the Anglican Church (and other denominations too) between those for whom the 'spiritual life' and the world are separate, and those for whom the 'spiritual life' is lived in the everyday world in communion with God. Therefore in reality worship is often affected by the privatization of faith, absence of any sense of God's purpose for the world, and even the severing of the act of worship from public issues altogether. Worship-on-Sunday may become separate from the everyday, and the act of going to church becomes a thing-in-itself. Within worship love is often a central theme – easily corrupted into a pink marsh mallow feeling by ignoring love's content of justice, a passionate concern for the deprived. Worship may become a period of fantasy when the worshipper who is inclined to idealism may withdraw into a dream world of religious symbols and language. The 'spiritual life' is lived (necessarily) in the world, but the world is treated as a transit camp for 'spiritual' behaviour, rather than as an intrinsic part of God's plan of creation.

Worship equips the people of God for their task in the world

'God does not choose the fit, he fits those whom he chooses' – by internalizing a sense of God's presence and a vision of God's kingdom of righteousness for all peoples. Therefore worship is part of an apprenticeship in the Christian life. For example it shapes the congregation's language, ways of thought and value system: it also Christianizes the way the members see the world – injustice comes to be seen as a blasphemy against God and his purposes.

In West Africa, on one occasion I was consulted by a student who could not read the blackboard in class. We obtained a pair of spectacles which did the trick. But more than that. She deliberately returned to thank me with the words 'I had no idea the trees in the compound were so beautiful.' Like a pair of spectacles, there is a sense in which the eucharist opens the eyes of those who share it. By celebrating the greatness of God in a particular place at a particular time our eyes are opened to see and celebrate God's handiwork in all other places and all other times. There is a pattern that connects everything: when we discover the pattern we give thanks to God.

Two writers, Nicholl and Solzhenitsyn, both describe such eucharistic moments in daily life. Nicholl,[306] who was out for a morning jog in the hills near Bethlehem, encountered four Muslim labourers on their way to work. As he ran swiftly past them the fourth man plunged a hand into his lunch bag and pushed a big handful of raisins into Nicholl's hand with the words 'You are sweating!' 'The word that came unbidden into my mind as I felt the soft skins of the raisins in my sweating palms was "Eucharist" – I felt instantly that the labourer and I had shared a moment of eucharist.'

Solzhenitsyn[307] was a political prisoner in the USSR and describes how he was being moved from one labour camp to another. He and his fellow prisoners were sitting in a group on a station platform under armed guard. He describes how embarrassed by their presence are the free citizens hurrying to and fro who 'drop their guilty heads and try not to see us at all, as if the place was empty'. But an old woman comes near, breaks off a piece of her bread and throws it to them. She is too weak to throw it far enough: the guards work the bolts of their rifles and point them at her – 'and the holy bread, broken in two, was left to lie in the dirt while we were driven off'.

Lambourne[308] has discussed the 'sacrament of mercy' symbolized by the giving of a cup of cold water. In pastoral care it is this sacrament of mercy which rends the veil between those who help and those who need; worship interpenetrates daily life. There is no more to be said or done except to acknowledge the gift and give '*eucharist*'.

Christ is not only present in the one who serves but is encountered in the sick, the poor and the prisoner.

Preaching to a congregation is part of the pastoral task of welding people into a community inspired for the work of the kingdom. We have discussed previously the gap that has developed in Western consciousness between left and right brain ways of thinking. The left brain has become dominant, and the relevance of this is obvious in pastoral care – most particularly in Western methods of preaching and counselling.

A parable is a beautiful example of whole brain thought. It is like a time bomb. Its purpose is to disturb its hearers out of their set ways of thinking.[309] The right brain creates images in which the left brain may delve again and again for insight to express in words. But misuse of the parable by the left brain can reduce a parable to two or three logical points plus an application to life. This can imprison the hearer in the preacher's own interpretation without kindling images in the right brain whence surprising insight and feeling may stir the whole person to respond to God's purpose in his/her own special way.

Some preachers use the sermon in worship for Christian instruction because many members of the congregation do not take other opportunities to read, study, learn and grow in the faith. Preaching can become a matter of information and exhortation. These have their place in equipping people for mission, but left brain activity *on its own* leaves people spiritually starved. It is not that what is said is wrong, it is simply boring. It stirs no passion (the word which combines both the meaning of feeling and suffering).

We have noted a withering in power and meaning of Christian symbols and images in a society whose thinking is shaped by scientific secularism. Preaching to the general public (as Lord Soper does on Tower Hill) is therefore a different matter from preaching to a congregation of the faithful in the context of worship.

It has been said that preaching should involve not only logical argument but also stirring statements. It is interesting to compare for example the style of Bishop Melito of Sardis (circa AD 170) in his homily on the Pascha. It begins:

The scripture from the Hebrew Exodus has been read
and the words of the mystery have been plainly stated,
how the sheep is sacrificed
and how the people is saved

and how Pharaoh is scourged through the mystery.
Understand, therefore, beloved
how it is new and old,
eternal and temporary,
perishable and imperishable,
mortal and immortal, this mystery of the Pascha:
old as regards the law,
but new as regards the word;
temporary as regards the model,
eternal because of the grace;
perishable because of the slaughter of the sheep,
imperishable because of the life of the Lord;
mortal because of the burial in earth,
immortal because of the rising from the dead.
Old is the law,
but new the word;
temporary the model,
but eternal the grace;
perishable the sheep,
imperishable the Lord;
broken as a lamb,
but resurrected as God.
For although as a sheep he was led to slaughter,
  yet he was not a sheep;
although as a lamb speechless,
  yet neither was he a lamb.
For the model indeed existed,
  but then the reality appeared.
For instead of the lamb there was a Son,
  and instead of the sheep a Man,
and in the Man Christ who has comprised all things.[310]

This is an example of a preacher using images to stir the whole being of his hearers, to kindle their love of tradition with its Christian images and stories: also to weld them into a community with belief and loyalties in common and to move them to obedience in the Christian way of life. Its style is poetic rather than analytical, and evokes passionate response from its hearers. He achieves an effect which a logical argument alone cannot do. How far such a style of preaching would be effective with a European audience today is

We can't keep living white Europeans!

questionable: we tend to look for the more logical discourse which is acceptable in our culture thanks to the shaping of the educational system. But it would be far more acceptable in an audience of black worshippers who look for a more holistic style of address, and would intersperse such an address with lively comments of 'Amen', 'Hallelujah', 'Praise the Lord'. A white European often finds this embarrassing both because the expression of strong feelings is not one of our characteristics, and because our behaviour in church is particularly restrained.

A poem or a sermon (unlike an advertisement) does not try to impose something on those who listen. Poets and preachers cannot *control* the response that people make to their words. A sermon is a work of art and the artist gives it a life of its own. If the congregation are reduced to spectators not participants, then this is a corruption whereby persons are treated as objects.

In catholic worship there tends to be more use of non-verbal symbols and ritual which communicate through the right brain. Protestantism tends to be more verbal and less visual (a historical protest against meaningless ritual), which is more congenial to a left brained Western culture and an articulate middle class. The style of the sermon can be very paternalistic, and can also be an example of theory divorced from relevance to practice. All these features make participation by members or visitors from other cultures less possible. Indeed the presence of other nationalities or denominations in worship helps to expose the grooves of worship and enrich it with different gifts.

Why don't we talk to the articulate!

Worship is a wholing activity

The opposite of a correct statement is a false statement. But the opposite of a profound truth may well be another profound truth (Niels Bohr).

I deliberately use the verb 'wholing' rather than the noun 'wholeness' because wholeness is an ideal towards which we struggle and grow, a pointer towards the kingdom yet to be completed, now partly visible. Worship is an activity which helps us individually and corporately to grow towards wholeness. In it we give ourselves to God and to a purpose which is worth living and dying for. Such an overmastering purpose integrates our thoughts, words and deeds: helps to integrate us as individuals and raises the morale of the congregation. (In the church where I worshipped as a boy it was customary to substitute the words 'overmastering life' instead of 'everlasting life' in public readings and prayers. The word conveys *quality* rather than timelessness.)

Worship also takes a whole view of life, giving us a larger context of joy in God's love and good purposes into which to put the tragedies and horrors of the world. To conduct intercessions for the sick with so many details about illness that we lose sight of God's healing grace is clearly to take a negative rather than a whole view.

Nevertheless there is a formalism and loss of wholeness in worship in many churches today. All other aspects of faith and life consequently disintegrate. Throughout this book we have noted various truths which have depended upon holding two aspects of life together and refusing to relinquish either aspect although they may seem alternative or contradictory. We can design worship in such a way as to make it possible to hold such differing aspects of reality together. For example we noted the way that Western society has overemphasized *individuality* at the expense of our belonging to one another: whereas Marxism and Fascism have both overemphasized *corporateness* at the expense of individuality. In worship we need to hold together both those aspects of the truth about human beings. Other twinned aspects of life and belief which tend to get separated are:

Active and Passive. It is essential to rely on the grace of God and to let him act in our lives: but on the other hand we ourselves must also respond and struggle to do his will, to resist injustice, and to bend every effort to further the values of the kingdom. Reed has described[311] the rhythm of utter dependence upon God in worship, and independent responsibility in our daily lives.

Holy and Homely. God is to be worshipped both as holy (in the sublime words of the Sanctus) and also as present in everyday and homely situations such as a family meal. In order to make a connection between the Holy Communion in church and our own family meals (that they too might be holy communion) my wife and I established a particular pattern of Grace before Sunday lunch. We share a piece of bread and pass it round, each member breaking a piece and saying 'One family'. Then a glass of squash (or water or whatever we are drinking) is similarly passed round and all share one glass saying again 'One family'. We then join hands and sing our usual daily Grace. If a guest is present they too are included in the one family. In a Grace before meal the general providence of God through nature, and the co-creative work of humankind as farmers, lorry drivers, millers and bakers, are brought together.

Matter and Spirit. We are creatures with very material needs if we are to live – food, water, warmth, vitamins and trace elements. But we are more than creatures, and to become fully human we need also 'every word that comes from the mouth of God'.[312] It is in the person of Jesus (and in the eucharistic bread) that spirit and matter exist in harmony. In the Lord's prayer there is also a balance between what we may describe as 'material' and 'spiritual' requests: in fact there is nothing unspiritual about bread (Berdyaev wrote: 'Bread for myself is a material question: bread for my neighbour is a spiritual question'[313]), and nothing immaterial about forgiveness of sins (which brought a paralyzed man to his feet).

Real and Ideal. It is important both to have a vision of the fullness of God's kingdom when his purpose reaches its end, and also to

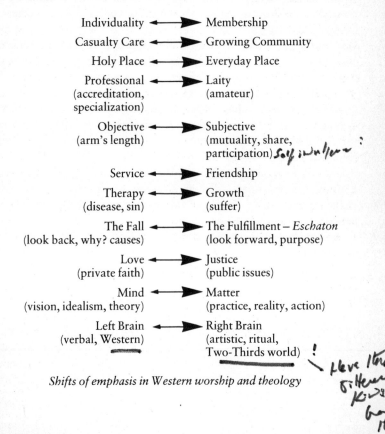

Individuality ⟶ Membership

Casualty Care ⟶ Growing Community

Holy Place ⟶ Everyday Place

Professional ⟶ Laity
(accreditation, (amateur)
specialization)

Objective ⟶ Subjective
(arm's length) (mutuality, share,
participation)

Service ⟶ Friendship

Therapy ⟶ Growth
(disease, sin) (suffer)

The Fall ⟶ The Fulfillment – *Eschaton*
(look back, why? causes) (look forward, purpose)

Love ⟶ Justice
(private faith) (public issues)

Mind ⟶ Matter
(vision, idealism, theory) (practice, reality, action)

Left Brain ⟶ Right Brain
(verbal, Western) (artistic, ritual,
Two-Thirds world)

Shifts of emphasis in Western worship and theology

remember that in the present life our real situation always falls short of our vision. We are given signs of the kingdom now, and a foretaste of the future fullness to come. The good news of the kingdom in the present is not sinlessness and perfection, but forgiveness and goodness enough.

It is possible to go on collecting twins such as Sacred/Secular, Acceptance/Confrontation, Peace/Disturbance, Unity/Diversity, Prayer/Work, Privacy/Publicity, Personal/Political, Sunday/Week-day, Holy/Everyday, Intellect/Feeling, Verbal/Non-verbal, Mind/Body, Thought/Deed, Care/Skill, and others which are important for a proper balance in both worship and daily life.

These polarities of truth represent a harmony of opposites in Christian worship and theology, but in our present situation in Western culture they have either got divided or out of balance. A shift of emphasis is now required. In the diagram above each aspect is connected to its opposite by a double headed arrow, the larger of which indicates the direction in which a shift of emphasis is required. This is a tactical situation: that is, the shift of emphasis is required during the last twelve years of the twentieth century in Western culture. The situation could well be different now in another culture: or could well be different in Western culture by the end of the century.

Worship celebrates the greatness of God and gathers into one great drama the themes of a shared vision and mission, worth, commitment, and apprenticeship in membership of the Christian community, giving a sense of purpose and high morale to both individual and congregation.

There is an ancient saying: A monk is at prayer; when he knows he is praying, he has ceased. When our whole attention is given to God we transcend those divisions and polarities, which we have described, in a foretaste of wholeness.

In worship together we are apprentices learning to 'see' and 'hear', and to live a life of worship:

> . . . and the holy bread, broken in two, was left to lie in the dirt while we were driven off . . . (p.214).

> I rebuked myself with the remembrance of Christ's word 'Ye did it unto me', and then it suddenly seemed that Christ was really and literally present under my hands in the form of a sick person. I saw him and I touched him (p.167).

> Let everything that hath breath, praise the Lord (Psalm 150).

Appendix 1

Primary Health Care in an Inner City (An Experimental General Practice)

After the 1939–45 war Dr Robert (Bob) A. Lambourne, a general medical practitioner (later a psychiatrist, theologian and university lecturer in pastoral studies), began to write articles[314] which were critical, from a Christian viewpoint, of the values and practice of medicine in Britain: and of the church's approach to healing. His friend and colleague, Dr James Mathers, and myself shared in his thinking and writing, and this Birmingham 'seethe' provided a focus for research and publications related to religion and medicine. The Rev. Anthony Bird, an Anglican priest, studied medicine and became a general medical practitioner in Birmingham. He also joined the explorations, writing[315] and researching[316] in his practice.

Appointed principal of The Queen's Theological College, Dr Bird established in 1977 an *experimental general practice* with the support of the College, the Department of Theology in the university, and the Christian Medical Commission of the World Council of Churches. Dr Malcolm Rigler pioneered the work for the first two years. Then Men had a row as Rigler left!

The selection of the site for what was seen as an adventure in 'medical mission' was guided by theological thought. The lay-out of the surgery and the style of practice were similarly theologized (there is some discussion of these matters in chapter 8, pp.71–74).

The practice was the first in Britain to have explored the role of the Nurse Practitioner.[317] The role of receptionist has also been researched (see discussion on pp.73, 84), and in 1980 the first receptionist received a 'Receptionist of the Year' award in the West Midlands.

A summary of the first four years of the practice has been written by Dr Bird.[318] In 1982 the practice acquired additional purpose-built premises in a new Health Centre. The team has grown to include a medical partner Dr Mohammed Walji, a midwife, health visitors, social worker, nurse practitioner, receptionists and inter-preter/receptionists: team meetings are held regularly to discuss and make decisions about the work.

In 1985 a research project[319] was carried out into the value of patients having access to their case notes, deliberately encouraging their use in interviews as health educational material. This research has focussed on the helpfulness or otherwise of this more cooperative style of health care for ethnic minorities in the inner city.[320]

A sense of wholeness has particularly influenced thought about health and illness in relation to patients' families and neighbour-hood. Home midwifery and care of the dying have therefore also been given attention.

The practice has had links with both the Department of General Practice and the Department of Theology in the university. It has therefore been a centre for education (as well as research), and students from several disciplines – medicine, social work, pastoral studies and theology – have worked and studied there.

It is a significant place, both in its own nature and in its educational work for professionals and patients, integrating theory and practice, faith and life, personal and public issues. The mutuality between patients and staff could be seen reflected in the smiling faces of local children waiting in the street outside the surgery for their party in July 1987 to celebrate the tenth anniversary of the opening of the practice.

Just a little romantic for there are bad human choices here also! – as I know well! It points to hopes to state that Drs Rigler & Bird violently disagreed & broke up which made things very difficult for the beginning.

Appendix 2

Education for Faith and Life
The Diploma in Pastoral Studies[321]

The Diploma in Pastoral Studies of the University of Birmingham (Dept of Theology) is a post-graduate course of one year's full-time study (or two years part-time). It is intended for men and women, lay and ordained, professional or not, whose pastoral concern stems from the nature of their work and/or their membership of a faith. Its purpose is to explore theological thought and human care in the context of a Western city. It was the first course of its kind in a university of the United Kingdom.

Dr Robert (Bob) A. Lambourne was the first tutor of the course. He ran a pilot course with the Rev. Dr Eric Fenn in Rubery Hill Psychiatric Hospital for students from a missionary training college. In 1964, appointed as Lecturer in Pastoral Studies, he took three students through the first year's course in the university. The course has now run for over twenty years, and more than two hundred and fifty students have shared in it.

Its title, 'Pastoral Studies', indicates one of its main concerns, namely *study*. By being located in a university it is a discipline within the Department of Theology in the Faculty of Arts, open to all the exacting demands – including examinations – of an intellectual milieu. It is a transdisciplinary course (studying, for example, psychology, sociology, social work and group work as well as theology) and has a major dimension of practical work (in such situations as industry, social work, probation service, hospitals, prison or counselling). Half the time is spent in the university, and half is spent in practical work in the city. Its aim could generally be described as *'the study of humankind in the light of faith in God'*. In order to integrate the study of theology and everyday theology, theory and practice, each student has to theologize their practical work with the help of the rest of the group.

Being a university course, it is open to all suitably qualified people. It is not sectarian like a theological college, nor is it concerned with training for the ordained ministry. Each year a group of about twelve post-graduate students take the course. They vary in age, sex, married and single, ordained and lay, professional and amateur, of various denominations, and are from many parts of the world both Western and Two-Thirds. Their academic qualifications are from various disciplines, including philosophy, theology, psychology, chemistry, sociology, modern languages, botany, English and applied biology among others. Their life experiences are varied: some are ordained ministers (men and women) either in training or of many years local church experience: others are housewives, missionaries, teachers, nurses, a social worker and a doctor. Over the years the number of teachers and the numbers of Two-Thirds world students have increased, and the proportion of women has also grown.

To build a community out of these diverse people was always a basic task: some details of how we tackled this are given in chapter 12 (pp.118f.).

The Diploma in Pastoral Studies has been and continues to be an educational venture for the democratization of theology, integrating both study and practice, faith and life, personal and public issues. It continues to explore a model of group apprenticeship in living and learning theology.

Notes and References

1. Edwin Smith, *Aggrey of Africa*, SCM Press 1929
2. J. Y. Bannerman, *Mfantse Akan Bbebusem*, Ghana Publishing Corporation 1974
3. The World Commission on Environment and Development, *Our Common Future*, Oxford University Press 1987
4. *The New Black Presence in Britain*, Statement by BCC Working Party on Britain as a Multiracial Society, Community & Race Relations Unit, BCC 1976
5. R. F. W. Nelson, *Thinking about the Future of Work*, Transformation Research Network Review, Ottawa 1983, p.62
6. J. Townroe, *Christian Spirituality and the Future of Man*, SSJE Centenary Lecture 1966, p.2
7. A. V. Campbell, *Rediscovering Pastoral Care*, DLT 1981, ch.3
8. W. A. Clebsch, C. R. Jaekle, *Pastoral Care in Historical Perspective*, Harper 1967, p.4
9. H.R.H. the Duke of Edinburgh, 'Universities and the Diffusion of Culture', *Frontier* 1974, 17, 3, p.137
10. Private communication
11. E. Bendall, *So You Passed Nurse*, Royal College of Nursing Research Series 1975
12. E. Bendall, *Learning for Reality*, cyclostyled summary of a research project 1972/3 carried out in a sample of nine nurse training schools in England, GNC. See also M. F. Alexander, 'Integrating Theory and Practice in Nursing,' *Nursing Times*, 1982, Occasional Paper, (1) Vol 78, 24, June 16, pp.65–68; (2) Vol 78, 25, June 23, pp.69–71
13. James 2.14–17
14. K. Koyama, *Waterbuffalo Theology*, SCM Press 1974
15. *Christianity and Nursing Today*, Report of a Working Party of the Nurses Christian Movement, Epworth 1964, p.2
16. P. Halmos, *The Personal and the Political*, Hutchinson 1978
17. *Faith in the City*, Report of Archbishop of Canterbury's Commission on Urban Priority Areas, Church House 1985
18. 'Ideal and Real', leading editorial, *Daily Telegraph*, Friday 24 December 1965, p.10
19. D. Tutu, quoted on a Christian Aid poster, 1985
20. F. Capra, *The Turning Point*, Wildwood House 1982
21. M. Ferguson, *The Aquarian Conspiracy*, Granada 1982, pp.326–7
22. W. J. Hollenweger, 'The Roots and Fruits of the Charismatic

Renewal in the Third World: Implications for Mission', *Research Bulletin*, Institute for the Study of Worship and Religious Architecture, University of Birmingham 1980, pp.125–43

23. M. Wilson, *Health is for People*, DLT 1975

24. R. F. W. Nelson, *The Illusions of Urban Man*, Ministry of State for Urban Affairs, Government of Canada 1977, pp.50–1

25. R. Titmuss, *The Gift Relationship*, Pelican 1973

26. W. Shakespeare, *The Merchant of Venice*

27. P. Webb (compiler), *Someone to talk to directory*, Mental Health Foundation 1985

28. I. Suttie, *The Origins of Love and Hate*, Kegan Paul 1935, p.2

29. K. Appiah–Kubi, 'The Church's Healing Ministry in Africa', *Contact* WCC, Geneva 1975, 29

30. M. Powell, *Patients are People*, Educational Explorers 1975

31. Poster, USPG, 157 Waterloo Rd, London, SE1 8UU

32. T. Roszak, *The Making of a Counter Culture*, Faber & Faber 1970, p.232

33. C. S. Lewis, *The Great Divorce*, Fontana 1971

34. The Hon. K. C. Norton, 'A Future for our Children', an unpublished address to a conference on *Current Issues in Child Psychiatry*, Lake Couchiching, Canada 1978. See acknowledgement

35. This section is based on an article, M. Wilson, 'The Winter of Materialism', *Community*, 1979, 23, pp.1–3

36. M. Wilson, 'Violence and Non-violence in the Cure of Disease and the Healing of Patients', *Christian Century* LXXXVII, 24, 17 June 1970, pp.756–8.

37. R. A. Lambourne, *Community, Church and Healing*, Arthur James 1987, pp.45ff.

38. M. Wilson, 'No Man is an Island', *International Review of Missions* LVI, 1967, 223, pp.344–54.

39. M. Balint, *The Doctor, the Patient and the Illness*, Pitman Medical 1957, pp.32ff.

40. H. Hellberg, 'Curing or Healing?', *Health in Medical and Theological Perspectives*, 'Tubingen 2', WCC, Geneva 1967, p.6

41. J. G. R. Howie, 'Research in General Practice: Pursuit of Knowledge or Defence of Wisdom?', *British Medical Journal*, 1984, 289, 6460, pp.1770–2.

42. Matt. 4.4

43. A. Siirala, *The Voice of Illness*, Fortress Press 1964

44. O. N. Mukuna, 'Salvation as a Process of Humanisation versus Separate Development as a Process of Dehumanisation', Unpublished paper 1973

45. Personal letter from the Rev. Phillip Than, Anglican priest in Brunei. See acknowledgment

46. Olayinka, in an interview with E. Rowe, 'A Fusion of Culture reflected in Art' *West Africa*, 10 Sept. 79, 3243, p.1648

47. J. Metge, P. Kinloch, *Talking Past Each Other*, Victoria University Press, Price Milburn, New Zealand 1978

48. V. J. Donovan, *Christianity Rediscovered*, SCM Press 1978

49. M. Wilson, 'No Man is an Island', see note 38 above

50. M. Dewey, *Thinking Mission*, USPG April 1986, 50, p.5

51. R. E. C. Browne, *Love of the World*, Churchman 1986, Introduction. The quotation is in an extended form from a personal communication

52. Acts 10. For an exploration of this encounter see W. J. Hollenweger, *Evangelism Today*, Christian Journals, Belfast 1976, p.11

53. Acts 11.4

54. Acts 11.18

55. C. Hughes Smith, *Open Cast Theology*, private publication 1986

56. W. J. Hollenweger, (1) 'Intercultural Theology at the University of Birmingham', *Research in progress, completed and planned*, 1985 (obtainable from the Dept of Theology, University of Birmingham, B15 2TT; (2) The Centre for Black and White Christian Partnership, see note 117 below

57. Acts 10.17, 19, 28, 29, 34, 35; 11.2–18

58. Mark 3.1–6

59. Mark 2.3ff.

60. Mark 2.12

61. J. A. T. Robinson, *Honest to God*, SCM Press 1963

62. D. Deeks, 'Some Reflections on Theological Education', *Facets*, Winter 1973, Issue 3, pp.3–10

63. K. Lorenz, *On Aggression*, Methuen 1966, p.205

64. L. Newbigin, *The Finality of Christ*, SCM Press 1969, p.75

65. M. Wilson, 'Exorcism: a clinical/pastoral practice which raises serious questions', *Expository Times* LXXXVI, July 1975, 10, pp.292–5

66. P. Valery, *An Anthology*, selected by James Lawler from Collected Works of Paul Valery, ed. J. Matthews, Routledge & Kegan Paul 1977

67. R. E. C. Browne, *Love of the World*, see note 51 above, p.3

68. P. Freire, *Pedagogy of the Oppressed*, Penguin 1972, preface

69. R. E. C. Browne, *Love of the World*, see note 51 above, p.2

70. M. Kane, *Theology in an Industrial Society*, SCM Press 1975

71. S. Barrington-Ward, *C. M. S. News-letter*, October 1979, 429

72. C. R. Avila, *Peasant Theology*, Book No 1, W.S.C.F. Asia, Hong Kong 1976, pp.22–3

73. A. P. Bird, *The Search for Health – A Response from the Inner City*, University of Birmingham 1981, p.107

74. (1) A. P. Bird, M. T. I. Walji, 'Our Patients have Access to their Medical Records', *British Medical Journal*, 1986, 292, pp.595–6; (2) M. E. Gittens, A. P. Bird, M. T. I. Walji, F. M. Hull, 'Does it Help Patients to Read their Medical Records?' *Allgemein Medizin*, 1985, 14, pp.146–8

75. Psalm 31.8

76. R. A. Lambourne, 'Models of Health and Salvation, Secular and Christian', *Explorations in Health and Salvation*, A Selection of Papers by Bob Lambourne, ed. M. Wilson, University of Birmingham 1983, p.202

77. J. Metge, P. Kinloch, *Talking Past Each Other*, see note 47 above

78. T. W. Manson, *The Teaching of Jesus*, Cambridge University Press 1931, pp.239–40

79. A. O. Dyson, 'Pastoral Theology – towards a new Discipline', *Contact* Edinburgh 1983, 1, 78, pp.2–8

80. Mark 9.28

81. Mark 9.33

82. Mark 9.9

83. John 9.2

84. Luke 9.10

85. Mark 10.13

86. J. Mathers, 'The Gestation Period of Identity Change', *British Journal of Psychiatry*, 1974, 125, pp.472–4

87. J.G.Colston, *Judgment in Counselling*, Abingdon Press 1969, pp.50ff.

88. Acts 10.9–20

89. John 14.6

90. Rom. 2.8

91. R. A. Lambourne, 'Models of Health and Salvation, Secular and Christian', see note 76 above, p.202

92. J. Mathers, 'The Pastoral Role: a Psychiatrist's View', *Religion and Medicine* 2, ed. M. A. H. Melinsky, SCM Press 1973, p.90

93. M. Wilson, *The Hospital – A Place of Truth*, University of Birmingham 1971

94. Michel Quoist, *Prayers of Life*, Gill & Son, Dublin 1963, pp.90–2

95. M. Wilson, *The Hospital – A Place of Truth*, see note 93 above, pp.118–21

96. H.Williams, *The True Resurrection*, Mitchell Beazley 1972

97. R. M. Pirsig, *Zen and the Art of Motor Cycle Maintenance*, Corgi 1976, p.284

98. D. Bonhoeffer, *Letters and Papers from Prison*, The Enlarged Edition, SCM Press 1971

99. J. G. Davies, *Every Day God*, SCM Press 1973

100. J. Pickard, '*Prayer Manual*', Methodist Church Overseas Division 1986–7

101. K. Burne, *The Life and Letters of Fr Andrew*, Mowbrays 1948

102. M. Wilson, the material in this chapter is based on 'Personal Care and Political Action', *Pastoral Studies Spring School*, Dept of Theology, University of Birmingham 1983, pp.33–40. Also in *Contact* Edinburgh 1985, 2, 87, pp.12–22

103. P. Halmos, *The Personal and the Political*, Hutchinson 1978

104. A. V. Campbell, 'The Politics of Pastoral Care', *Contact* Edinburgh, 1979, 1, 62, pp.2ff.

105. The founding of the Catholic Crusade is described in C. Noel, *Autobiography*, Dent 1945, p.107

106. C. Noel, *The Battle of the Flags*, Labour Publishing Company 1922

107. F. D. Maurice, *The Kingdom Of Christ*, Dent 1837, 2 vols

108. A. Ecclestone, *The Parish Meeting at Work*, SPCK 1953

109. J. V. Wilson, *The Redemption of the Common Life*, Dobson 1950

110. Ibid. p.83

111. Ibid. p.168

112. Ibid. p.164

113. Ibid. p.176

114. W. Ferrier, *The Life of Kathleen Ferrier*, Hamish Hamilton 1955

115. Hans-Ruedi Weber, *Experiments with Bible Study*, WCC, Geneva 1981, Study 15, pp.180ff.

116. W. J. Hollenweger, *Conflict in Corinth/Memoirs of an Old Man*, Paulist Press 1982

117. Centre for Black and White Christian Partnership, Library Extension, Selly Oak Colleges, Birmingham B29 6LQ

118. A. Andresen ed., *The Danish Folk High School*, Hojskolernes Sekretariat, Vartov, Farvergade 27,G, DK–1463 Kobenhavn K, Denmark

119. The United World Colleges, International Office, London House, Mecklenburgh Street, London, WC1N 2AB

120. B. Mazibuko, 'Centre for Black and White Christian Partnership', *Second City Soundings*, ed. F. Young, G. Wakefield, Methodist Conference 1985, p.71. See also note 117 above

121. V. J. Donovan, *Christianity Rediscovered*, see note 48 above

122. *Faith in the City*, see note 17 above, paras 3.22–23

123. J. McGilvray, 'The Church and Health: Reflections and Possibilities', *Contact*, WCC, Geneva Oct. 1984, 81, p.8

124. R. A. Lambourne, 'Health Today and Salvation Today', *Explorations in Health and Salvation*, see note 76 above, pp.234ff.

125. M. Wilson, *The Hospital – A Place of Truth*, see note 93 above, pp.293ff.

126. Matt. 25.37–40

127. P. C. W. Bellamy, 'The Contemporary Relevance of Bob Lambourne's Writings', *Religion and Medicine* April 86, Vol. 2, 1, p.134

128. Matt. 25.31ff.

129. D. Bonhoeffer, *The Cost of Discipleship*, SCM Press 1959, p.230

130. Gen. 1.28

131. Luke 22.25

132. *Activities Report of the Christian Medical Commission*, WCC, Geneva Jan 1983–June 1984, p.14

133. Matt. 6.33

134. W. Mandela, *Part of my Soul*, Penguin 1985

135. P. Welch, 'Encountering Other Faiths: the Theology of Neighbourhood', *Second City Soundings*, see note 120 above, p.65

136. Mark 4.26–32

137. J. G. Davies, *Worship and Mission*, SCM Press 1966, p.130

138. P. J. Palmer, 'A Place Called Community', *Christian Century*, 16 March 1977, pp.252ff.

139. Jean Vanier, *The Challenge of L'Arche*, DLT 1982

140. J. Mathers, 'The Pastoral Role: a Psychiatrist's View', *Religion and Medicine* 2, see note 92 above, p.88

141. C. D.Kean, *Christian Faith and Pastoral Care*, SPCK 1961, p.42

142. E. W. Southcott, *The Parish Comes Alive*, Mowbray 1956

143. Catholic Crusade, see note 105 above

144. A. Ecclestone, *The Parish Meeting at Work*, see note 108 above

145. G. Dix, *The Shape of the Liturgy*, Dacre Press 1945, pp.82–102

146. B. Reed, *The Dynamics of Religion*, DLT 1978

147. R. K. Orchard, *Servants of Life*, Conference for World Mission (BCC) 1979, ch. 10

148. M. Ramsey, Debate on 'Church and State', General Synod of the Church of England, *Report of Proceedings*, 17 Feb. 1971, Vol.2, No.1, p.68. See acknowledgement

149. D. Clark, *Basic Communities: Towards an Alternative Society*, SPCK 1977

150. *Community*, published by The National Association of Christian Communities and Networks (=NACCAN), Westhill College, Weoley Park Road, Selly Oak, Birmingham, B29 6LL

151. D. Clark, *The Liberation of the Church*, NACCAN, Birmingham 1985. See note 150 above

152. J. Mathers, 'The Authority of the Pastor', *Contact* Edinburgh, Summer 1975, 49, pp.25–31

153. R. A. Lambourne, 'Authority, Personal Knowledge and the Therapeutic Relationship', *Contact* Edinburgh, Nov 1968, 25, pp.22–40. This special number on 'Authority' contains six articles by various contributors (including B. Palmer and B. Reed *inter al.*) responding to Lambourne's main paper

154. S. Windass & M. Chance, *The Social Atom*, unpublished paper. See acknowledgment

155. Matt. 8.9

156. Poem quoted in P. Lomas, *True and False Experience*, Allen Lane 1973

157. D. Martin, *Adventure in Psychiatry*, Bruno Cassirer 1962

158. D. Martin, *The Church as a Healing Community*, Guild of Health, London 1958, p.7

159. W. D. Wills, *Spare the Child*, Penguin Educational 1971, pp.34–5

160. Luke 9.10

161. John 13.1–16

162. Luke 22.25–7

163. Mark 11.28

164. Mark 2.1–12

165. Matt. 25.31–46

166. J. Mathers, 'The Authority of the Pastor', see note 152 above, p.31

167. P. White, *Voss*, Penguin 1960, p.147

168. C. Berhorst, 'The Chimaltenango Development Project – Guatemala', *Contact* WCC, Geneva 1974, 19

169. J. R. Sibley, 'Kodje Do, S. Korea', *Contact* WCC, Geneva 1971, 5

170. Luke 3.8

171. F. E. Schumacher, *Good Work*, Cape 1979

172. United World Colleges, see note 119 above

173. A. S. Maslow, *Motivation and Human Personality*, Harper & Row 1970

174. John 15.13

175. J. W. Revans, (1) 'Structures and Obstructions', *Religion and Medicine*, ed. M. A. H. Melinsky, SCM Press 1970, p.93; (2) *Standards for Morale*, OUP 1964

176. J. W. Revans, 'Management, Morale and Productivity', *Proceedings of the National Industrial Safety Conference*, ROSPA 1963, p.84

177. Development of this line of thought owes much to: *The Church for Others: the Church for the World*, Report of West European Working Group of the Department of Studies in Evangelism, WCC, Geneva 1963

178. Luke 10.29–37

179. John 13.1–16

180. Matt. 12.17–21; Deut.Isa. 52.13–53.12

181. Matt. 25.31–46

182. Luke 15.4–7

183. R. Titmuss, *The Gift Relationship*, see note 25 above

184. Simone Weil, *Waiting on God*, Fontana 1959, p.97

185. L.Van der Post & J. Taylor, *Testament to the Bushmen*, Penguin 1985

186. M. Dewey, 'Dialogue with those of Other Faiths', *Thinking Mission*, USPG 1986, 50, p.7

187. Mark 14.34–42

188. A. F. Young & E. T.Ashton, *British Social Work in the Nineteenth Century*, Routledge, Kegan and Paul 1956, pp.67–78

189. J. Rimmer, *Troubles Shared, The Story of a Settlement 1899–1979*, Phlogiston 1980, p.145

190. See note 180 above

191. Matt. 8.16–17

192. J. Macmurray, *Ye are my Friends & To Save from Fear*, Quaker Home Service 1979

193. James 2.23

194. Ex. 33.11

195. Matt. 11.19

196. John 15.13–15

197. Eph. 5.21

198. A. V. Campbell, *Moderated Love*, SPCK 1984

199. B. J. Easter, 'Communication and Community: a study of Communication with special application to a Community for the Mentally Handicapped from a Theological and other perspectives,' PhD. Thesis, University of Birmingham 1983

200. P. Sarpong, 'Answering Why? – the Ghanaian Concept of Disease', *Contact* WCC, Geneva, April 85, No. 84

201. H. S. Kushner, *When Bad Things Happen to Good People*, Avon, New York 1981, p.136

202. John 9

203. S. Carter, 'Friday Morning', *Salvation Today and Contemporary Experience*, ed. T. Wieser, WCC, Geneva 1972, p.105

204. Job 21.7–26

205. R. Fung, 'Evangelism Today', *A Monthly Letter about Evangelism*,

Commission on World Mission and Evangelism, WCC, Geneva, July 1979, No. 7/8

206. Dan. 12.2

207. Julian of Norwich, *Revelations of Divine Love*, ed. G. Warnack, Methuen 1901

208. T. D. Hunter, 'Self-run Hospitals', *New Society*, 14 Sept. 1967, pp. 356ff.

209. M. Wilson, *The Hospital – A Place of Truth*, see note 93 above, section 1, Essay 1

210. Job 36.22

211. A. Solzhenitsyn, *The Gulag Archipelago*, Vol.2 1918–1956, Parts III–IV, Collins Fontana 1975, pp.638ff.

212. 'Possum', (P.O.S.M. = Patient Operated Selector Mechanism), 'a device that enables severely paralysed patients to use typewriters, adding machines, telephones and a wide variety of other machines', *Concise Medical Dictionary*, OUP 1980

213. For example: R. A. Lambourne, *Community, Church and Healing*, see note 37 above; F. Wright, *The Pastoral Nature of Healing*, SCM Press 1983; H. Booth (ed.), *In Search of Health and Wholeness*, Workbook of Dept of Social Responsibility, Methodist Church 1985 (suitable for group study); *The Healing Church*, 'Tubingen 1', WCC, Geneva 1965; M. Wilson, *The Church is Healing*, SCM Press 1966

214. Matt. 5.39; John 18.23

215. John 10.17–18; 10.39; 11.53–4

216. J. K. Baxter, *Jerusalem Daybook*, Price Milburn, Wellington 1971, pp.2–3. See acknowledgment

217. J. R. Sibley, 'Kodje Do, S. Korea', see note 169 above

218. A. Ecclestone, *Yes to God*, DLT 1975, p.131

219. W. H. Vanstone, *The Stature of Waiting*, DLT 1982

220. John 13.31

221. John 12.24

222. Rom. 6.3–4

223. I John 3.14

224. Col. 1.13–23; Eph. 1.3–10

225. II Cor. 5.17

226. Rom. 8.19

227. Deut. Isa. 42.6

228. J. A. T. Robinson, 'God is to be found in the cancer as in everything else', *St Martin's Review*, Jan. 84, 1314, p.2–4

229. Acts 17.28

230. Matt. 25.31–46

231. M. Wilson, 'Violence and non-violence in the Cure of Disease and the Healing of Patients', *Christian Century*, see note 36 above

232. W. H. Vanstone, *The Stature of Waiting*, see note 219 above

233. D. Soelle, *Suffering*, DLT 1973, pp.61ff. and pp.145ff.

234. Matt. 25.40

235. M. Wilson ed., *Explorations in Health and Salvation*, see note 76 above, p.176

236. Matt. 15.22

237. M. Wilson, 'All the Way back to Billesley?', *St Martin's Review*, Oct. 1976, 1227, pp.1–4

238. A. van Soest, 'Sermon at Bob Lambourne's Memorial Service', *D.P.S. Spring School Papers*, Theology Dept, University of Birmingham 1972

239. M. Thornton, *English Spirituality*, SPCK 1963, pp.44ff.

240. W. H. Vanstone, D. Soelle, see notes 219 & 233 above

241. F. Y. Young, *Can These Dry Bones Live?*, SCM Press 1982, pp.60–1

242. B. Proctor, *Counselling Shop*, Burnett Books 1978

243. T. D. Vaughan ed., *Concepts of Counselling*, Bedford Square Press 1975, survey pp.90ff. British Association of Counselling, 37a Sheep St, Rugby, CV21 3BX

244. Various Contributors, *Constitutional Papers*, Association for the Promotion of Pastoral Care and Counselling, address as for the B.A.C. see note 243 above

245. M. Jacobs, *Swift to Hear*, SPCK 1985

246. J. Mathers, 'The Accreditation of Counsellors', *British Journal of Guidance and Counselling*, VI, 2, July 78, pp.129–39

247. Y. Craig, 'Mediation – a Way of Healing', *The Way of Life*, Guild of Health, London, Oct./Dec. 85, Vol 17, 4, p.110

248. E. Y. Lartey, *Pastoral Counselling in Intercultural Perspective: a study of some African (Ghanaian) and Anglo-American views on human existence and counselling*, Verlag Peter Lang, Frankfurt 1987

249. J. Ferguson, 'Communication with the Divine World: Oracles', *The Religious Perspective: African Religion*, Open University 1978, A101, 19 & 20, pp.84–7

250. M. Wilson, 'Should the Patient be Told the Truth?', *Patient Counselling & Health Education*, 1978, Vol 1, 2, p.74

251. R. A. Lambourne, 'Counselling for Narcissus or Counselling for Christ?' *Explorations in Health and Salvation*, see note 76 above, pp.152–3

252. R. A. Lambourne, 'Counselling for Narcissus or Counselling for Christ?', see note 76 above, p.136

253. R. A. Lambourne, 'An Objection to the Proposed National Pastoral Organisation', *Explorations in Health and Salvation*, see note 76 above, pp.125ff.

254. R. A. Lambourne, 'Talk at Carr's Lane Church', *Explorations in Health and Salvation*, see note 76 above, pp.162ff.

255. T. C. Oden, *Game Free*, Harper & Row 1974, pp.35–44

256. C. Truax, R. Carkhuff, *Toward Effective Counselling*, Aldine, Chicago 1967

257. H. Eysenck, 'The Effects of Psychotherapy: an Evaluation', *Journal of Consultative Psychology*, 1952, 16, pp.319–24

258. C. Truax, R. Carkhuff, *Toward Effective Counselling*, see note 256 above, p.100

259. G. Goodman, *Companionship Therapy*, Jossey-Bass 1972

260. J. Mathers, 'The Accreditation of Counsellors', see note 246 above

261. R. A. Lambourne, 'Personal Reformation and Political Formation in Pastoral Care', *Explorations in Health and Salvation*, see note 76 above, p.189 ref.2

262. K.Crossley-Holland, *The Norse Myths*, Penguin 1982, 6, The Mead of Poetry, p.26

263. Homer, *The Odyssey*, Trans. W. Shewring, OUP 1980

264. S. Suzuki, *Nurtured by Love*, Exposition Press, New York 1977

265. D. Shepherd, *The Man who Loves Giants*, David & Charles 1975

266. A. Milavec, *To Empower as Jesus Did: Acquiring Power through Apprenticeship*, Toronto Studies in Theology, Vol.9, Edwin Mellen Press, Toronto 1982

267. M. Polyani, *Personal Knowledge*, Routledge & Kegan Paul 1958

268. J. Crewdson, 'Review Article: Christian Apprenticeship', *Modern Churchman*, XXVII, 1985, 2, p.53

269. John 12.21

270. F. R. Kinsler, *Ministry by the People*, WCC, Geneva, & Orbis, New York 1985

271. Information from (1) AVEC, 155A King's Road, London, SW3 5TX; (2) The Grubb Institute, Group and Organisational Studies Unit, E.W.R. Centre, Cloudesley St, London, N1 OHU

272. M. V. Woodgate, *Father Congreve of Cowley*, SPCK 1956, p.33

273. E. Berne, *Games People Play*, Andre Deutsch 1966

274. *All are Called: Towards a Theology of the Laity*, Working Party of the General Synod, Board of Education, Anglican Church, Church Information Office 1985 , p.3

275. R. Moss, 'Whatever happened to the Discredited Laity?' *Pastoral Studies Spring School Papers*, Dept of Theology, University of Birmingham 1980–1981, pp.39–47

276. The word 'disable' is taken from: I. Illich, *The Disabling Professions*, Boyars 1977

277. Quoted by C. Saunders, *Care of the Dying*, Nursing Times Reprint, Macmillan 1959, Introduction

278. S. Pattison, 'Images of Inadequacy: an examination of some theoretical models of Hospital Chaplaincy', *Contact* Edinburgh, 1980, 4, 69, p.10

279. C. K. Hamel Cooke, 'The Role of Lay Visitors', *Contact* Edinburgh 1980, 4, 69, pp.21–3

280. Ecumenical Commission of *The New Initiative*, Birmingham Christian Council of Churches 1972

281. H. A. Eadie, (1) 'Health of Scottish Clergymen', *Contact* Edinburgh, 1972, 41; (2) 'Psychological Health of Clergymen', *Contact* Edinburgh, 1973, 42

282. R. K. Orchard, *Servants of Life*, Conference for World Mission 1979, esp. chs. 9 & 10

283. John 15.19

284. R. K. Orchard, *Servants of Life*, see note 282 above, ch. 3

285. M. Wilson, *The Hospital – A Place of Truth*, see note 93 above, p.41

286. John 12.31–32

287. Ezek. 3.18–21; Jonah 1.1ff.

288. A. V. Campbell, 'The Politics of Pastoral Care', James Blackie Memorial Lecture, *Contact* Edinburgh 1979, 1, 62, pp.2–15

289. (1) M. Stocks, *A Hundred Years of District Nursing*, Allen & Unwin 1960, pp.22–3 and index; (2) E. Platt, *The Story of the Ranyard Mission 1857–1937*, Hodder & Stoughton

290. Matt. 5.14–16

291. Matt. 13.33

292. Matt. 5.13

293. M. Wilson, *Health is for People*, see note 23 above

294. R. F. W. Nelson, *Thinking about the Future of Work*, see note 5 above, esp. Section IV

295. R. F. W. Nelson, op.cit. p.88

296. *Ethical Reflections on the Economic Crisis*, Episcopal Commission on Economic Affairs, Canadian Conference of Catholic Bishops 1983

297. D. P. Killen, 'Theological Reflection – a necessary skill in lay ministry', in F. R. Kinsler, *Ministry by the People*, WCC, Geneva, and Orbis, New York 1985, p.226

298. C. Elliott, *Praying the Kingdom*, DLT 1985, esp. ch.6, pp.80ff.

299. Mark 3.1–6

300. M. Wilson, 'Seminars in the School of Nursing', *Nursing Times*, 12 Feb. 1970, Occasional Paper

301. W. J. Hollenweger, *Jungermesse/Gomer: Das Gesicht des Unsichtbaren*, Zwei szenische Texte, Chr. Kaiser, Munich 1983

302. M. Buber, *The Knowledge of Man*, Allen & Unwin 1965, pp.67ff. and 181ff.

303. D. Bonhoeffer, *Letters and Papers from Prison*, The Enlarged Edition, SCM Press 1971

304. S. Kierkegaard, (1) *Journals and Papers*, ed. A. Dru, OUP 1938, p.153; (2) *Journals and Papers*, ed H. V. Hong and E. H. Hong, Indiana University Press 1975, Vol.3 L–R, 3403, p.558

305. James 2. 14–17

306. D. Nicholl, *Holiness*, DLT 1981, pp.149–50

307. A. Solzhenitsyn, *The Gulag Archipelago*, 1918–1956 Parts I–II, Collins Fontana 1974, p.525

308. R. A. Lambourne, 'The Cup of Cold Water and the Cup of Blessing', *Explorations in Health and Salvation*, see note 76 above

309. D. Oliphant, 'Motives for Metaphor', *Pastoral Studies Spring School Papers*, Theology Dept, University of Birmingham 1983, pp.21–32

310. Bishop Melito of Sardis, *On Pascha*, ed. S. G. Hall, OUP 1979, pp.3–4, verses 1–5

311. B. Reed, *Going to Church*, Grubb Institute of Behavioural Studies, London 1970, pp.13ff.

312. Matt. 4.4

313. N. Berdyaev, *The Fate of Man in the Modern World*, University of Michigan Press 1961, p.124

314. R. A. Lambourne, e.g.(1) 'The Daily Round of Suffering and

Healing', *The Wonder of Divine Healing*, ed. A. A. Jones, Arthur James 1958; (2) *Community, Church and Healing*, see note 37 above

315. A. P. Bird, (1) 'Wholeness – the Response of the Weak', *Regina*, Queens College, Birmingham 1975; (2) 'Participative Medicine', *Crucible*, Board for Social Responsibility of the General Synod of the Church of England, Jan./March 1980; (3) 'The Human Face of Medicine', *Regina*, Queens College, Birmingham 1976, pp.8–10

316. T. W. B. Cull and A. P. Bird, 'Patient/Doctor Seminars', *Journal of the Royal College of General Practitioners*, 1974, 24, pp.247–50

317. B. Stilwell, (1) 'The Nurse Practitioner at Work', *Nursing Times*: (a) 'Primary Care', 27 Oct. 1982, pp.1799–1802; (b) 'The American Experience', 3 Nov. 1982, pp. 1859–60; (c) 'Clinical Practice', 10 Nov. 1982, pp.1909–10; (2) 'Extending the Nursing Role in Inner City General Practice', *Journal of Community Nursing*, (a) Vol.5, no.3, Sept. 1981, pp.17–18; (b) Vol.5, no.4, Oct. 1981, pp.8–11

318. A. P. Bird, *The Search for Health*, see note 73 above

319. A. P. Bird, M. T. I. Walji, 'Our Patients have Access to their Medical Records', see note 74 above

320. (1) A. P. Bird, Ombersley Road (Birmingham) Project 1985–6, Protocol, June 1985, limited publication; (2) A. P. Bird, M. Walji, J. Cobb and other Practice Staff, Ombersley Road (Birmingham) Project, Mid Term Report, Nov 1985 (revised Feb 1986), unpublished

321. Current information on the course is available from the Secretary, Dept of Theology, University of Birmingham, B15 2TT

Index